S0-CVF-158

IN SEARCH OF EUROCOMMUNISM

IN SEARCH OF EUROCOMMUNISM

edited by
Richard Kindersley

St. Martin's Press
New York

St. Martin's Press, Inc., 175 Fifth Avenue, New York, NY 10010
Printed in Hong Kong
First published in the United States of America in 1981

ISBN 0–312–41114–6

Library of Congress Cataloging in Publication Data

Main entry under title:
In search of Eurocommunism
Based on papers from two seminars giveat
St Antony's College, Oxford, in 1978.
Includes index.
1. Communism—Europe. 2. Communist parties—
Europe. I. Kindersley, Richard.
HX238.5.15 1980 335.43'094 80–5073
ISBN 0–312–41114–6

Contents

Preface

Apart from the contributors themselves, I am glad to thank those who have helped in various ways with the compilation of this book: Isaac Aviv and Alyson Price for translating Jean Elleinstein's and Giuseppe Vacca's papers respectively; and Alberto Chilosi, for advice on some terminological points in the latter. Janet Caldwell, Pat Kirkpatrick, Mary Oxford, Clare Powell and Elizabeth Stevens typed the final drafts. Most of all I wish to thank my wife, who, in spite of illness, showed the greatest patience and understanding while I was working on this book.

R. K. K.

Notes on the Contributors

ISAAC AVIV has been Lecturer in History at the Hebrew University of Jerusalem and Senior Associate Member of St Antony's College, Oxford. He completed his doctorate at the University of Paris with a thesis on the PCF in the 1960s, and has published various articles on the history of the French and Spanish working class movements.

MANUEL AZCÁRATE is a member of the Executive Committee of the Communist Party of Spain, with special responsibility for foreign relations. He is joint author (with José Sandoval) of *Spain 1936–1939* (London, 1963).

JEAN ELLEINSTEIN is a prominent member of the French Communist Party and Maître-assistant in Contemporary History at the University of Poitiers. He was Joint Director of the Centre for Marxist Studies and Research in Paris. His publications include *Histoire de l'URSS* (4 vols, Paris, 1972–5), *The Stalin Phenomenon* (London, 1976) and *Le P.C.* (Paris, 1976).

RICHARD KINDERSLEY is a Fellow of St Antony's College and Faculty Lecturer in International Communism at Oxford University. He is the author of *The First Russian Revisionists* (Oxford, 1962).

PAUL PRESTON is Reader in Modern History at Queen Mary College, London. He is author of *The Coming of the Spanish Civil War* (London, 1978) and he edited *Spain in Crisis: the Evolution and Decline of the Franco Regime* (Hassocks, 1976).

BRANKO PRIBIĆEVIĆ is Professor of Political Science at the University of Belgrade. He has published, among other things, *The Shop Stewards' Movement and Workers' Control, 1910–1922*

(Oxford, 1959) and a major study of contemporary communism and socialism, *Socijalizam – svetski proces* [*Socialism – a world process*] (Belgrade, 1979).

CHRISTOPHER SETON-WATSON is a Fellow of Oriel College and Lecturer in Politics at Oxford University. His publications include *Italy from Liberalism to Fascism, 1870–1925* (London, 1967).

GIUSEPPE VACCA is a member of the Central Committee of the PCI and Consigliere di Amministrazione at Radiotelevisione Italiana. He was previously Docente in the History of Political Thought at the University of Bari. His publications include *Marxismo e analisi sociale* (1969) and *Scienza, Stato e critica di classe* (1970), and he has edited *Politica e teoria nel marxismo italiano 1959–69* (Bari, 1972) and *PCI, Mezzogiorno ed intellettuali, dalle alleanza all'organizzazione* (Bari, 1973).

H. T. WILLETTS is a Fellow of St Antony's College and Faculty Lecturer in Russian History at Oxford University. He has published numerous articles on Russian history and related subjects, and his translations include volume III of Alexander Solzhenitsyn's *Gulag Archipelago* (London, 1978).

Introduction

This book arose from two seminars given at St Antony's College, Oxford, in 1978: one primarily devoted to Eurocommunism as such, and the other to communism in Southern Europe. In the former, speakers from the main Eurocommunist parties – the French, Italian and Spanish – were invited, and contributions from them are included in the book. For the rest, most of the papers are drawn, with varying degrees of revision, from the seminars. Conversely, a number of seminar talks have been omitted, as much for reasons of space as for any other.

The resultant work consists of nine papers in all, including a tailpiece by the editor. Each of the three Eurocommunist parties is covered by a contribution from a prominent member, followed by a paper by a British (or in one case Israeli) scholar on some aspect of the party concerned. These papers are, however, in no sense comments on the Eurocommunists' contributions, but stand on their own feet. These are framed between two papers on aspects of Eurocommunism in general, namely "The USSR and Eurocommunism" and "Eurocommunism and the New Party".

No effort has been made to standardise the contributions. The result, plainly, is a certain heterogeneity of approach. I do not believe that this is necessarily disadvantageous; rather does it allow the real difference between the parties to find the analysis best suited to them, instead of suffering the imposition of a grid which, for all its regularity and utility for comparativist purposes, might well miss something essential to an understanding of the particular party.

H. T. Willetts's opening paper is mainly centred on Eurocommunist–CPSU relations, but raises all the major issues of Eurocommunism. Manuel Azcárate and Jean Elleinstein, for the PCE and PCF respectively, offer what are essentially political statements; but Elleinstein (speaking at a time when he was somewhat at odds with the PCF leadership) makes it clear that he is not *representing* the PCF. Giuseppe Vacca, on the other hand, reflects the intellectual heritage of the PCI with a genealogy of the *idées maîtresses* of Italian communism today. This does not mean that ideology is not an important force outside Italy, as Isaac Aviv makes plain in his study of the PCF as an ideological community, nor that it is exclusively predominant in Italy, as emerges from Christopher Seton-Watson's examination of the PCI's position in current Italian politics. Paul Preston deals with the Spanish party mainly through an analysis of Carrillo's victory over other factions in the party. This is appropriate to a party just emerged from a long period of suppression, when the removal of the containing bonds of persecution allows such differences not merely to come to light, but to affect party policy.

There are, of course, differences of judgement and interpretation among the contributors. It is no part of an editor's duty to arbitrate between them or award them marks, which could only be on a scale constructed according to his own predilections. In my own contribution, therefore, although I have used points made by the contributors, I have dealt with a few selected themes which, it seems to me, have not been covered elsewhere.

1 The USSR and Eurocommunism

H. T. WILLETTS

Invented (hopefully? mischievously?) by a journalist of Yugoslav origin writing for an Italian paper,[1] ignored or repudiated at first by the Western European communist parties, then adopted in turn by Berlinguer, Carrillo and Marchais, the term "Eurocommunism" describes the latest recrudescence of a secular tendency in the international communist movement.

The trend of course had reappeared long before it found this new name. President Giscard d'Estaing has teased the PCF by saying that they should more properly speak of "Italocommunism", and Togliatti's comrades are right to claim that his was a decisive contribution to the process of ideological *aggiornamento*. No less justified, however, were the Chinese ideologists in whose early law suits against "revisionism" Togliatti stood proxy for Khrushchev. From 1956, at any rate, Togliatti was engaged in giving political body (rather more body, to be sure, than the CPSU could have wished) to Khrushchev's "ideological innovations": the authorisation at the XX Congress of the "peaceful path" to socialism, the insistence on the need for foreign communists to adapt their policies to the special circumstances of their own countries, the renunciation of Soviet claims to hegemony within the world communist movement. These were old themes reworked, and Soviet exegetes were quick to delimit their implications. Not only Czechoslovakia in 1948 but the Baltic States in 1940 proved to be examples of countries which had taken the "peaceful path" to socialism.[2] The adaptation of policy to local circumstances, it was found, extended only to tactics, not to the final aim (establishment of proletarian dictatorship), nor to the decisive stage in its achievement (exploitation of a "revolutionary situation" to "smash the old state apparatus"). Soviet renunciation of hegemony did not release other communist parties from the obligations of "proletarian internationalism", which included acceptance of Leninism as the common ideology, recognition of Soviet society as a model susceptible of only minor adjustments to local conditions, and unqualified support for Soviet foreign policy.[3]

None the less, the CPSU did not, could not attempt to force conformity on the PCI or other parties which showed revisionist velleities. The breach with China was one of the factors which imposed restraint (a simultaneous schism within Europe was unthinkable) and another was the potential importance of the PCF and PCI to the achievement of Soviet aims in Western Europe. The Sino-Soviet quarrel, and their success in remaining aloof from it, emboldened the PCI and some other parties to enlarge the area of independence, and to reinforce at international gatherings the principle of non-interference in the affairs of fraternal communist parties.[4] The CPSU suffered more or less silently, and not only for diplomatic reasons. Khrushchev's innovations sprang from a realistic recognition that the communist parties in advanced capitalist countries could not, any more than the CPSU itself, remain paralytically fixed in an anachronistic stance. A "revolutionary situation" leading to "proletarian dictatorship" on the classical Marxist–Leninist model was a remote contingency in modern Western Europe, imaginable indeed (like the "revolutionary crises" which had brought the Eastern European communist regimes into being) only as the result of war – and the elimination of all danger of war from Europe was a prime aim of Soviet policy. Discipline in the communist movement was weakened by the relaxation of international tensions, but the USSR itself, moving from "cold war" via "peaceful competition" to détente, did not want a relationship with Western communist parties so tight and intimate that it might inhibit or complicate Soviet relationships with Western governments. From the Soviet point of view, then, the European communist parties could make themselves most useful by broadening their appeal and building up their electoral strength; by exerting pressure in support of Soviet initiatives without behaving so provocatively as to damage relations between "their own" governments and the USSR; and by postponing grander ambitions until the CPSU judged them timely. For the present, the communist parties in advanced capitalist countries would not be expected to advance the interests of world communism by challenging initiatives, but only to play a discreet and not too tightly controlled auxiliary part in assisting Soviet manoeuvres in the international arena.

For its part, the USSR did not fuss too much about the heretical pronouncements, or silences, of Western communist parties (about, for instance, the abandonment of "dictatorship of the proletariat" as its declared aim by the PCI or that party's readiness to admit non-Marxists as members)[5] provided none of these had clearly anti-Soviet implications; about their incongruous friendships; or about their occasional impertinences in interparty dealings. Life, as someone in the International Department of the Central Committee must have said, would apply its correctives.

This *modus vivendi*, never an entirely happy one, broke down under the impact of three events: the Soviet reconquest of Czechoslovakia, the intensification of Soviet action against dissidents after Khrushchev, and the publication of *Gulag*. (*Gulag*'s revelations, as the author himself has said,[6] should not have come as news to Western European readers, but no previous exposure of the camp system has stirred such deep disgust and anger.) It is unfair to suggest that electoral calculations alone decided the PCI, PCF and PCE to dramatise their disapproval of Soviet abuses, past and present, and their renunciation of doctrines which have always served to justify those abuses. The strain and embarrassment of defending, or tacitly condoning, Soviet behaviour which the Western public at large found detestable had proved too much for many party members in the past, and was bound, sooner or later, to prove too much for any political leadership operating in a democratic milieu. But it was the almost simultaneous evolution of the *compromesso storico*, the *Union de la Gauche*, and Santiago Carrillo's hopes of a place for his party in a coalition government after Franco, which enabled the three parties to make common cause against the CPSU. Their alliance was reinforced by joint resistance to the CPSU in the 18 months of troubled preparation for the Berlin Conference of Communist and Workers' Parties, and at the conference itself (June 1976).

No guesses will be made here as to whether the three parties may some day regret the pledges they gave in the years 1975–6. What seems undeniable is that these pronouncements have opened up an ideological rift far wider and deeper than that between the USSR and Yugoslavia (which finds it expedient to approve of any show of independence from the USSR, but has considerable reservations about the ideas of the Western European parties), or than that between the USSR and China. This is not to say that relations between the USSR and the Western parties will necessarily be bad, or that they need ever be as bad as the USSR's relations with China: communists are the first to accept the possibility of tactical co-operation with ideologically incompatible partners. But it is difficult to imagine in what circumstances the ideological pledges of the PCI, PCF and PCE could ever be retracted: and the very fact of their existence must tend to strengthen the hand of elements in the parties determined to live up to them, must attract support which is conditional on their preservation, must preclude uncritical support of Soviet ideas and actions for the future.

Parties which for decades had more and more improbably pretended that the USSR was a humane workers' democracy, while "bourgeois democracy" was fraudulent and inhuman, suddenly began to speak not only of the need to preserve the relative freedoms of a "pluralist" system under socialism but, from the Soviet point of view more insultingly and alarmingly, of the need to introduce those freedoms into Soviet society. They were intent, as a spokesman for the PCE put it,[7] on realising a conception of socialism:

> strikingly different from *totalitarian* [my emphasis] socialism as it came into being in the East European countries . . . in historical circumstances entirely different from those of today.

This improved modern variety, "vigorously defended also by the Italians and French at Berlin" and

> unanimously supported also by the British and Swedes . . . realises itself in democracy, in the full exercise of individual rights, in a pluralism [*sic*] of political parties, ensuring the possibility of a change of government according to the will of the people expressed in general elections.

It further insists on intellectual and religious freedoms, recognises the right to strike and renounces the imposition of any official ideology by the state. Devotion to these principles had already been jointly proclaimed by the PCI and PCF before and after their talks in Rome in November 1975: in particular the parties pledged support for "the plurality of political parties, the right to existence and activity of opposition parties, democratic alternation between the majority and the minority", and vowed not merely "further to democratise economic, social and political life" (these are also the words of a hoary and hollow Soviet cliché) but "to guarantee . . . *existing bourgeois liberties*" [my emphasis].[8] In its "Declaration of Freedom" (May 1975) the PCF had not only sanctified the right to strike, but with unmistakeable anti-Soviet innuendo condemned arbitrary internment in medical institutions, banishment, invasion of privacy, bugging, the keeping of secret dossiers on citizens, exile, anti-Semitism, the death penalty. . .[9]

The CPSU probably found the (often only implicit) criticism of Soviet society in these Italian and French programmatic documents more offensive, and certainly harder to acknowledge, than the exuberant ruderies of Carrillo's *Eurocomunismo y Estado* (1977). Acceptance, by the PCI and PCF as well as the PCE, of the term "Eurocommunism" to describe the reformed creed compounded the insult. If its sole intention had been to hurt Soviet susceptibilities no more effective word could have been chosen. "Eurocommunism" can only exist as the antithesis of "Russocommunism" – even if this term is never used. The USSR has always resented not only the accusation that its socialism is perverted by Russian backwardness, but, no less, patronising tolerance of its shortcomings in consideration of the Russian past, or even the mere suggestion that Soviet society, for good or ill, shows characteristics which are more easily explained by the character and history of the Russian people than by the history of European socialism at large or Marxism in particular. There is no denial of Russia's pre-revolutionary backwardness, no pretence that it did not have its effect. The "objective" – economic and institutional – conditions in Russia were not, it is admitted, propitious for the building of socialism. Lenin, no one denies, took advantage of favourable "subjective" conditions – the inability of the old rulers to rule, the eagerness of the people for change – to seize power first and create the preconditions (as defined by classical Marxism) afterwards. The economic backwardness and the international weakness of old Russia meant that socialism could only be built at the cost of great hardship and heavy sacrifices. But the CPSU will not and cannot admit that this backwardness, this terrible struggle have permanently distorted Soviet socialism, or left on it any specifically Russian mark. It insists that the difficulties were triumphantly overcome, that the USSR has succeeded in constructing the most advanced society on earth, a model for communists everywhere – though their problems will be smaller, and the solutions to them in certain respects different – simply because it is the first country of "realised socialism", of "working socialism", of "socialism in action". (The translations of "real'ny sotsializm" favoured by Western writers – "existing socialism", "realistic socialism", etc. – do not convey the full force of the original.)

Equally, suggestions that Leninism is an adaptation or perversion of Marxism to fit Russian circumstances, or that its most distinctive features are inherited from some earlier, non-Marxist strain in Russian political thought (the "Russian Jacobinism" of Tkachev and some members of the Narodnaya Volya is most often invoked), are fiercely resented. Leninism is not the Marxism of Russia, but "Marxism in the age of imperialism and proletarian revolution". The international authority of the CPSU rests as much on its claim that Leninism is universally valid as on its pioneering work in the "building of socialism".

> Leninism is the highest stage in the development of Marxism. All the basic regularities of development in a new historical epoch are reflected in it. . . Rejection of Leninism is a rejection of internationalism.[10]

One after another, the Eurocommunists have rejected Leninism – not indeed as a fund of ideas on which they may draw when it suits them, but as the prism through which Marxism must be viewed.

The hottest of the ideological arguments between the CPSU and the Eurocommunists centres around the inevitability of the use of force and of the transition from parliamentary to dictatorial methods at some stage on the way to socialism. The Soviet view has long been that there is indeed "in a number of capitalist countries . . . a prospect of the more or less gradual and relatively peaceful conquest of power by the working class".[11] Two main reasons are usually given for this view. One is that the "objective conditions" for the establishment of socialism are fast maturing in these countries. (Here Soviet writers have in mind particularly the rapid growth of the public sector of the economy, and of state intervention in economic and social life generally, and they sometimes make a point of the divorce of ownership from management even in the private sector.) The second is that the might of the Soviet Union can protect a nascent socialist regime from any attempt by international capitalism to suppress it. The working class can travel a long way towards socialism by the parliamentary route. But however gradual the process a sharp dividing line is sooner or later reached.

> The prerequisite of the conquest of power will be a revolutionary situation and a general national crisis. . . . Only the forms in which they arise are changing – there is a smoothing out of the transitional process from the normal political situation to crisis.[12]

Communists must

> not yield to illusions and lose sight of the probability that at the critical moment the development of events will demand from the working class and the masses under communist leadership actions which while remaining profoundly democratic in form will necessarily be combined with open violence[!].[13]

The disagreement on this point stems partly from a difference of opinion about the character and role of the state in advanced capitalist societies. In the Eurocommunist view the state apparatus can be taken over and democratised under parliamentary control. In the Soviet view:

> the influence of the democratic forces on the state apparatus does not change its character. The growing role of the state apparatus as a result of the development of state monopoly capitalism makes smashing it a matter of still greater urgency.[14]

Perhaps to reassure the bureaucrats whose support they regard in other contexts as potentially a great advantage to the communist cause, perhaps also to distance themselves from the neo-Bakuninism of the ultra-left, Soviet writers feel the need for a gloss on the traditional metaphor: while "smashing" the state apparatus communists must "provide for preservation of those mechanisms for the regulation of production and other social processes which have taken shape under capitalism".[15] "Smashing", on this interpretation, comes to mean little more than breaking the hold on policy and administration of "representatives of the ruling class" in high bureaucratic posts who identify the nation's interests with those of capitalism.

It is, of course, the coercive apparatus of the state which must be most thoroughly smashed, for "even where the peaceful path is possible the workers will collide at every step with savage resistance from the bourgeoisie backed by the military".[16] (But even in this context, Soviet writers can speak of winning over rational elements in the officer corps.) The Chilean débâcle is often invoked by supporters of the Soviet viewpoint as an awful warning of what awaits regimes which set out to build socialism without smashing the old apparatus of coercion,[17] and fashioning weapons of their own, or in other words, proceeding from the "formal democratic to the revolutionary stage". In Chile "an absolute was made of one [the parliamentary] path"; ". . . the masses found their hands tied"; ". . . many regarded preparations for an eventual change of path as absolutely unacceptable"; ". . . the atmosphere of legality" had "an ambiguous effect". Whereas the coalition parties should have realised that "there was no reason to feel bound hand and foot by legality like a Gulliver", that "the revolution can do without bloodshed only if the majority impose this [*sic*] and the minority cannot prevent them", that "our advance must be safeguarded not only by popular but by adequate military support", that "the balance of forces is not established once and for all except when revolution having consolidated its positions . . . eliminates antagonistic classes to build a classless society". Cunhal no less than Corvalan has outraged Eurocommunists by his fundamentalism. "In Portuguese conditions", he has said, "there is no room for a Western European type of democracy." And if the Portuguese Communist Party has removed the term "dictatorship of the proletariat" from its programme, this is, he tells us, "a matter of expediency", and it "changes nothing in our conceptions or our doctrines".[18]

"Smashing the state apparatus" is a formula susceptible of endless casuistic refinement. If certain other requirements were met Western European communists in power might reduce it to limited measures of reorganisation and remanning without incurring Soviet displeasure. It is, however, on the most important of these other requirements that the Eurocommunists (and here we must remember that the term awkwardly embraces some communist parties outside Europe, notably the Japanese) are hopelessly at odds with the CPSU and its East European congeners, and for that matter, with the Yugoslavs, the Third World parties apparently without exception, and not least the CPC. I refer of course to the Leninist requirement that the working class and its allies under communist leadership must establish their power irreversibly by suppressing "hostile parties, and the rule of the ballot box".[19] It is unthinkable that a regime which has taken power to build socialism should submit its policies to the judgement of the people in open and freely contested elections, and that if defeated it should yield power to enemies intent on dismantling its work. Whatever is done with the old bureaucracy, one institution must be utterly and uncompromisingly "smashed": parliament in its bourgeois form.

On this point Rosa Luxemburg, whose eloquent prophecies of the inevitable dictatorial degeneration of Lenin's party are so often quoted by his critics, can be summoned to his support. *Kommunist*,[20] clearly addressing itself to the Eurocommunists though without mentioning them, recently quoted at some length from her *Russian Revolution* (1918):

> Those who try to introduce into revolutionary tactics the homespun methods of the parliamentary war of mice and frogs only show that the psychology of the revolutionary is alien to them, that both the living principle and the whole historical experience of revolution are to them a book with seven seals.
>
> Kautsky and those likeminded Russians who wanted to preserve the bourgeois character of the Russian revolution are an exact copy of the German and British liberals of last century who distinguished the good revolutionary period, the Girondiste period [of the Great French Revolution] from the bad period

> beginning with the Jacobin coup. . . . But for the coup by the wild Jacobins even the first timid and inchoate achievements of the Girondist period would have been buried. . . .
>
> The Bolshevik Party was the only one which was conscious of the mission and duty of a truly revolutionary party, and with its slogan "all power to the proletariat and the peasantry" it ensured that the revolution would advance. . . .
>
> The Bolsheviks thereby solved the celebrated problem of the "majority of the people" which has weighed so long and so heavily on the German Social Democratic Party. It [the SDP] sucked in parliamentary cretinism with its mother's milk, and it tries to introduce into revolution the primitive recipes of the parliamentary kitchen: "to achieve anything at all you must first win a majority". The real dialectic of revolution refutes these parliamentarian imbecilities. The way forward leads not via a "majority" to revolutionary tactics but on the contrary through revolutionary tactics to a majority. . . .
>
> Not the observance of bourgeois democracy, but the dictatorship of the proletariat, is destined to realise the building of socialism.

In August 1975, an anniversary article on Lenin's "Two Tactics of Social Democracy" by Konstantin Zarodov[21] (editor of *Problems of Peace and Socialism*) was sharply critical of "modern compromisers" who ignore the Leninist distinction between a "political majority" (which a communist party cannot do without) and an "arithmetical majority" (which is inessential). Eurocommunists, and particularly the PCF, saw in this a hostile reference to themselves, and Brezhnev, by demonstratively honouring Zarodov soon afterwards, authorised them to do so.[22] Yury Krasin, perhaps the most skilful of contemporary apologists of Leninism, has enlarged on this theme in various contexts. Lenin, he reminds us, held that though a revolutionary party needed at decisive moments the support of a majority of the population this cannot always be taken to mean an "arithmetical majority" obtained by "election, referendum or the counting of heads". To make revolutionary action conditional on the results of elections in fact condemns the movement to inaction. This is because within the arithmetical majority the preponderance will almost certainly be on the side of "those who doubt, vacillate, show indecision and timidity in the fact of abrupt changes". The proletarian avant garde can win to its side an enduring majority only by convincing the waverers in practice that proletarian rule serves their interests. And this it can do "only by means of such an instrument as state power, that is only after overthrowing the bourgeoisie and destroying its state apparatus".[23]

Can any political sociologist, or indeed any casual observer of the Western political scene, deny the force of Krasin's observations? Even within the working class itself, as he says elsewhere, there are such "negative phenomena" to be taken into account as "exclusive concern for short term needs, a variety of conformist attitudes, political instability, susceptibility to bourgeois influences".[24] Give or take a loaded term or two, his is an acceptable description of the most obvious obstacle to rapid and radical reconstruction of a free society: as long as the people are free to dismiss governments, how can they be induced to make present sacrifices for the sake of future advantage, be firmly attached to leaders who must make mistakes and irksome demands, and be prevented from switching their allegiance to a political opposition which promises relief from burdens, or simply voting "agin the government", whatever its complexion, on principle? What indeed is to prevent the majority from switching its vote from election to election, so that successive governments might endlessly put down and tear up and put down again the foundations of a socialism which would never come close enough to completion to prove itself once and for all?

There may be those who expect frank scorn for the "counting of heads" as a method of forming governments from right-wing or technocratic elitists rather than from communists. Leninists, unlike the elitists, cannot of course openly base their objections on an assertion that the mental and moral limitations of the masses are incorrigible and permanent. The masses – the arithmetical majority – *will* some day realise their interests and rally to communism. But only when they are converted by socialism in action. In the meantime the avant garde, which knows better than the masses what is best for them, the "political majority" in Lenin's sense, must concentrate all power in its hands.

Eurocommunists will have none of this. The genuine political democracy, which is, they insist, as important a feature of socialist society as public ownership, demands the preservation of "bourgeois" freedoms, their supplementation but not their replacement, and in particular the maintenance of a sovereign parliament freely elected. The suggestion that this will materially slow down progress towards socialism, that hostile governments elected with the help of timid, vacillating, ideologically unstable workers will periodically undo the achievements of their communist predecessors, is dismissed as unreal. Experience indeed tells us that in advanced societies democratically elected governments rarely find it practicable, or for that matter desirable, to repeal the whole legislative programme of their predecessors. But this is, of course, because free elections in such countries tend to produce moderate "middle of the road" consensus-seeking governments. A government which ventured far to left or right and was dismissed by a rebellious electorate might see its work systematically demolished. But the Eurocommunists do not in any case rely merely on the gradual accretion of institutional changes which it is impractical to unscramble. They rely on an ever securer hegemony of socialist ideas, not only amongst the workers but amongst other large sections of the population. In spite of the ups and downs in its electoral fortunes, the political formation engaged in building socialism can expect to become the normal party of government.

To Leninists this can mean only one thing: that the Eurocommunists, loth as they are to admit it, are latter-day Mensheviks, or mere social-democrats. All the symptoms are present: gradualist opportunism, a hankering after impure alliances, "parliamentary cretinism". Was not the very word "pluralism" coined by the arch social democrat, H. J. Laski?[25] The Eurocommunist, the Menshevik, the social democrat, all believe that the builders of socialism must have the understanding and assent of the majority of the people at every stage. A Leninist is ready – in Lenin's own phrase – to have his revolution first and create the preconditions afterwards. The assent of the majority is amongst the preconditions which may have to be created retrospectively. But in any case – and support for this view can be drawn from bourgeois writers[26] – Soviet democracy is in many respects superior to bourgeois democracy.

It is easy to understand the reluctance of Eurocommunists to wear the social-democratic label. Their parties, after all, were born by fission from the "discredited" social democratic parties of the 2nd International. Their very name – "communist parties" – is that chosen by Lenin to replace the supposedly tarnished appellation "social democratic parties". Periodic cooperation or alliance with socialist parties makes it even more important for them to preserve that distinctive "communist", non-social-democratic identity. (And furthermore, "social-democratic" is increasingly used in some countries to distinguish the right wing from the left within socialist parties.) The Eurocommunists themselves look for their ideological roots in the history of their own parties: not only Gramsci but the great figures of the Popular Front period (even, with no apparent humorous intent, G. Dimitrov) are called in to help. In the present writer's view, the Eurocommunists would be wise to avoid a duel with the Leninists in which the weapons were quotations from these avatars. It is, on the other hand, difficult to see what any Eurocommunist could find to criticise (except, occasionally, the outmoded terminology) in the propositions which follow.

> The object of socialism is the abolition of all forms of exploitation and oppression, political and economic. Full socialisation of production is possible without democracy, and democracy is possible without socialism. Only a solution at once socialist and democratic can eliminate exploitation and oppression. Ripeness for socialism depends in part on the degree of concentration of the economy, in part on the acceptability of the socialist idea to society at large, including groups outside the proletariat. Of course, the workers may need to resist attempts by the former ruling class to overthrow their government. But if the time for socialism has come such attempts can best be resisted within an ultra-democratic system. It is nonsense to suggest that in a developed modern democracy the bureaucracy at large would side with the dispossessed class against a proletarian party supported by the majority of the electorate, or that the party through parliament would not be able to control the armed forces. Even in a country where it constitutes the majority of the population the proletariat must induce the intermediate classes to identify their interests with its own, not with capitalism. Class and party must not be confused. A class may be divided between different parties, a party may control members of different classes. If the majority in a parliamentary election votes against socialism, socialists must bow to its will.

> There are only two ways of maintaining a dictatorship against the will of the majority: Jesuitism [the author has in mind "Jesuit socialism" in Paraguay] and Bonapartism.

These were the views of Karl Kautsky, summarised here from *Democracy or Dictatorship* (1918),[27] a less successful politician than Lenin to be sure, but arguably a more scrupulous Marxist, who from its inception decided that the Soviet régime could hardly escape the deformities now so obvious to Eurocommunists. He saw no good reason to cease calling himself a social democrat. Are the Eurocommunists closer to the Kautsky who wrote "[our aims] remain the conquest of state power by winning a majority in parliament and converting parliament into the master of the government" or to the Lenin who commented (in *State and Revolution*) that "this is the purest and most vulgar opportunism"?

Magistral exposition of Leninist fundamentals is the genre which the CPSU favours in its running argument with Eurocommunism. Except under provocation particular Eurocommunists are not named. In public Soviet and East European commentators do not pin the Eurocommunist label on whole parties. They are careful to suggest that the phenomenon is not a spontaneous development within the parties but a "cuckoo's egg", an injection of poison, a bacillus introduced by the subversive agents of capitalism. As a rule, they prefer to avoid the word Eurocommunism altogether, speaking instead of the "social democratic" or "reformist" or even "so-called democratic communist"[28] trends, "in some sections of certain parties". None the less, *Kommunist* may gratefully publish independent testimony that Eurocommunism belongs in the Pandemonium ruled over by the CIA.

> We are faced with an ideological front of imperialism, fascism, racism, militarism . . . which are our obvious foes, and also with the crypto-capitalist forces of Maoism, Trotskyism, reformism, revisionism, Eurocommunism, and social-democratism. These all strive to keep imperialism alive. Bernstein, Kautsky, Trotsky and Mao are all spiritual ancestors of this movement, and its aim . . . is to wreck real Marxism–Leninism, as the Socialist Revolutionaries and Mensheviks tried to do during the Great October Revolution.[29]

The CPSU, while leaving no doubt about its views, is anxious to avoid an open clash with the leadership of Western Communist parties and the leaders of the PCI and the PCF at least have of late been careful not to provoke the Soviet establishment unnecessarily. The most violent Soviet reactions, naturally, are to direct criticism of the CPSU and Soviet society as they now are, whether their shortcomings are attributed to some congenital flaw, to degeneracy or to arrested development. The CPSU, even after its attempt to overthrow him, must have been astonished and dismayed to read in Carrillo that it is the duty of Western communists to help the USSR and other socialist states overcome the "alienation of the working class", and those features of "totalitarian socialism" in which it "resembles fascism" or "the monstrosities of imperialism".[30] More moderately worded Eurocommunist strictures are not necessarily less infuriating: Lombardo Radice's talk, for instance, of "persistent conservatism" (in the USSR and Eastern Europe) "and immobilism stemming from fear of change", of the need for foreign comrades to deliver them from "that crisis of uneven growth" which has left them with "enormous heads intellectually, technologically and economically" unsupported by "commensurate bodies in terms of political structure, cultural emancipation, and so forth".[31] Very carefully weighed critical utterances from very high quarters are perhaps most wounding of all: J. Kanapa's laconic mention, for instance, of "continuing lack of democratic progress in some socialist countries".[32] The same authority offered this lapidary characterisation of the "real socialism" which the PCF rejects:

> It is considered necessary to ban opposition, introduce censorship, take away freedom of expression, assembly and demonstration from one section of the people. And we are supposed to tell the workers, the French people, that these are among the consequences of what the French communists propose to you . . .[33]

We may be sure that Eurocommunist intervention on behalf of individual dissidents, open or tacit encouragement of opposition groups like the Workers' Defence Committee in Poland or Charter 77 in Czechoslovakia, the regular commemoration (especially by the PCI) of the martyred Dubček (a Eurocommunist without knowing it, according to Carrillo), are all insults which set pulses angrily racing in Eastern Europe, though there is as a rule no retort in print. Perhaps most keenly resented of all are systematic attempts by Eurocommunists to strike a balance between the negative and positive results of the Soviet experiment. Four leading Soviet authorities, "challenging", in number and eminence, the five French authors of *L'URSS et nous*[34] (recommended by G. Marchais at the Congress of the PCF in May 1979)[35] were outraged by the very suggestion that a reassessment was necessary, but also (not altogether impertinently) enquired why writers who until recently had leaned if anything too heavily on the positive side, who had been exaggeratedly and unrealistically uncritical of the USSR, had now suddenly toppled over in the other direction.

Soviet and East European reactions to Eurocommunist criticism and interference are of course not just a matter of wounded vanity. The behaviour of the Eurocommunists is potentially a disruptive force in those societies. And in this context we can see why the measured strictures of a Kanapa might seem more fearful than the fulminations of a Carrillo. If the USSR and its like are at once primitive, degenerate and stagnant, reforming and modernising them is a daunting task. But to say that they have great achievements behind them, and that though they are now marking time or have lost their way they can, with comradely help from outside, recover their impetus and sense of direction, perfect their socialism by democratising it – this is an encouragement, an incitement even, to the forces of democratic opposition, by no means negligible in those countries.[36] The phenomenon of Eurocommunism perhaps already inhibits the Soviet and Eastern European regimes to some extent in their choice of counter-measures. If there were a major upheaval in Poland, for instance, Soviet (and Bulgarian, and perhaps even Czech) tanks might roll. But the damage to the USSR would be much deeper and more lasting than that inflicted by the invasion of Czechoslovakia in 1968: there is an inevitable progression in these matters. With the greatest goodwill, I cannot understand the explanation sometimes offered by French communists of the different attitudes adopted by their party (not all of it!) to Soviet intervention in Hungary in 1956 and to the reconquest of Czechoslovakia in 1968. Intervention in Hungary, we are told, was justified *because* socialism was not firmly established there, whereas in Czechoslovakia it was unnecessary because socialism could stand on its own feet. (Is this argument compatible with Eurocommunist respect for the will of the majority?) But whatever their views in the past, very many Western European communists would surely feel that a third Soviet military action of the same type was the occasion for a definitive break with the CPSU. It is of course because the Western European parties can urge restraint on the USSR that not only the Yugoslavs, who have an imperfect sympathy with Eurocommunism, but Ceauşescu, who has no ideological affinity with it at all, have developed strong links and regular contacts with them.

It is none the less likely that the Western Communist parties will try not to aggravate the internal difficulties of the Eastern European regimes, and will see their role as that of discreet mediators and counsellors of moderation. They seem ready, sometimes too ready, to discern signs of progress, assurances of amendment, in the behaviour of their Eastern comrades. Obviously there is a limit beyond which publicising Eastern scandals, even by deprecating them, could damage party unity, diminish the appeal of communism to the electorate, and for both these reasons, reduce the bargaining power of a communist party in search of an electoral alliance with other parties.

Some Western commentators already see Eurocommunism as a flash in the pan. It has, they would have us believe, no future except as a source of inspiration to party ad-men at election times. For one thing, the communist parties cannot afford to encourage too much debate in their own ranks. Internal democracy in the Western parties, it is often suggested, would make it more difficult for the leaders to enforce the democratisation of party programmes. Then again, they themselves would be unbearably embarrassed – and the writings to date of even the least inhibited Eurocommunists seem to bear this out – by a truly rigorous and detailed scrutiny of the Soviet record and the history of European communism at large.

That the Eurocommunist parties diverge from the USSR, each at its own characteristic angle, on some matters of foreign policy, is well known. Thus, the PCI would not wish to upset the balance in Europe by taking Italy out of NATO prematurely, and in this context its spokesmen have sometimes mentioned the possibility of a Soviet-dominated Yugoslavia after Tito's death.[37] Lombardo Radice has set out the PCI's position in some detail. It "could not be expected to work against the general interests of the Soviet Union", and would be compelled to take the Soviet side if there were

> imperialist aggression with the avowed objective of rolling back socialism [but] Italy, France and the other European members of NATO must be prepared to be loyal to the common defence policy of the alliance if that policy is based on common decisions . . . their obligation lapses if the U.S. ceases to respect the defensive character of the alliance . . . and imposes decisions without the concurrence of the other signatories. . . .[38]

The PCF often seems intent on showing itself truer to the Gaullist heritage than its rivals: determined that France must not draw closer to NATO, it deplores Giscard's "Atlanticism", but it is also committed to the preservation of a French *force de frappe*.[39] The PCE is against the accession of Spain to NATO, but for a Europe "independent both of the USSR and of the USA", for a world no longer bi-polar (since the hegemony of each superpower in its own bloc has become intolerable) but multi-polar. On the way to this objective, and before general disarmament, regional defence arrangements (including a Western European alliance) may be necessary. And in the immediate future nothing should be done to upset the existing equilibrium, which alone guarantees peace. The appropriate time for the USA to withdraw from Spain, for instance, might be when the USSR withdraws from Czechoslovakia.[40] The PCI, PCF and PCE are all in favour of the EEC, though the views of the PCF on the forms of association are quasi-Gaullist, and those of the PCI enthusiastically internationalist. No common Eurocommunist policy towards the EEC is discernible beyond vague declarations of intent to "democratise the community" and "impart a new content to integration".

From the Soviet point of view there is perhaps little cause for immediate alarm in the patriotic declarations of the Eurocommunist parties. They are, essentially, an assurance that communists in power, or sharing power, would be in no hurry to change the status quo in Europe. But is the USSR itself eager to do so? Not, we may suppose, while its overriding preoccupations are the actual contest with the USA, and the contest, perhaps soon to begin in earnest, with China; and while the "status quo" is defined partly by the chronic failure of Western Europe to achieve political cohesion, genuine economic integration, or a substantial defence capacity. The antipathy of the European communist parties towards the USA is ineradicable. They can be relied on to remain hostile to American cultural as well as economic inroads into European countries, and to what they see as the neo-imperialism of transnational corporations. (Even though Carrillo, for instance, reserves a role for international capitalism in the economic development of Spain.) They can probably be relied on, too, to improve on the already considerable contribution which Western Europe is making to the modernisation and expansion of the Soviet economy. Economic integration, and even an inevitably underfunded and inadequate common defence programme in a Western Europe from which communist electoral successes had accelerated the withdrawal of the USA, need hold no fears for the USSR. A likely pattern of events would, of course, be an initial communist success in one major European country, which would aggravate divisions in Western Europe, but would give the USSR an opportunity to show its detachment and its impartial interest in good relations with capitalists and communists alike.

It may, then, seem to the CPSU that Eurocommunism holds, for the time being, no great dangers. But it is the habit of Soviet policy-makers and their advisers to think farther ahead than is usual amongst their Western counterparts, and they must at least allow for the possibility that in a longer perspective the consequences of Eurocommunism could be very damaging to their interests.

Let us note once again that although the leaders of the Eurocommunist parties may see the need to rein in their overeager progressives, to call a halt or even order a tactical retreat, they cannot retrace their steps very far. Once heretical ideas are now the starting point from which its fresher and bolder members can always urge their party forward again. Though the process of internal change, the democratisation of party life, proceeds sluggishly, it will go on. In the past no European communist party could have carried out a revirement of the sort which we have recently seen without a disastrous split. Not the least interesting and impressive aspect of the Eurocommunist episode is the way in which strongly differentiated *correnti*, as the Italians call them, have succeeded in coexisting, in the PCF as well as in the PCI. (The CPGB is one of the parties which has been less fortunate, but then sectarianism is a natural result of chronic insignificance.) Obviously, disgruntled factions may still break away, or be expelled, but if, as seems likely, no major split occurs in the PCF or the PCI, we must take this as a sign that they are maturing as political parties of the European type, or perhaps we should in fairness say reverting to the shape which was theirs before Bolshevisation. But internal diversity, internal pluralism, would be a guarantee of continued independence, would hold the promise that objective and critical attitudes towards Soviet-style socialism and to international actions governed solely by Soviet self-interest, will be certain of a hearing. Increasingly, in the course of internal debate and of adaptation to a broad electorate, the Eurocommunist parties may be expected to reinforce the contrasts between themselves and their former Soviet mentors, to identify themselves more and more clearly with genuine national interests which more than ever in a world of sharpening competition for shrinking resources will often be incompatible with bogus Soviet internationalism. The USSR has, to put it at its lowest, lost some of its ability to interfere in this process. Marchais' suggestion that the Berlin conference of 1976 might be the last of its kind invites the retort that never is a long time. If the CPSU should consider arranging another big international gathering, it could surely no longer hope to involve the communist parties of advanced capitalist countries in rituals of assent or collective shaming, as it did in the past. It must deal with their leaders on a footing of equality and with diplomatic discretion.

Nothing alarms the CPSU more than the feeling that it is not in complete control of a situation: of a once firmly held instrument. This vertiginous sensation must be what the Eurocommunist episode has induced in the Soviet leaders. It represents – as Djilas has said – a dizzy drop in Soviet influence.

NOTES

1. Frane Barbieri in *Giornale Nuovo*, 26 June 1975.
2. See article "Fevral'skiye Sobytiya 1948 v Chekhoslovakii" in *Sovietskaya Istoricheskaya Entsiklopediya*, vol. 14 (Moscow, 1973), p. 999.
3. For a subtle formulation of present requirements see Kadar's article in *World Marxist Review*, no. 1, 1977, together with his remarks at the Berlin Conference quoted in *World Marxist Review*, no. 3, 1977, p. 77.

4. T. Timofeyev's post-Berlin Conference article "Novoye i staroye v anti-kommunizme", *Kommunist*, no. 16, 1976, is interestingly confused on the subject of Soviet claims to leadership.
5. According to Lucio Lombardo Radice the term "Marxism–Leninism" has now "disappeared from the party vocabulary in a natural way, like dictatorship of the proletariat". He would prefer to speak of "a party that grew out of Marx", not "a Marxist party" (quoted in *The Times*, 16 October 1977).
6. In A. I. Solzhenitsyn, *The Oak and the Calf* (London and New York, 1980).
7. J. B.: "Berlin – Conferencia de partidos comunistas", in *Mundo Obrero*, 7 July 1976.
8. *L'Humanité* and *L'Unità*, 18 November 1975.
9. *L'Humanité*, 20 May 1975.
10. See review of K. Zarodov, *Sotsializm, mir, revolyutsiya* in *Voprosy filosofi*, no. 3, 1979.
11. See review of Yu. Krasin, *Teoriya sotsialisticheskoy revolyutsii* in *Voprosy filosofii*, no. 5, 1978.
12. Ibid.
13. Zarodov, op. cit.
14. Krasin, op. cit.
15. Ibid.
16. Ibid.
17. See in particular articles by V. Teitelboim and Orlando Millas in *World Marxist Review*, nos 1 and 2, 1977.
18. A. Cunhal, "Results and prospects of the Portuguese revolution", in *World Marxist Review*, no. 1, 1977. See also his speech of 6 May 1978, reproduced in *Kommunist*, no. 14, 1978.
19. Zarodov, op. cit.
20. "Iz istorii rabochego dvizheniya", *Kommunist*, no. 1, 1979.
21. *Pravda*, 7 August 1975.
22. *Pravda*, 18 September 1975.
23. Yu. Krasin, "Problema bolshin'stva v sotsialisticheskoi revolyutsii", *Kommunist*, no. 11, 1977.
24. Ibid.
25. Mentioned by Shakhnazarov in an article on "Democratic centralism and political pluralism", *Kommunist*, no. 10, 1979.
26. Shakhnazarov refers to L. Churchward, *Contemporary Soviet Government* and D. Lane's *The Socialist Industrial State*. Professor Churchward is quoted as saying that mass participation in the process of administration in the USSR is something considerably bigger than the participation of the majority of the population in elections in many parliamentary states, and Dr Lane as holding that the absence of private property in the USSR opens greater opportunities for popular participation in political life than in the West.
27. Karl Kautsky, *Demokratie oder Diktatur* (Berlin, 1918).
28. Review of Zarodov's *Sotsializm, mir, revolyutsia*, in *Voprosy filosofii*, no. 3, 1979.
29. Letter from D. Pifis, Greek producer, to *Kommunist*, no. 14, 1978. The preceding issue of the same journal, no. 13, 1978, carried an article by the

Finnish communist, Willi Pessi, in which he referred to his party's rejection of "attempts undertaken under the various slogans of 'Eurocommunism' to toss aside the experience of realised socialism, absolutise national peculiarities, oppose them to the general laws of socialist revolution and oppose the communist movement in capitalist countries to the communist parties of socialist countries".

30. Carrillo, *Eurocomunismo y Estado* (Barcelona, 1977), pp. 167–8, 199, 202.
31. In an interview with Radio Free Europe (!), reproduced in *Encounter*, April 1977.
32. J. Kanapa, in *France Nouvelle*, 18 October 1976.
33. J. Kanapa, in *France Nouvelle*, 4 October 1976.
34. A. Adler, F. Cohen, M. Decaillot, C. Frioux and L. Robet, *L'URSS et Nous* (Paris, 1978). Reviewed by Krasin and others in *Kommunist*, no. 5, 1978.
35. *Le Monde*, 10 May 1979.
36. See H. Timmermann, "Moskau und der europäische Kommunismus nach der Gipfelkonferenz von Ost-Berlin", *Osteuropa*, no. 4, 1977.
37. See C. L. Sulzberger, "NATO vis à vis Eurocommunism", *International Herald Tribune*, 5/6 February 1977.
38. "Communism with an Italian face?" Conversation between Lucio Lombardo Radice and George Urban, in G. Urban (ed.), *Eurocommunism* (London, 1978).
39. The Common Programme of the PSF and PCF in 1972 rejected a French independent deterrent. The PCF changed its mind on this subject in the summer of 1977, and it is one of the many issues on which French communists and socialists are now at odds.
40. Carrillo's suggestion, in *Eurocomunismo y Estado*.

2 The Present State of Eurocommunism: its Main Features, Political and Theoretical*

MANUEL AZCÁRATE

I will deal first with political definition, secondly with historical aspects, thirdly with some theoretical questions and fourthly with international aspects of the subject.

What, then, is Eurocommunism? It is in my opinion a new current in the communist movement and in Marxist thinking. In a period when there is no more monolithism in the communist movement, when there are other currents, in China for instance, Eurocommunism is one such current. It is not only a current of ideas, but already a political force in Europe exercising a certain influence on the destinies of the Western parts of our continent. Secondly, it is a new strategy for the transformation of society and a new conception of what socialist society can be and should be in advanced industrialised countries. The essential points of Eurocommunism could be summed up as follows: capitalist society should be transformed into socialist society with full respect for political freedoms, human rights, trade union freedom, religious and cultural freedom. . . . Moreover, this change should be made through universal suffrage, which means obviously that if a coalition government in favour of socialism is defeated in elections, it must resign. Indeed this seems to me a quite probable eventuality; it is very likely that there will be difficulties and that such a coalition in favour of socialism will make mistakes. The

*A lecture delivered at St Antony's College, Oxford, on 22 May 1978.

socialist state which we favour will have no official ideology. It is a pluralistic conception including the idea that different parties will take part in the advance towards socialism. In Spanish conditions, for instance, such an advance, without the collaboration of communists, socialists and groups or sectors of Christian inspiration, is in my opinion inconceivable. This plurality will continue in socialist society where there will be free play of parties and a free contest of ideologies.

The economic transformation we envisage will be based on the coexistence of a public sector and a sector of private enterprise consisting mainly of small and medium-sized enterprises. This is not a tactical attitude for electoral purposes, because these small and medium-size enterprises are economically necessary to satisfy the needs of the population; without these sectors of private enterprise, certain products and services necessary for life could not be efficiently produced and therefore the standard of living would fall. That is why we favour this coexistence. But the socialist transformation would put an end to the domination of the economy by a small oligarchy controlling the banking and financial systems. Thus we conceive socialism as the enlargement and development of democracy, bringing democracy into the field, not only of politics, but of social and economic life. We believe that this type of socialism will allow the citizens much more real participation in the enterprises where they work, in the districts where they live, in the town and in the affairs of the country through elections and parliament.

One must surely admit that the capitalist system does not guarantee the stability of democracy, and not only because the system has in quite a number of cases promoted fascist forms of terrorist oppression of the people. One could say that these are exceptional; but in fact there is a tendency in monopoly capitalism today to centralise, to increase the powers of the high bureaucracy and the executive organs of government, to diminish the powers of elected bodies. Our conception aims at a society in which democracy will be more effective, the state will be more decentralised and in which together with forms of representative democracy, elections, parliament, etc., there will develop forms of direct democracy in the enterprise, in the educational system, in the health system and in others, so that every day the citizen can participate more and more in decisions which influence his own life. We aim for what might be called a self-managed life, and we look for forms of self-management.

The question arises whether Eurocommunism exists or not. Even some members of very important Eurocommunist parties, like Amendola, have said that Eurocommunism does not exist, and that all that exists is the national phenomenon, that is the position of the Spanish Communist Party, the Italian, the French, but that there is no Eurocommunism as such. Now the French, Italian, Japanese or Spanish political situations are very different; and it would be a mistake to think that Eurocommunism means that all the Eurocommunist parties have the same policy. They are different not only because their situations are different, but also ideologically. Nevertheless there is a common phenomenon, and a new phenomenon, and if there is a new phenomenon it should have a new name. This general phenomenon is that in these parties, and in some others, there has been a profound change from a dogmatic conception of socialist revolution, based on the idea that the Russian example must be followed, that only violent revolution is possible, and that the dictatorship of the proletariat is the only possible form of state; a change towards the ideas I have expressed above. There are thus both differences and common ideas in the principal parties of Western Europe and also in Japan, because it too is a highly developed industrial country with a communist party which has roots in society.

I will now pass on to some historical aspects of the subject. Where does Eurocommunism come from and why has it appeared? It is not realistic to present Eurocommunism as if communist party leaders all of a sudden discovered the virtues of democracy. Let us recall briefly the historical reason for the foundation of the Communist Party. In the First World War the international links that existed between the parties that belonged to the Socialist International were broken. Then in Russia the Bolsheviks led by Lenin realised the first revolution to destroy the capitalist system in any country. This example had a very strong influence on some socialists, anarchists, trade unions and groups of revolutionaries in Europe of that period. But it is important to stress that the Russian revolution was not the only one to occur after the First World War. There was a revolution in Germany. The Kaiser was defeated and the Social Democratic Party of Germany took power and crushed the Spartakist insurrection. In that period in Germany, and especially with the ideas of Rosa Luxemburg, there was a possibility of another sort of socialist revolution not of the Soviet type; but this was crushed by the socialist party in Germany, which preferred to build the Weimar Republic with all the tragic consequences that we know of. All the conflicts in that period helped to polarise the most radical sectors of the Labour movement, and of the youth and so forth, round the Russian example. In itself the Russian example could not be useful for a socialist transformation in the West, because it was based on very exceptional conditions in a backward country. Very soon, Stalinist degeneration turned the Communist International and the communist parties into sectarian bodies in which truth came only from above, in which Moscow was a sort of Mecca, in which there was monolithic discipline and in which Marxist theory was transformed into dogma, losing its essential character as scientific method. This process was facilitated and accelerated by the objective situation, in which the Soviet Union was surrounded by capitalist countries which intervened at first militarily, and later economically. This Stalinist degeneration was increased by this mentality of a besieged fortress. Nevertheless, almost from the beginning, contradictions appeared between the interests of an anti-capitalist policy in the West and the directives and dogmas of the Communist International centralised under the leadership of Stalin. We cannot now go into the history of this contradiction but one name, that of Gramsci, may be mentioned as an example of a theoretical development, inside this process, but with a much more advanced approach from a Marxist point of view to the realities of Western Europe.

Further, Soviet foreign policy interests *vis-à-vis* the menace of Hitler obviously lay behind the policy of the Popular Front. But there was also strong pressure from the workers and popular masses for anti-fascist unity, and in that period some communist parties were able to express and to a certain extent to become champions of this mass pressure. It was an interesting time in the history of the Communist International and I will allow myself a brief digression on this point in connection with the lecture given by the Foreign Secretary of Great Britain in November 1977 in Cambridge. I think it is important to have a serious debate on these matters among people with a general interest in history, among communists, socialists, and others; but a serious debate needs to avoid over-simplification of history, and all the more falsification of it. Dr David Owen presented the policy of the Popular Front in the following terms:

> We have instead to ask ourselves what the attitude of these Communist Parties really is to democracy and to the ballot box. At the Seventh Congress of the Comintern in 1935, Georgi Dimitrov, the Secretary General, said in launching a popular front policy: "Comrades, you will remember the ancient tale of the capture of Troy. . . . We, revolutionary workers, should not be shy of using the same tactics." [Now Dr Owen continues] "Is Communism in Europe a latter-day Trojan Horse for dictatorship and totalitarianism? Or has there been a qualitative change. . ."[1]

Well, I think that in history quotations are a very important matter, and the quotation of Dimitrov (and I am not here to defend Dimitrov) is wrong. In this passage, Dimitrov was referring to the mass organisations which the fascists had in various countries, the Hitler Youth, the "Kraft durch Freude", the Dopolavoro in Italy, and their cooperatives, and trade unions. And it is there that he speaks about the Trojan horse and that he says that "revolutionary workers should not be shy of using the same tactics". But then, where in Dr Owen's text there is a full stop and quotation marks, Dimitrov continues ". . . the same tactic against our Fascist enemies as they use against us".[2] That is to say, the quotation is incorrect. The sentence of Dimitrov was about the problem of tactics *inside* the fascist organisations, the sort of things that we in Spain were obliged to do in the vertical trade unions and so on. It has nothing to do with the problem of democracy or ballot box.

In general, I think that Popular Front policies cannot be understood in such a Manichean form. The interest of the Popular Front policy is that it began to put in question some of the positions that were typical of Stalinism. In Spain there was cooperation in the government between communists, socialists, Catholics and bourgeois parties, which had never happened before in the history of communist parties; and this is an experience in which we still find ideas for the elaboration of our policies today. When we say this, we do not try to hide the errors we committed in this period, for instance in the persecution of Trotskyism and so on. But it is not possible to put it in black and white: it is necessary to examine all the various aspects.

After the Second World War there was again a beginning of original thinking in some communist parties that were in coalition governments on the basis of the struggle against Hitler's occupation of Western Europe. This was cut short by the creation of the Cominform which was created precisely – or at least one of its main aims was – to put an end to this beginning of original thinking. Then, with the XX Congress of the Communist Party of the Soviet Union, came the end of the myth, and from then on some communist parties began to think for themselves and to differ, on certain issues, from the Soviet communist party. Soon we in Spain saw not only the insufficiency, but I would say the falsehood of the thesis of the "cult of personality". It was soon very clear (I think Togliatti was the first to stress it) that the problem was not the "cult of personality" but that the whole political system of the Soviet Union was an authoritarian system, anti-democratic and despotic, in which power was in the hands of a very small nucleus of persons who used repression as a fundamental way of keeping power. The basis of Stalinism is the cult of the state as an apparatus of bureaucratic repression of the population. This realisation led to the process of self-criticism, very dissimilar in different parties, and to the elaboration of new ideas.

If the question is put, "what is the point of departure of Eurocommunism?" I would give the year 1968. In 1968 we have the convergence of at least three factors. First, the Paris May, which up to a point put an end to the illusion of a "neo-capitalism" capable of solving the contradictions of capitalism. It marked the appearance of new revolutionary factors in Western society and the need for fresh Marxist thinking on these problems which the Communist Party had until then not been able to understand or even recognise. Secondly, there was the Prague spring which meant looking for a new relationship between socialism and democracy. This experience was watched with enthusiasm, for instance, by us and other communists in the West. The third factor was the Soviet invasion which put in a very acute form the need for the independence of communist parties from the Soviet Union, and for the condemnation of a major political act of the Soviet Union. It was, of course, a great shock for a large number of communists, but in spite of the tragedy for the Czechoslovak people, it also helped them to overcome the deeply rooted attitude of apologetic admiration for the Soviet Union.

This was the origin of the rejection of the Soviet model, of critical study of the Soviet experience, and of the central idea that communist parties in the West must present another draft, another proposal of socialism, and not the socialism which exists in the Soviet Union. It is important to note that this change was not made by some theoreticians or some party leaders; it was a change in the minds of thousands and thousands of people who had been deeply influenced by the first period in which the Soviet model was considered as the only example to follow. Eurocommunism is really a process in which people are participating in very large numbers and in different degrees in various countries. For instance, in the preparation of the IX Congress of our party in Madrid, many tens of thousands of persons participated in discussion, voted, and so on. It is a real change of attitude in which a very large number of people participated.

We may now turn from historical to some theoretical issues. The question is sometimes put whether Eurocommunism is a return to Social Democracy. Even President Brandt, commenting on Eurocommunism, asked why they do not change their name, and call themselves socialists? Is it a return to Social Democracy? In our opinion this is a matter of substance, because for nearly a hundred years Socialist and Social Democratic parties have been in government, sometimes for long periods, in most of the countries of Western Europe, and in no case has the capitalist system been changed; and in no case has a socialist society been created. The attitude of Eurocommunists is that we do not want to go on like this. We consider that we are a real alternative to this attitude of Social Democracy, which means, in effect, administering capitalist society. The old communism, if I may be allowed the term, was an ideological alternative, not a real alternative; but we think that Eurocommunism is a real alternative for the present situation. Especially we believe that in Eurocommunism there is an answer to some new problems that did not exist when the European labour movement was divided after the First World War. We believe that Eurocommunism can offer a way to overcome the division of 1919 and to create a common pluralism in which everyone will keep his own personality, in which we can move together towards a democratic and socialist transformation in Western Europe.

Among these new problems which did not exist and which are fundamentally important to Eurocommunism, I will stress three. First of all, the relationship of socialism and democracy is objectively different today from what it was in other periods. There have been changes in the social structure of society. The number of wage earners today represents the great majority of the population in industrialised countries. There is also a qualitative change in the role of technicians, scientists, professionals and intellectuals. They now tend to live on wages, and they come into contradiction with monopoly capital not only economically (though that contradiction exists), but also by virtue of their creative work. That is why they tend to become today one of the active forces, together with the working class, of the advance to socialism. Therefore in the Spanish Communist Party we believe that the strategic alliance for the advance towards socialism is no longer what Lenin defined as an alliance of workers and peasants; it is what we call *the alliance of the forces of labour and culture*, which includes, basically, the workers, peasantry and the technical, professional and scientific intellectuals. Moreover, small and medium-sized enterprises now also come into contradiction with the domination of monopoly capital. Even executives in enterprises, and in the public sector of economy, develop attitudes which do not coincide with that of the oligarchy of owners, which has the supreme control of the economy. From this we conclude that the possibility of a very big majority in favour of a socialist alternative has increased considerably.

Nor is the content of socialist transformation the same today as it was. The development of the productive forces has raised new problems which capitalism cannot solve. So the advance towards socialism today means not only to put an end to the system of capitalist exploitation but to solve such problems as the liberation of women, and to achieve a real equality for women in work, culture, social life, the family, sexual life. It must solve the problem of a new place for culture and education in society. So too with the problems of ecology and town planning. In a word, new social needs have been generated, and on the basis of these new social needs new mass movements, together with the working-class movements, now also have a socialist vocation. In that sense, one may say that socialism becomes an objective need for the great majority of the population. From this we may also conclude that in conditions of democracy it will be possible to convince people, that is, to create large zones of ideological hegemony for socialist solutions.

The second problem is the problem of the state. We Eurocommunists are subjected to criticism on this score, especially by Mandel and others. Their idea is, more or less, that a democratic advance will always be destroyed by the state apparatus. However, to understand this problem fully it is worth seeing if there is not an important difference between the theory of the state in Marx and in Lenin. Of course there are common aspects, the idea that the state is a dominating apparatus, what Harold Laski, whose disciple I was in my youth in London, called the supreme coercive power. Lenin saw *only* this aspect of the state; but in Marx, and Gramsci, there is a much more complete theory of the state which takes account of its necessary mediating role in society. Lenin's conception leads to the strategy of destroying the state apparatus and creating a new power outside it: this is the theory of dual power; destroying one apparatus and establishing a new apparatus. But Eurocommunism has to face a different reality. The state of today is not the same; it is involved in economic life, it has inside it thousands and thousands of civil servants who are technicians, scientists and workers who tend to create their own trade union organisation. Even the problem of the army must be reconsidered; we should see in what sense scientific attitudes increase their role in the army, and what are its new relations with the rest of society. By this we do not mean to deny the danger for democracy of an instrument of violence based on discipline. But in order to take account of these new tendencies, and to understand this new reality, we think that Lenin's theory is not useful; we must go back to Marx and to Gramsci. If we study them we come straight to the possibility of transforming the state, of democratising the state, and of conceiving the struggle for socialism outside and inside the state. In this conception the advance to socialism will go together with efforts to give a decisive role to the most democratic part of the state, to democratically elected bodies, to the defence of liberties and to the decentralisation of the state.

My third point is the problem of the party. We in Spain are seeing many changes in the Communist Party. First, we have emerged from a long period of illegality. This is a historic change for us, because of our 58 years of existence we have had about 50 of illegality (even before the Franco dictatorship, there was Primo de Rivera's dictatorship and a period of reaction under the Republic). So we are really beginning something new. We are trying to create a party of a new type, a mass party, a democratic party, able to convince and therefore be a protagonist in a democratic advance to socialism: a protagonist together with other protagonists. I insist on our pluralistic attitude; and for that we need a profoundly democratic internal party life. We suppressed the cell system a full year before our legalisation. At our last congress, there were big differences of opinion, which were expressed in votes; and the discussion was public. Inside the party there is a diversity of cultural currents. Today we have achieved something which in Spanish conditions is very important; the presence of Christians, of Catholics in the communist party has become something normal and there are well-known Catholic personalities even in the leadership of the party, in the executive committee. I personally am not a Christian, but a Catholic could speak with the same right as I am speaking now in the name of the Communist Party of Spain. We have retained, by the decision of the Congress, democratic centralism in the sense that majority decisions are obligatory for the whole of the party, and that the central organs elected at the congress represent the party and speak in its name. (Sometimes we have the impression that the situation with democratic centralism is a little like that of Monsieur Jourdain in the Molière comedy, who spoke in prose without noticing it: many political parties apply democratic centralism, or even not very democratic centralism, without mentioning it.) There is the problem of fractions. We have decided, again by decision of the Congress, that fractions are not a positive way of developing the struggle of opinions, discussion and democratic life in the party, because fractions personalise the discussion. We admit free discussion in journals and publications, but not fractions, for fractions are the beginning of different parties and that, in our opinion, is not useful for democratic party life. We believe that we are eliminating the remnants of Stalinism. There was an interesting amendment on this point. We had put in the draft that the Spanish Communist Party has eliminated Stalinism, but after the amendment we said that *fundamentally* we have eliminated Stalinism and that we must continue in that way. We are very conscious that you cannot change things immediately. We decided that we are not a Leninist party, and that Leninism is not our theoretical basis. We decided to define our party as Marxist Democratic Revolutionary. We have a great admiration in general for Lenin, just as we have for other revolutionaries like Rosa Luxemburg, Trotsky, Mao, Gramsci and others. But our strategy is different from that of Leninism. Much of Lenin's theory was influenced by his historical situation, and has lost its relevance to the present day. So we say in the theses that we are recovering the democratic and anti-bureaucratic essence of Marxism. The Communist Party of Spain rejects every dogmatic conception of Marxism, since Marxism has a scientific non-dogmatic character. The Spanish Communist Party will make continual efforts to increase its theoretical capacity so as to assimilate the objective changes in society, the new achievements of science and the experiences of revolutionary practice, and absorb in a critical spirit new developments in Marxism.

Let us now consider the role the Communist Party is playing in Spain today. I think there is general agreement that its role is increasing. When the general elections of June 1977 took place, in which we had only 9.5 per cent of the vote, we had just come out of illegality, and still suffered from the severe handicap of those 40 years of anti-communist propaganda which portrayed us as common criminals or something of the sort. I myself campaigned in the peasant province of Leon and I must say that in some villages the thing that most surprised people was that I was a normal human being. This was the first surprise. Next, in the partial elections in the two very important provinces of Asturias and Alicante there were interesting changes. We were the only party which increased its votes: in Asturias we passed from 60,000 to 87,000, while in Alicante we gained 7000. At the same time the socialist party lost; the surprising thing was that although they were in the opposition, they still lost more than half of their votes. Our share of the vote rose to 23 per cent in Asturias and 16 per cent in Alicante. Of course all this is influenced by the fact that there was a very high abstention rate, which complicates the matter: nevertheless it is absolutely clear that the Communist Party increased its vote in absolute terms in a period of very high abstention. The important point is that there were much more normal, free elections, which convincingly demonstrated our strength. The fundamental thing in Spain is to have a policy of democratic concentration, to have a consensus so as to get a constitution on which there will be very broad agreement; and we believe that the Communist Party, on the basis of the ideas outlined in this paper, will contribute to that end.

Finally a brief word about some international problems. We are in favour of European economic and political integration and we think that the question of integrated defence must also be considered. We believe that the democratic left-wing labour movement of Western Europe must unite in order to overcome the Europe that is today under the domination of the big monopolies. We are in favour of a united Western Europe which will be subordinate neither to the Soviet Union nor to the United States but will have good relations with them, will cooperate and have good relations with China and especially with the Third World (which we think will be one of the main problems of future international relations). This united Europe can be an independent factor of world politics and therefore help to overcome the present bipolar situation in which two superpowers decide on many matters and can create very dangerous situations of conflict. In that sense Eurocommunism makes a clear political choice for a Europe beyond the present division into military blocs.

As Eurocommunists we are attacked by the Soviet Union for two reasons: first, for our attitude in foreign policy, which goes against the continued status quo under the hegemony of the superpowers. Secondly, we are attacked because we represent a socialism, or an outline of socialism, which I believe may be worthy of the last decades of the twentieth century. Probably this attack is due to the fact that the ideas of Eurocommunism have an influence that goes beyond Western Europe. We are also attacked by the USA, notably in the declaration of the Carter administration against the possible participation of Eurocommunist parties in government. We believe that this represented something of the old attitude of American imperialism, claiming a sort of right of intervention in European affairs; but it is in the interest of all left-wing and democratic forces not to accept such a situation.

The fact that we are attacked in this way is not surprising; but we feel that there is an increasing interest in Eurocommunism among socialist parties and movements, in the trade union movements, in the Christian world, and in youth organisations. The present period of economic crisis in Europe is not *only* economic; it is also a crisis of politics and ideology. Eurocommunism can be one of the factors of renovation in Western Europe. The resolution of the present crisis cannot be a return to the previous situation. Eurocommunism offers ideas and proposals that can help to open the door to a future system of more liberty and more social justice.

NOTES

1. Dr David Owen, Hugh Anderson Memorial Lecture, Cambridge Union Society, 18 November 1977.
2. Jorge Dimitrov, *Seleccion de trabajos* (Sofia, 1977), p. 108.

3 The PCE's Long Road to Democracy 1954–77*

PAUL PRESTON

On 29 and 30 June 1976, a Conference of Communist and Workers' Parties was held in East Berlin. Although the meeting had been jointly inspired by the Italian Communist Party and the Polish United Workers' Party, the dominant note was struck by the Spaniard Santiago Carrillo. The speech made by the Secretary General of the Partido Comunista de España expressed a commitment to a liberal, pluralist view of socialism and affirmed roundly that Europe's communists were subject to no central authority and followed no international discipline. Much as it caused chagrin to comrades who still recognised the guiding role of Moscow, Carrillo's speech was hardly surprising. He and his party had long been groping towards such positions, with tentative uncertainty in the mid-1960s and with resolute determination after the Russian invasion of Czechoslovakia in 1968. What was extraordinary, in retrospect, was his contemptuous dismissal of the journalistic label "Eurocommunism" for such communist moderation. "The term is most unfortunate", he declared. "There is no such thing as Eurocommunism."[1]

Hindsight made that rejection seem distinctly ironic since, at the time of making it, Carrillo was writing two works which were, in their different ways, to become fundamental texts of the Eurocommunist doctrine. From 1970, the PCE had been involved in a process of "capturing democracy". The return to the surface after more than 30 years of clandestinity was conceived in terms of party

*I would like to acknowledge the assistance of the Central Research Fund of the University of London in the preparation of this paper, an earlier version of which was read to a seminar at St Antony's College, Oxford, on 30 January 1978.

militants, lawyers and workers, acting increasingly as if democratic rights already existed. The consequent challenge to the regime's cosmetic reform schemes was speeded up after the death of Franco on 20 November 1975. Well-known party leaders began to appear in public and long-exiled figures began to return openly to Spain. In February 1976, Carrillo himself entered the country secretly to participate in the transition to democracy and to try to keep the PCE out of the political ghetto to which its enemies hoped to consign it. Forced to spend much time in hiding, he used his enforced idleness to prepare a book, *"Eurocommunism" and the State*, and a long report, *From Clandestinity to Legality*.[2]

That report, read to a plenum of the PCE held publicly in Rome from 28 to 31 July 1976, constituted a direct application to Spain of the ideas and ideals associated with "Eurocommunism". Less theoretical and less universal than the book, the report was a clear statement of how the PCE wished to be seen in Spain: as a party totally independent of Moscow, committed to a pluralistic model of socialist democracy and to peaceful and democratic means of obtaining it, and willing to respect ideological and religious differences and even hostile verdicts of the electorate. By the time he was arrested by the Spanish police on 22 December 1976, Carrillo had changed his mind about allowing these positions to be labelled "Eurocommunist". The journalistic value of such a modern and un-Russian sounding term was not lost on the intensely propaganda-conscious Carrillo.

For nearly 40 years, the Franco regime, with some not inconsiderable help from the Catholic Church and the Western media, had denounced the communists as torturers and assassins at the orders of the Kremlin. If the PCE were to play a role in Spain's new democracy, Carrillo had to convince the world that he and his followers were not simply waiting for the chance to build a Mediterranean Gulag. The publication of his book in the spring of 1977 went a long way towards solving the PCE's credibility problems. The favourable impression that it had created in the bourgeois press was increased a hundredfold when Carrillo and his book became the targets for a series of savage and anonymous articles in the Soviet journal *Novoye Vremya* (*New Times*). It did the PCE's Secretary General no harm at all in Spain for the Russians to accuse him of waging "a determined and crude campaign against the Soviet Union and the CPSU" and of being at the service of "the interests of imperialism and the forces of aggression and reaction".[3]

What particularly infuriated the Russians was Carrillo's open insistence that the success of democratic socialism among the Western communist parties would have a great impact on the Eastern bloc and lead to a number of Prague springs.[4] Carrillo pushed this view in interviews with the press in various European countries and in speeches made at Queen Mary College, University of London, and at Yale University.[5] Russian displeasure was made clear not just in the Soviet press. According to veterans of the Abraham Lincoln Brigade, Americans who fought in the Spanish war, an attempt was made by the fiercely pro-Moscow Communist Party of the USA to frame Carrillo as a strike-breaker.[6] The intensity of the split between Moscow and the PCE made headline news throughout Europe and the USA, and the PCE even published a substantial dossier of newspaper reactions.[7]

By the autumn of 1977, his own "Eurocommunist" pronouncements and the Kremlin's hostility were beginning to roll back the Spanish press's distrust of Carrillo. Just when his image was reaching a peak of popularity, he received what could only seem like a stab in the back. The seeming treachery was the publication in November of the memoirs of Jorge Semprún, recalling his time in the 1950s and early 1960s as organiser of the PCE's clandestine network inside Spain. Semprún was expelled from the party in April 1965 along with PCE's major theorist, Fernando Claudín. Their crime was to have postulated prematurely the positions now associated with Carrillo and "Eurocommunism". A few perceptive readers of *"Eurocommunism" and the State* had already noted that Carrillo's enthusiasm for political and philosophical pluralism was expressed more by repetition of the word "liberty" than by close reasoning. Now Semprún's book argued that the PCE's adoption of "Eurocommunism" was merely tactical and rendered valueless by the continuing existence within the party of basically Stalinist attitudes.

In *Autobiografía de Federico Sánchez* – the name had been his pseudonym in clandestinity – Semprún repeated some of the accusations first made by Claudín in the early 1960s. The most damaging of Claudín's criticisms was that the PCE was out of touch with reality and incapable of flexibility of self-criticism. He claimed that it was characterised by *triunfalismo*, a kind of dogmatic self-congratulation which had confidently predicted the imminent downfall of the Franco dictatorship from the early 1940s and interpreted every labour dispute in Spain as the work of the PCE and the confirmation of the correctness of its line.[8] To a certain extent, it might be argued that the trauma of the expulsion of Claudín and Semprún, and the party's gradual adoption of their ideas, went some way towards remedying the condition of rigid *triunfalismo*. Semprún, however, now went much further. To Claudín's criticisms, he added others.

The charge that the PCE had consistently falsified its history in creating a democratic image and was a servile lackey of the Kremlin had hitherto only been heard on the lips of Francoists. However, even more hurtful to the Spanish communists were a number of accusations that had previously been made by General Enrique Líster, an unrepentant Stalinist who was expelled from the PCE in 1970. These included claims that the PCE was dominated by the personality cult of Carrillo and the suggestion that party dissidents had been disposed of by the simple expedient of denunciation to the police.[9] More dramatic was the insinuation that the death of the PCE's last great martyr, Julián Grimau, executed by the dictatorship on 20 April 1963, had in some way been manipulated by Carrillo.[10]

Such accusations were normally ignored by the communist leadership. However, the repercussions in this case were so enormous that some reaction was called for. Before December was out, *Autobiografía de Federico Sánchez* had sold over 150,000 copies and was the centre of frantic press and media interest. As author of novels such as *Le grand voyage* and *La deuxième mort de Ramón Mercader* and of the scripts for films such as *Z*, *L'Aveu* and *Un état de siège* for Costa Gavras and *La guerre est finie* for Alain Resnais, Semprún was already a major celebrity. More importantly, he was a party hero. The son of a Spanish diplomat exiled in France, he joined the resistance at the age of seventeen in 1940. Captured by the Gestapo in 1943, his linguistic abilities not only helped him to survive Buchenwald but also to organise the communist network within the camp. After the war, he joined the PCE and, as Federico Sánchez, he carried out clandestine work in Spain with panache, courage and intelligence, eventually being co-opted on to the politburo.

Under the circumstances, Semprún's accusations could not be

ignored, although Carrillo himself never admitted to having read the book. After 37 years of persecution in the struggle against the dictatorship, it was understandable that Semprún's attacks should be felt by the PCE to be a blow below the belt. The consequent hurt reaction came over as a rather ham-fisted attempt to ensure that past issues would not tarnish the party's newly won image. At first, a party journalist, Manuel Vázquez Montalbán, stated in the PCE newspaper *Mundo Obrero* that, if the party was really committed to internal democracy, it should come to terms with the accusations made and with its own past mistakes.[11] That intelligent tolerance was quickly swamped by a furious reply from Fernando Soto, communist deputy for Seville, who denounced Semprún's book as "a load of rubbish dumped on the highest peaks of human dignity".[12]

Shortly thereafter bigger guns were brought into action. Manuel Azcárate of the party executive produced a reply to Semprún in a national newspaper.[13] While more diplomatic in tone than Soto's intervention, it proved little more successful in achieving its aim. Indeed, Azcárate's refutation inadvertently went some way to substantiating Semprún's original case. Semprún accused the PCE leadership of being *desmemoriado*, of having blotted out its collective memory. Admitting his own defective recollections and claiming not to have the time necessary to check the documents, Azcárate began by presenting the issues of the 1964 schism so as to imply that Claudín had been proposing collaboration with the dictatorship. He went on to give a controversial account of the democratic procedures which accompanied the Claudín–Semprún expulsions. Finally, he accused Semprún of simply repeating the worst kind of Francoist propaganda. It was not difficult for Semprún to demolish these arguments a few days later.[14] Nor was he seriously challenged by the declarations made on 8 January by the President of the Partit Socialista Unificat de Catalunya, Gregorio López Raimundo. The Catalan Communist leader explained Semprún's motives as

> pure and simple envy. Carrillo is so superior to everyone else. Carrillo's political creativity is beyond any of us. The trouble with Semprún and Claudín is just bad-tempered jealousy of the political, ideological, moral and intellectual superiority of Carrillo. They should be humble and accept reality.[15]

In the short term, the damage done to PCE credibility by the scandal surrounding the Semprún book was considerable. To such an extent, indeed, that Claudín himself and the ex-Claudinista, Javier Pradera, one of the *Autobiografía*'s dedicatees, felt obliged to dissociate themselves from some of its wilder accusations.[16] Among the charges hurled at the PCE in the ensuing media coverage, the one which hit hardest was that Carrillo's "Eurocommunist" positions reflected not democratic conviction but opportunistic tactics. In consequence, Carrillo himself was eventually forced to enter the arena. By comparison with the efforts of Soto and Azcárate, his intervention was masterly. He diverted attention away from the specific accusations of the *Autobiografía* to a wider consideration of the disproportionate damage that they were doing. Justifiably stressing the PCE's paramount role in the struggle for democracy in Spain, he claimed that the press campaign surrounding the book was an orchestrated offensive against "Eurocommunists" in general and ultimately against the new-born Spanish democratic regime.[17] The implication that Semprún was somehow darkly linked with Kissinger and Brezhnev in a global anti-Eurocommunist plot was absurd. None the less, Carrillo's remarks served to put the polemic into a more reasonable perspective.

In fact, the assertion that recriminations about the PCE's internal history unfairly obscured the communists' role in the fight for democracy underscored the ambivalence of the entire polemic. Much of what Semprún said was true but that did not obliterate the PCE's central contribution to the struggle against Franco. The communist defence against accusations of internal authoritarianism is that such things were caused by the clandestinity imposed by the dictatorship. Accordingly, complaints that Semprún's view was a partial one might have been made more effectively with documents rather than with insults. If that did not happen, it was because Carrillo was understandably reticent about certain details of his stewardship of the party. The long battle to win democratic credibility had been won and Carrillo was not overkeen to risk his fragile triumph by disinterring regrettable incidents from the past.[18]

The PCE's enemies would argue that if, as Semprún maintains, "Eurocommunist" positions are not a fundamental aspiration of the entire party but simply a tactic imposed from above, the commitment to a pluralist, democratic socialism is highly suspect. On the other hand, it might well be countered that if, in trying to make his party seem democratic, Carrillo has been forced to give it a democratic structure and objectives, the fact that he used Stalinist methods to do so ultimately does not matter. Moreover, the PCE's reluctance to publicise the more unsavoury elements of its past does not mean that the party is incapable of change. Carrillo has claimed that changes of strategy are in themselves a form of self-criticism.[19] Semprún, however, would argue that such changes were no more than desperate measures to cover the party's failure to make any correct analyses of political and economic development in Spain since the Civil War.

In the view of Semprún, the only real achievement of Carrillo and his entourage is to have survived the consequences of their mistakes. It is possible to contrast this damning vision with Carrillo's own perception of his achievements as party leader because, in his report to the Rome meeting of the Central Committee in 1976, he actually drew up the balance sheet of his leadership.[20] Recognising, without going into details, that mistakes had been made, the Secretary General highlighted the five areas in which he thought his work had had most positive results:

1. to have kept the party alive during the period of clandestinity and to have left it solidly organised for the democratic process;
2. to have increased the party's links with the working class;
3. to have elaborated the programme of national reconciliation and of the unity of democratic forces which effectively forestalled attempts to isolate the PCE;
4. to have won the party's independence from Moscow, to have asserted its right to elaborate its own road to, and model of, socialism and to have been in the front rank of the movement to renovate the world communist movement;
5. to have avoided conflicts between militants in the interior and the exiled leadership and between generations.

Some at least of Carrillo's claims have a basis in fact. For them to be accepted without qualification is, however, rendered difficult by Semprún's accusations and the party's feeble response to them. An assessment of the sincerity or validity of the PCE's "Eurocommunism" requires that Carrillo's public commitment to democracy be balanced against Semprún's allegations of the survival of undemocratic practices within the party. An examination of the process whereby the PCE was democratised suggests, paradoxically, that the debate which led to Semprún's expulsion and which is the source of his bitterness against Carrillo was a significant step on the road to real change for Spanish communism.

The PCE in the 1940s displayed many of the characteristics highlighted by Semprún. Indeed, with the leadership exiled in Moscow and totally dependent on Russian charity, the Spanish communists could hardly be anything other than the most hard-line orthodox Stalinists.[21] An understandable tendency to a mimetic loyalty to the Moscow line was exhibited during and immediately after the period of the Nazi–Soviet pact. Spaniards were at first urged to have nothing to do with a reactionary, imperialist squabble and then suddenly exhorted to join together to stop Franco taking part in the war against the Allies.[22] In a similar fashion, the exiled leadership made desperate attempts to justify its own existence by maintaining the most rigid control over the militants in the interior. Even the most heroic party members were likely to be accused of being agents of the Gestapo if their line was too independent.[23]

Mimesis of the Russians perhaps reached its height when PCE members who returned from German concentration camps were not treated as heroes, as was the case with their French and Italian comrades, but interrogated and then kept away from positions of responsibility in a kind of political quarantine.[24] Further evidence of a slavish dependence on the Kremlin was revealed in the PCE's response to the Soviet attack on Tito. Carrillo himself has claimed that the Spaniards acted "like a herd of sheep" in mounting the most vituperative attacks on the Yugoslavs and in seeking sacrificial victims, in the form of Catalanists, within the PCE.[25]

It is ironic that the PCE was set on the long road to independence of Moscow by Stalin himself. From 1944, the centrepiece of PCE policy inside Spain was a guerrilla war against the dictatorship inspired by hopes of restoring the defeated Republic. By 1948, however, the guerrilla groups were increasingly on the defensive in their isolated struggle against the police, the Civil Guard and the Army. Their immediate objective had been to prepare a national uprising to coincide with Allied intervention against France. With the intensification of the Cold War, not only was that clearly not going to take place but Stalin was loath to risk an international incident over communist activity in Spain. Accordingly, in September 1948, the PCE leadership was advised by Stalin to withdraw the guerrilleros and to begin a long-term policy of infiltration into legal *sindicatos* and other organisations within Spain.[26] A corollary of the abandonment of violence was a heightened commitment to the view that the dictatorship could only be overthrown by a broad alliance of opposition forces. With the rest of the Spanish democratic forces widely influenced by the Cold War atmosphere and smouldering resentment of PCE high-handedness during the Civil War, the creation of a wide front obliged the Communists to show credible moderation. And that was to involve a degree of de-Stalinisation.

After the death of Stalin in March 1953, a slow and grudging effort was made to liberalise. Within 18 months, the party held its V Congress in Prague. The proceedings there revealed a willingness to change but also indicated how painfully gradual de-Stalinisation was likely to be. The PCE Secretary General, Dolores Ibárruri, presented a long report whose main theme was the need for democratic unity against the Francoist clique. There were several aspects of it that were unlikely to seduce the socialists, republicans and anarchists with whom unity was proposed. Not only did she accuse them of responsibility for Franco's victory in 1939 but she also implied that they were lackeys of American imperialism. A previous attempt at unity, the Alianza Nacional de Fuerzas Democráticas, sponsored by them in 1944, was declared to be a police montage.[27] Language reminiscent of the Stalinist purges was used to denounce 'degenerate' elements within the PCE itself. Like the victims of the Rajk and Slansky trials, they were accused of contact with Noel Field. If such references preoccupied socialists, republicans and anarchists, their effect was hardly minimised by reiterated admiration for Eastern bloc countries and declarations of intent to follow the example of the CPSU.[28]

La Pasionaria's report scarcely concealed the conviction that the leaderships of the other left-wing groups could be by-passed and their rank-and-file members simply absorbed into the PCE.[29] On the other hand, by comparison with the virulent sectarianism which had characterised the communist attitude to socialists and anarchists since the departure of the PCE from the republican government-in-exile in August 1947, Dolores Ibárruri's language represented a significant effort at moderation. Indeed, she spoke at length of the need to eliminate sectarian attitudes within the party. However, her tentative steps towards liberalisation were surpassed by those of the PCE's organisation secretary, Santiago Carrillo.

As organisation secretary, Carrillo was a powerful figure in the party hierarchy, with responsibility for the interior apparatus. His spectacular rise to prominence in the PCE between 1936 and 1944, and his career thereafter, had been marked by strict adherence to Moscow. However, by 1954, influenced by his links with cadres inside Spain, he had come to feel that the PCE's operational centre in Paris, directed by Vicente Uribe, was rigidly Stalinist and out of touch with the interior. The Civil War leadership of the PCE – La Pasionaria, Uribe, Antonio Mije and Enrique Líster – tended to think in terms of a wide front of democratic forces to re-establish the Republic. Carrillo felt that the PCE should cast its net even wider in search of allies against Franco and should come to terms with the fact that there could be no return to 1936. He had allies on the politburo, in the persons of Ignacio Gallego and Fernando Claudín, but they were of secondary status by comparison with Uribe, Mije and Líster. Carrillo was thus faced with a delicate problem. Dolores Ibárruri, resident in Moscow, was the grand arbiter and was likely to favour the old guard. Accordingly, Carrillo's report to the V Congress, on party statutes and internal organisation, was cautious and technical. Nevertheless, it did imply a call for a renovation of party structures. In consequence, cadres from the underground, including Jorge Semprún and Simón Sánchez Montero, were incorporated into the central committee, although not into the politburo.[30] The party would continue to be ruled by the politburo, but Carrillo's reforms were not entirely superficial. The extension of the central committee not only implied an intention to democratise the inner workings of the PCE but also strengthened Carrillo's position in the latest power struggle.

A show-down was to come within 12 months; probably sooner than Carrillo had anticipated. Towards the end of 1955, with the bulk of the party leadership in Bucharest for La Pasionaria's 60th birthday celebrations, the Paris operational centre was being run by Carrillo, Claudín and Gallego. News came in that the United

Nations, including the Soviet Union, had voted in favour of the entry of 16 new members, including Spain. The reaction of the PCE's Paris group was positive. Apart from the fact that the Russian vote had secured the addition of Hungary, Bulgaria, Rumania and Albania to the UNO, Spain's inclusion was seen as more than a tit-for-tat and as part of the post-Stalin quest for peaceful coexistence. An inevitable recognition of the reality of the Franco regime's stability, it was a gesture to the West. In addition, there was a feeling among the PCE's "young lions" that the end of international isolation would favour the spread of democratic ideas in Spain by increasing cultural, commercial and political relations with democratic countries. This impression was confirmed by Jorge Semprún who returned from a mission in the interior to report on growing anti-regime feeling among university students, dissident Falangists and Catholics.[31]

Carrillo quickly produced a lengthy and enthusiastic article on the UNO vote. Hailing it as a victory for the USSR's peaceful policy, he went on to point out that it prevented the Francoists depicting their international isolation as the result of a communist conspiracy. Carrillo hoped that it would lead to the Spanish bourgeoisie moving on from the false dilemma "Francoism or communism" to the true one "Francoism or democracy".[32] This positive view was not shared by the old guard in the politburo. Without criticising the Soviet Union, they issued a savage denunciation of the UNO admission of Francoist Spain, which was broadcast over the party's transmitter, Radio España Independiente. Their affront at the betrayal of "republican legality" revealed a rigid exile mentality in contrast to the notably more flexible and realistic stance of the younger group. But it had not been Carrillo's intention to provoke a conflict. Only when it turned out to be impossible to retrieve his text from the printers did he take up the cudgels in earnest.

Jorge Semprún was sent to Bucharest to put the Paris group's case. Uribe and Líster, who received him, were shocked at the potential rebellion, especially when Semprún cited his experiences as Federico Sánchez to criticise the rigidity and irrelevance of party policies. When it was finally possible to speak to La Pasionaria, Semprún found her ready to listen, but hostile. Anxious not to precipitate a major split in the party, she said that she would consider his views. Plans were then made to divide the Paris group. Claudín was included, with Uribe, Mije, Líster and Pasionaria, in the PCE delegation to the XX Congress of the CPSU in February 1956. The intention was to "recuperate" him prior to denouncing Carrillo for social democratic reformism and opportunism. Claudín had, however, agreed with Carrillo that they would both go down in the fight to renovate the party. In the intervals of the sessions of the Moscow Congress, Claudín resisted the blandishments of the old guard and forcefully put to Dolores Ibárruri his group's views on the poor showing of the PCE in the interior. At first, she sided with Uribe and things looked bleak for the liberalisers. Then suddenly, having had a preview of Khrushchev's secret report denouncing Stalinism, she decided that the views of Claudín and Carrillo were in line with the new currents of liberalism emanating from the Kremlin. Carrillo was sent for. Mije and Líster saw what was happening and Uribe was isolated. Shortly afterwards, he was replaced as director of the Paris centre by Carrillo, who was now virtually acting secretary general.[33] Thus, in both the provocation and the resolution of the conflict, the de-Stalinisers found their aspirations paralleled by those of the Russian leadership.

In fact, Carrillo was delighted by the policies of Khrushchev, apparently coinciding as they did with his own desires to renovate the PCE. The revelations of the XX Congress were satisfactory evidence for him that the USSR was on the road to democratisation. For Claudín, they were profoundly disturbing and set him off on a long intellectual pilgrimage to understand the way the socialist ideal had been deformed by the Stalinist experience. The events in Hungary in October 1956 were to exacerbate Claudín's doubts even further while Carrillo and the rest of the leadership were confident that Khrushchev was in the right.[34] These divergences were eventually to lead to the traumatic crisis within the PCE in 1964. In the meanwhile, however, Carrillo was pressing home his victory over the Stalinists.

The first fruit of the newly won flexibility in the politburo was the elaboration of the policy of national reconciliation. Free of the Stalinist stranglehold, it was now possible to meet the demands of the interior for efforts to find common ground with the new opposition to Franco emerging among students and Catholics. After lengthy discussions during the spring of 1956, the PCE issued a major declaration in favour of burying the wartime hatreds fostered by the dictatorship. The new policy not only expressed communist readiness to join with monarchists and Catholics in a future parliamentary regime but also indicated a commitment to peaceful change.[35] In August, a plenum of the central committee was held near Berlin to ratify the new policy. It was to witness a dramatic extension of the process of liberalisation tentatively begun at the PCE's V Congress.

The two principal reports were presented by Dolores Ibárruri and Santiago Carrillo. They both reflected a desire to emulate the example of the CPSU, a further indication of the influence of Moscow over the PCE's democratisation. Nevertheless, the two reports also heralded important changes in the party's methods. La Pasionaria paid tribute to the CPSU for its courage in publicly recognising its errors and for pointing the way to different roads to socialism. She went on to speak of the need for alliances with conservative and liberal forces in Spain in order to secure a pacific transition to democracy.[36] This clearly represented a new departure from past sectarianism but it was mild by comparison with what Carrillo had to say. His report was an intensely critical survey of the defects of the party leadership. Pungent and lucid, it indicated his resolve to complete the process begun in 1954. He began by denouncing the cult of personality in the PCE, albeit absolving Dolores Ibárruri of complicity therein. He criticised the exiled leadership for subjectivism, sectarianism and isolation from the realities of the interior. And when he spoke of the narrow authoritarianism of the politburo, he specifically blamed Uribe for being an obstacle to collective leadership and self-criticism. Both Uribe and Mije were to be sacrificial victims, making public confessions of their errors to the plenum. The two main reports were unanimously approved by the central committee. The autocritiques and the unanimity may have suggested that little had changed. Similarly, the leadership's renewed commitment to the rules of democratic centralism was somewhat devalued by the fact that central committee members were still co-opted by the politburo. Nevertheless, the airing of a critical spirit and the expanded membership of the politburo and central committee promised, in theory at least, steady progress towards democratisation. This was particularly true of the move to incorporate leaders working in the interior, such as Semprún, Simón Sánchez Montero and Francisco Romero Marín, into the politburo.[37]

Perhaps surprisingly, 1956 was to be the apogee of Carrillo's efforts to liberalise the party until the events of 1968 provoked a further surge of democratisation. It would be wrong to underestimate the changes which took place between 1954 and 1956. By comparison with other opposition forces, and in particular with the socialists and anarchists, the PCE was relatively strong, united and with meaningful links between the interior and the exiled leadership. However, the hard-won flexibility of 1954 and 1956 was soon somewhat stultified by the party's rigid reaction to the fact that the national reconciliation policy did not achieve the immediate overthrow of the dictatorship. The PCE had always been blessed by a generous component of subjective optimism. This was especially true of Carrillo; indeed, it was one of his greatest strengths. When it became apparent that the dictatorship was not tottering before a nationwide opposition, the PCE leadership reacted by intensified optimism and hostility to cadres with the temerity to point out the unreality of the party line.

Carrillo owed his rise to the party to, among other things, his capacity for hard work and his strength of personality. After 1956, he began to concentrate power in his hands in an unprecedented way. The job of organisation secretary passed to Eduardo García, an unquestioningly loyal cipher, and the powers of the position effectively remained in Carrillo's hands. Between 1956 and 1964, the central committee only once opposed Carrillo's wishes and even then it was to deny him permission to risk his person on a clandestine mission to Spain.[38] The enormous amount of work of an organisational kind undertaken by Carrillo left him with little time to study the real situation in Spain. Members of the central committee tended to produce reports which conformed to the party line rather than to concrete reality. The conditions of clandestinity exacerbated this problem in the interior. PCE agents entered Spain with instructions from the Paris centre and handed them on to their contacts on a kind of chain basis. Inevitably, the creativity of the rank-and-file was stifled by the simple transmission of abstract orientations or slogans. Reports from cells in the interior tended to be efforts to prove the validity of the party line.[39]

The problem was highlighted by the practical application of the policy of national reconciliation. In 1957, as a response to the harsh conditions created by the government's stabilisation plan, there was a series of strikes in northern Spain. The Communists were blinded by their own optimism, hailing the strikes as the fruit of their new policy. Simón Sánchez Montero reported to a plenum of the central committee in May 1957 that the strikes were "a plebiscite against the dictatorship, living examples of national reconciliation among Spaniards and demonstrations of the real possibility of the pacific overthrow of the dictatorship".[40] Accordingly, a day of national reconciliation was called for 5 May 1958. Its effects were minimal yet Carrillo, who was the prime mover behind the idea, declared it a successful rehearsal for a great national movement against the dictatorship.[41] Such a movement, denominated the "national pacific strike", was thus planned for 18 June 1959. Within Spain, it was organised by Sánchez Montero, Romero Marín and Semprún. Claudín and Ignacio Gallego made clandestine visits to take part in the preparations. They all had some fears that the overthrow of the regime was not as imminent as the PCE regularly declared. However, Carrillo was determined that the strike should go ahead, despite a number of letters opposing the idea from Dolores Ibárruri in Moscow. In the event, the Huelga Nacional Pacífica was a failure. With unemployment increasing and workers unready to risk their jobs, that was hardly surprising.[42] What was more unexpected was the way in which Carrillo asserted his authority and ensured that the PCE accepted that the strike had been a success. He put his case to a meeting of party leaders held at the end of July 1959 at Uspenskoie, near Moscow. Only Claudín opposed his interpretation of the strike. The shock of the meeting was Dolores Ibárruri's announcement of her resignation as Secretary General. It is probable that, faced with the strength of Carrillo's position, she decided to put an end to a false situation in which she was Secretary General in name only.[43]

The failure of the Huelga Nacional Pacífica and Carrillo's suppression of the failure were to have far-reaching consequences within the PCE. Both Fernando Claudín and Jorge Semprún had started to reflect on the inadequacies of the party's analysis of the social and political development as the key to the inefficacy of the official line. When faced with a mendacious interpretation of the débâcle upheld by all Carrillo's considerable authority, they were impelled to a wide-ranging examination of the question of internal democracy in the PCE. The consequences of their reflections were not to hit the party for another four years. In the meanwhile,

Carrillo remained fully committed to the idea of a national general strike and reacted to the failure of 1959 with organisational measures aimed at ensuring success next time. Changes aimed at giving the PCE interior apparatus more flexibility were introduced at the VI Congress, held from 28 to 31 January 1960, in Prague.

The VI Congress saw Carrillo formally confirmed as Secretary General and Dolores Ibárruri "elevated" to the newly created post of party President. As part of the modernisation of the party, the politburo was converted into the executive committee and its membership expanded to 15. The central committee was also increased in size. This formal democratisation was countered by the creation of a five-man party secretariat. Consisting of the Secretary General, Fernando Claudín, Ignacio Gallego, Antonio Mije and Eduardo García – the last three being unconditional Carrillo supporters – the secretariat was considerably narrower than the politburo had been.

Given Carrillo's commitment to the idea, the Huelga Nacional Pacífica was confirmed by the Congress as the party strategy to overthrow Franco. However, changes were to be made to ensure its success. Implicitly the failure of the 1959 strike was admitted but attributed to organisational deficiencies. Semprún, as Federico Sánchez, delivered what was tacitly an inquest on the 1959 disaster. Highlighting the rigidities of the clandestine cell structure, he called for wider recruitment and a more democratic committee structure. The Congress recognised that the policies of reconciliation and the national strike would involve opening up the PCE to the middle and professional classes. To make possible the transition from a party of cadres to a mass party, PCE statutes were modified to admit looser conditions of membership and a decision was made to intensify recruiting efforts.[44]

Reconciliación Nacional, the Huelga Nacional Pacífica and the partido de masas were substantially correct, but somewhat premature, concepts which were only finally to come to fruition between 1975 and 1977. Not only did they put the PCE firmly in the vanguard of the anti-Franco struggle, but they also constituted irreversible steps towards the opening up of the party. In the short term, however, discrepancies were emerging between rhetorical liberalisation and the real lack of internal democracy. The noisiest manifestations of dissidence came from a number of pro-Chinese ultra-leftist groups which denounced Carrillo as a bourgeois revisionist. If anything, they wished to turn the clock back on the organisational and tactical reforms made in the PCE since 1954.[45] These "Marxist–Leninist" fractions deprived the party of some revolutionary students but probably contributed to the PCE's growing image as a serious and moderate party. Far more serious were the divergences which were to lead to the expulsion of Claudín and Semprún.

The PCE's optimistic view that the end of the dictatorship was nigh was based on the assumption that a narrow Francoist clique ruled over a backward agrarian economy on the point of social explosion. That view was plausible given the appalling social conditions in Spain in the early 1960s. Claudín and Semprún, however, saw signs that a major process of industrialisation was starting and began to call for a readjustment of the party's analyses on the basis of that changing reality. The distance between their convictions and the official line was starkly revealed in 1962. A series of strikes in northern Spain in the spring resulted in significant wage increases. Carrillo hailed this as the confirmation of the correctness of the Huelga Nacional Pacífica policy. He thereby failed to see that the strikes were essentially economic in motivation and that the apparent capitulation of the industrialists reflected their desire not to have production disrupted during an incipient boom. Far from examining the changing situation, executive committee members sought to defend the existing party line. Claudín and Semprún, on the other hand, argued between 1962 and 1964 that changes were taking place in Spanish capitalism which would alter the nature of working class discontent and ultimately of the regime itself.

Carrillo was hostile to their position in part because he did not take kindly to criticism under any circumstances and also because, if they were right, it meant that the policy of national reconciliation would be a long time in maturing. With economic development on the horizon, the bourgeoisie was hardly likely to join with the PCE against Franco. As Claudín implied, and events were to show, the party's policy would become relevant only at the point when a new burgeoning industrial bourgeoisie found the political mechanisms of Francoism to be a hindrance to their prosperity. Accordingly, Carrillo used his control of the party apparatus, rather than intellectual arguments, to defeat criticism. After airing the polemic at an executive meeting in March 1964, it was agreed that Claudín and Semprún should be suspended from the executive until all the documents in the case had been put before the central committee. Without doing this, Carrillo circularised party leaders inside Spain with a highly tendentious account of the debate which accused Claudín and Semprún of fractionalism. Then, on 19 April 1964, Carrillo made an emotionally charged speech to party militants in Paris which revealed that attempts were being made to split the party. He did not mention Semprún and Claudín by name, although that job was apparently done by party cadres planted in the crowd. Effectively excluded from the party, Claudín prepared a lengthy statement of his position in the hope of re-opening the debate. It was delivered to the executive in December 1964. In January, the PCE journal *Nuestra Bandera* reprinted Claudín's text with a tendentious commentary (in much larger print) under the heading "Document – Fractional Platform of Fernando Claudín". The debate never took place. Letters were received from inside Spain supporting the party. In April 1965, Claudín and Semprún read in *Mundo Obrero* that they had been expelled.[46]

The Claudín schism revealed the extent to which Carrillo was skilled in the Stalinist arts of party manipulation. Francesc Vicens, the Catalan Communist leader who was expelled for siding with them, claimed that, given Carrillo's grip on the party, it was tactical lunacy for Claudín to have raised the issue at executive committee level. In his view, the tactic which should have been applied was for Claudín and Semprún to persuade Carrillo privately that the official line was in error and that he should push the new orientation as his own. That would hardly have favoured the creation of a more flexible and democratic structure which was partly the point of the exercise. Nevertheless, it seemed to be more in sorrow for their tactical naivety than in anger that Dolores Ibárruri referred to Claudín and Semprún at the April 1964 meeting as "cabezas de chorlito" (bird brains).[47]

Events, and indeed Carrillo's later policies, have suggested that Claudín's analysis of Spanish capitalism was correct. Yet there is a more positive way to interpret Carrillo's behaviour. Claudín and Semprún were expelled as right-wing defeatists partly because their views implied that the Franco regime could well last another 25 years. Gregorio López Raimundo pointed out, at the time of the polemic over *Autobiografía de Federico Sánchez*, that the adoption of such an objectively pessimistic view could have had gravely depressing effects among militants who had already suffered 25 years of Francoism. Indeed, in the letters sent to the party in 1964, admittedly in response to a deformed version of Claudín's theses, there were clear implications that only big doses of subjective optimism made it possible to keep up the long, depressing and uneven struggle with the dictatorship.[48] Viewed in such a context, it is arguable that Carrillo used his control of the party apparatus to ensure that the new line could be imposed gradually without risk of damaging divisions. Even that, however, could not justify the methods used by Carrillo to suppress the ideas elaborated by Claudín and Semprún.

Indeed, it was revulsion against those methods which led them to ignore advice being given them by friends inside the Italian Communist Party to remain inside the PCE by means of a judicious auto-critique. Giancarlo Pajetta and Rossana Rossanda tried to persuade them to fight for their ideas from within. The Italians were convinced that the Claudín/Semprún theses coincided with a new current within the Communist movement. In fact, Semprún had already prepared a report on the situation in the PCE for Togliatti, at the request of Rossana Rossanda. And while Claudín and Semprún were being execrated in the PCE during the summer of 1964, Togliatti was preparing his testament which, in its recognition of the growing strength of European capitalism and its call for communism to adopt peaceful, independent roads to socialism, tended to coincide with their views.[49]

Whether Carrillo was more influenced in the later 1960s by the strength of Claudín's arguments or the moral authority of Togliatti's *Promemoria* is not clear. The fact remains, nevertheless, that in a number of articles and two books, *Después de Franco, ¿ qué?* and *Nuevos enfoques a problemas de hoy*, Carrillo gradually came to adopt the positions for which Claudín and Semprún were expelled. Another visible change in Carrillo's views related to the USSR. Some of the most virulent criticisms directed at Semprún and Claudín in the 1964 conflict resulted from their attempts to question the socialist nature of the Soviet regime. In his 19 April speech in Paris, Carrillo declared indignantly that the PCE would never be found expressing anti-Soviet opinions merely to curry favour with the Spanish bourgeoisie.[50] At that time, he still had total faith in Khrushchev's ability to correct the bureaucratic degeneration of Stalinism. Having based his own brand of tightly controlled and limited reform on that of Khrushchev, Carrillo was seriously disorientated by the unexpected disgrace of the Russian leader in October 1964.[51] Thereafter, and until 1968, a certain ambiguity is discernible in his many references to the Soviet Union. On the one hand, the habits of 30 years of unqualified support of Moscow prevailed, most notably in Carrillo's vituperative attacks on the Chinese.[52] On the other, there began to emerge glimmers of independence. Feeling that he had been betrayed regarding Khrushchev, Carrillo was uneasy with the new Soviet leadership. Moreover, the PCE policy of national reconciliation required that potential allies within Spain be convinced that the party did not share the dictatorial characteristics of the CPSU. Accordingly, Carrillo began trying to establish the differences between the PCE and the CPSU.

With the PCE still in clandestinity and persecuted by the Francoist police, with its leadership in exile and dependent on international, and particularly Russian, solidarity, Carrillo's early efforts were tentative and ambiguous. In 1966, he cautiously criticised the trial of the writers Sinyavsky and Daniel. In 1967, he tried to explain away the lack of democracy in the Eastern bloc in terms of the exigencies of the Cold War.[53] It was thus with great relief that the PCE seized on the developments in Czechoslovakia after the fall of Novotný as proof that socialism and liberty were compatible. Enthusiasm for the Prague spring was combined with praise for the tolerance of the USSR.[54] In fact, Carrillo's optimism was short-lived. By the end of July, the Spanish leadership was informed that the Soviet Union intended to put a stop to the Czech experiment.[55] The Spaniards thus had three weeks in August to reflect on how to react when the inevitable blow fell. The glare of publicity given to the 21 August Soviet invasion was seriously damaging to the PCE's reconciliation strategy. If the Claudín/Semprún schism had had any effect on the party leadership, it was to have made it more sensitive to developments in the interior. Thus, there was little unexpected about Dolores Ibárruri's condemnation of the invasion at the Kremlin on 21 August. Nevertheless, La Pasionaria's action required great courage given the PCE's dependent position, something of which both she and Carrillo were brutally reminded by Mikhail Suslov, in front of Luigi Longo and Giancarlo Pajetta of the PCI, on the following day.[56] Perhaps the insulting reminder that his was a small party spurred on Carrillo to stick to his guns.

On 28 August, the PCE executive committee met to condemn the invasion, although its communiqué also condemned "any attempt to use the tragic error committed in Czechoslovakia to denigrate the glorious history of the CPSU and the Soviet people".[57] In September, the central committee met to discuss the executive's action and voted by 66 to 5 in its favour. The two most notable members of the five were both noted Russophiles, Eduardo García, the party's organisation secretary, and Agustín Gómez, a central committee member who had been evacuated as a child to the USSR during the Civil War and was even a soccer international for Russia. On agreeing to abide by the rules of democratic centralism, they were both allowed to keep their posts. Although there seems to have been considerable rank-and-file sympathy for the Russian invasion, both inside Spain and among the exiles, the dissidents were given no official opportunity to air their views or rally support.[58]

Although denied access to *Mundo Obrero* and *Nuestra Bandera*, García and Gómez were able to circulate their views among party militants. They seem to have been relatively well received among PCE members resident in the Eastern bloc and among older militants who recalled Russian aid to Spain during the Civil War. Carrillo was furious at what seemed clearly to be Soviet-sponsored fractional activity. Since Gómez and García had some potential backing within the party, Carrillo used his skill in controlling the internal organisation to silence them. On 22 May 1969, a meeting of 27 central committee members, out of a total of 89, voted to exclude Agustín Gómez. In July, Carrillo forced García to resign from the secretariat and the executive by threatening him with expulsion from the party. The pro-Soviet dissidents responded by stepping up their activities, sending a number of documents to central committee members accusing Carrillo of being anti-Soviet, a revisionist, a liquidationist, an opportunist and an anti-Marxist. At the same time, more pressure was brought to bear on Carrillo by the Russians. He was "punished" for his attitude by the sale of Polish coal to Spain during the December 1969 Asturian miners' strike. On 30 December, the central committee formally expelled Gómez and García from the PCE, despite the resolute opposition of Enrique Líster.[59]

The PCE's original criticism of the invasion of Czechoslovakia had not been intended to provoke an all-out confrontation with the CPSU. However, the crudity of the Russian response, especially in challenging Carrillo's internal authority in the PCE, was pushing him ever more to outright independence. Forced away from the CPSU, the PCE moved correspondingly nearer to the Italian Communists, a development which was to have a liberalising effect on the Spaniards. Similarly, as Russian-inspired attacks on Carrillo continued, he responded by gradually eliminating the Stalinist elements from his own party and thereby accelerating the process of modernisation. Even though this was achieved by what can only be described as Stalinist methods, it had the effect of opening up the party, making it more attractive to intellectuals and students, and reducing the average age of militants. The reforms begun by Carrillo in the early 1950s in response to developments within the CPSU were thus consolidated nearly 20 years later by the same methods but in reaction against the Russians.

After the expulsion of García and Gómez, the pro-Soviet banner was taken up by Líster. He campaigned actively, through a stream of letters, to have the García/Gómez expulsions revoked and to have Carrillo's stewardship of the party examined. Two things sealed his fate: Carrillo's control of the apparatus and the attitude of La Pasionaria. Despite a number of pleas for Dolores Ibárruri to denounce Carrillo, she threw her weight behind the Secretary General. Despite her own pro-Soviet sympathies, she presumably was reluctant to preside over the distintegration of the PCE and was also fully aware that the party's survival lay in the more modern positions associated with Carrillo. The Secretary General in any case took no chances. Líster was simply not informed of the times or places of executive and central committee meetings. Finally, in September 1970, the central committee was convened to resolve the question of Líster's dissidence which had grown more hysterically anti-Carrillo. To ensure a majority in his favour, Carrillo co-opted 29 new members onto the central committee. Líster claimed that his supporters were not told when or where the session was to be held, that he was informed at such short notice as hardly to be able to prepare his case, that two of his supporters were physically prevented from entering the plenum and that he himself was physically threatened. The meeting ended with the expulsion from the party of Líster and four other pro-Soviet dissidents.[60]

Líster, Gómez and García formed their own PCE with its own *Mundo Obrero* and *Nuestra Bandera*. Consisting of veteran members, it had little future. Carrillo had the party organisation and the support of La Pasionaria. Accordingly, the pro-Soviet fraction eventually broke up into fragments led by García and Líster. Carrillo had won, not least because of his iron grip on the apparatus. That was made clear by the report to the expanded plenum of Ignacio Gallego, who replaced García as organisation secretary. In the face of the evident uneasiness of some central committee members regarding the expulsions, Gallego declared:

> Each one of us has the right to express and defend his opinion on any problem but here we are not concerned with that right. What we are concerned with is the unity of the party, of its principles of organization, of the attitudes that a militant, and particularly that a member of the central committee, should have towards an attempt to divide the party. In a clandestine party, it is impossible to accept ambiguity regarding a question of this kind. Anyone who fails to condemn and combat the fraction is in fact helping it, an attitude incompatible with their presence in the central committee. . . . In these conditions, we cannot allow ourselves to be carried away by an absurd liberalism.[61]

The clear implication that there could be no toleration of any deviation from the leadership's line lies at the heart of the accusations made by Semprún. In 1970, Claudín pointed out that the pro-Soviets could have been defeated in open debate and the PCE would have been healthier for the experience.[62] On the other hand, leaving aside Carrillo's evident tendency to authoritarianism, the risks involved in dealing with a challenge sponsored by the Russians in a party with a high proportion of Stalinist veterans constitute a degree of justification for the methods used.

In any case, Stalinist methods or not, the PCE was changing in such a way as to make a return to the past difficult. The removal of the Stalinists obviously made the party less rigid, a development symbolised by the replacement of the rather sinister Eduardo García by the urbane Ignacio Gallego. But it was only one of a number of changes. Throughout the 1960s, the party was extending its membership in the universities and the factories. The presence of students and the growth of the Workers' Commissions imposed upon the rank-and-file and the middle cadres a sense of realism and flexibility regarding the realities of Spanish society. This was a result both of the reforms introduced at the VI Congress and of the lessons taught by Claudín and which had been gradually assimilated by Carrillo. In fact, Claudín and others thought that Carrillo went too far in his search for alliances to overthrow the dictatorship.[63] However, the fact remains that the reconciliation strategy, renamed in 1969 the Pact for Liberty, was now being pushed by a party far more modern, moderate and responsive to social change than the narrow Stalinist organisation of the early 1950s.

The growth of student movements and powerful semi-clandestine unions was largely a reflection of the vertiginous economic growth of Spain in the 1960s. Yet no other opposition group reacted to the changes as effectively as the PCE. As the Communists became increasingly involved in the mass struggle against the regime, Carrillo began to talk of conquering "zones of liberty" and "bases for democratic struggle". By 1968, such "zones" were to be found in the increasing frequency of strikes, demonstrations and meetings held in the face of continuing police repression. At the same session of the PCE central committee which saw the expulsion of the Stalinists, Carrillo reported on the party's "salida a la superficie" or return to the surface.[64] It was the beginning of the "capture of democracy". In 1970, the PCE had launched a massive recruiting drive called the Promoción Lenín which saw the party swell not only in the big industrial areas but also in the countryside.[65] Simultaneously, PCE members became more involved in legal associations – housewives' groups, consumer pressure groups, parent–teacher associations, neighbourhood groups – and party lawyers were prominent in the defence of trades unionists on trial for their activities. All of this constituted, within the limits of the dictatorship, an attempt to emulate the successes of the Italian communists in municipal government, a demonstration that communists were efficient and reliable.

In 1973, the final crisis of the Franco regime began. The energy crisis began to take its toll of the prosperity which was the dictatorship's main claim to the loyalty of industrialists and bankers, and with the working class moving towards the kind of mass action long predicted by the PCE, the Francoist elite was shattered by the assassination of Admiral Carrero Blanco. The Pact for Liberty suddenly acquired wider relevance than it had had before. Spurred on by the example of events in Greece, Portugal and Italy, many of Spain's economic elite began to consider that an understanding with the communists could play a part in their own strategy for survival. The liberalisation of the PCE over the previous 20 years and the well-publicised estrangement from the USSR were finally paying dividends. Yet perhaps even more crucial than the negotiations between party leaders and representatives of progressive capitalist groups was the massive popular pressure in favour of democracy. All over Spain, democratic round tables and juntas sprang up, and everywhere communists were active in them. It was the fruition of the policies of returning to the surface and of capturing democracy. When the party leadership announced the formation of the Junta Democrática on 30 July 1974, it was the existence of the local organisations which gave significance to what might otherwise have been an empty gesture. In a similar fashion, it was the mass strikes and demonstrations of 1975 and 1976, in which the communists were prominent, that facilitated the unity of the Junta Democrática with the socialist-dominated Plataforma de Convergencia Democrática. The PCE was thus assured participation in the negotiations between government and opposition in late 1976 and early 1977 which prepared the way to the democratic elections of 15 June 1977.[66]

Under such circumstances, Santiago Carrillo's claims of five major achievements, made to the Rome meeting of the central committee in July 1976, are comprehensible. Twenty years after he took control, the party was well organised, with a strong working class base, armed with a relevant programme of democratic unity, independent of Moscow, and enjoying a high degree of internal unity. On the other hand, the foregoing examination of the years of Carrillo's leadership suggests that Semprún's accusations of authoritarianism and Stalinist manipulation were not without substance. Whether the PCE would be stronger had Carrillo used democratic methods is a matter for counter-factual speculation. In the case of the Claudín/Semprún schism, had Carillo and his supporters won their case in open debate, the PCE would probably have been more democratic and certainly theoretically more sophisticated. But it is impossible to say what would have been the effect on the rank-and-file of their immediately pessimistic line. In the case of the García/Gómez/Líster schism, it is arguable that, given the weight of residual Stalinism among the older membership backed by the Russians, only the use of debatable techniques could guarantee victory for Carrillo and the modern orientation.

The problem is considerably distorted by an examination of the PCE in isolation. Throughout the 37 years of anti-Franco resistance, there is hardly any group, whether socialist, anarchist, Maoist fraction or Christian Democrat, that did not succumb to depression and diversion. Despite astonishing examples of individual heroism, the non-communist opposition was characterised by inefficacy and fragmentation. In such a context, Carrillo's defence of the communists' self-deceptive optimism becomes comprehensible, seen as a crucial way to maintain morale.[67] An even more essential perspective is provided by recalling that, until 1976, the PCE was engaged in a mortal struggle with a savagely anti-communist dictatorship. The arrest of delegates to the V and VI Congresses on their return to the interior supported Carrillo's often repeated assertion that inner democracy and an open structure would have been luxuries facilitating the work of the police. On the other hand, as Claudín has pointed out, that does not justify the stifling of debate among the exiled leadership. Clandestinity imposed a rigid structure of co-opted cadres dependent on orders transmitted from above. Despite the difficulties, serious efforts were made, in the 1960s and after 1970 especially, to switch to a more flexible organisation based on committees and assemblies. Even if Carrillo's motives for adopting the rhetoric of "Eurocommunism" were proved to be only tactical, and therefore suspect, the fact remains that the PCE has now been set on a road from which it will be difficult to turn back. The adoption of democratic rhetoric and the turn to democratic internal organisation have encouraged an influx of young members who are increasingly swamping the older rank-and-file. Whatever his motives or his methods, Carrillo now finds himself at the head of a party substantially different from the PCE which expelled Semprún.

NOTES

1. For the Conference and its preparation, see Vadim Zagladin, *Europe and the Communists* (Moscow, 1977), pp. 15ff. For Santiago Carrillo's speech, see the supplement to *Mundo Obrero*, 14 July 1976.
2. Santiago Carrillo, *"Eurocomunismo" y Estado* (Barcelona, 1977) [hereafter *"Eurocomunismo"*] and *De la Clandestinidad a la Legalidad* (Cheratte, Belgium, 1976) [hereafter *De la clandestinidad*].
3. Comisión de Información y Propaganda del Comité Provincial de Madrid del PCE, *Dossier sobre la polémica en torno al artículo de la revista soviética TIEMPOS NUEVOS* (Madrid, 1977), pp. 5–16, 55–60.
4. *Il Manifesto*, 1 November 1975.
5. See especially *Der Spiegel*, 16 May 1977.
6. A letter by Saul Wellman alleging that Carrillo was being unjustly smeared for crossing a picket line at Yale was duplicated and distributed among Abraham Lincoln Brigade veterans. That the Chairman of the CPUSA, Henry Winston, was committed to attacking Carrillo was made clear in Julio Luelmo and Henry Winston, *"Eurocomunismo" y Estado o la desintegración del PCE y la ruptura con el movimiento comunista internacional* (Madrid, 1978). Cf. *Comment*, 4 March 1978, p. 77.
7. *Dossier* cited in n. 3.
8. Fernando Claudín, *Las divergencias en el partido* (Paris, 1964), pp. 10–26 [hereafter *Las divergencias*].
9. Enrique Líster, *¡Basta!* (n.p., n.d. [Paris, 1972?]), pp. 13, 21–7, 31, 45–9; Jorge Semprún, *Autobiografía de Federico Sanchez* (Barcelona, 1977), pp. 13–21, 111–14 [hereafter *Autobiografía*].
10. Semprún, *Autobiografía*, pp. 206–11. The Francoist version of the Grimau case is to be found in Servicio de Información Español, *¿Crimen o castigo? Documentos inéditos sobre Julián Grimau García* (Madrid, 1963). See also Amandino Rodríguez Armada and José Antonio Novais, *¿Quién mató a Julián Grimau?* (Madrid, 1976).
11. *Mundo Obrero*, 24 November 1977.
12. *Mundo Obrero*, 8 December 1977.
13. *El País*, 4 January 1978.
14. *El País*, 8 January 1978.
15. *Cambio 16*, 8 January 1978.
16. Interview with Pradera in *Por Favor*, 16 January 1978 and with Claudín in *Cambio 16*, 8 January 1978.
17. *Mundo Obrero*, no. 3, 19/25 January 1978; interview with Carrillo in *Cuadernos para el Diálogo*, no. 245, 7/13 January 1978.
18. For a general account of the PCE since the Civil War, see Guy Hermet, *Los comunistas en España* (Paris, 1972) [hereafter *Los comunistas*] and Paul Preston, "The dilemma of credibility: the Spanish Communist Party, the Franco regime and after", in *Government and Opposition*, vol. 11, no. 1, 1976.
19. Carrillo, *"Eurocomunismo"*, p. 133.
20. Semprún, *Autobiografía*, p. 39, Carrillo, *De la clandestinidad*, pp. 40–1.

21. See José Díaz, *Las enseñanzas de Stalin, guía luminoso para los comunistas españoles* (Mexico, 1940), passim.
22. José Díaz and Dolores Ibárruri, *España y la guerra imperialista: llamamiento del PCE a la emigración española* (Mexico, 1939), pp. 5–12; PCE, *¡Por la Unión Nacional de todos los españoles contra Franco, los invasores germano-italianos y los traidores!* (Mexico, 1941), pp. 3–7.
23. Líster, *¡Basta!*, pp. 146–9; Semprún, *Autobiografía*, pp. 123–5.
24. Semprún, *Autobiografía*, pp. 111–14; Santiago Carrillo, 'La situación en España y nuestras tareas después de la victoria de las Naciones Unidas', in *Nuestra Bandera*, no. 2, June 1945, p. 19.
25. Carrillo, "*Eurocomunismo*", p. 143; Carrillo, "Las tendencias liquidacionistas en nuestro partido durante el período de la Unión Nacional en Francia", in *Nuestra Bandera*, no. 28, June–July 1948, pp. 495–516; Vicente Uribe, "La penetración imperialista norteamericana pone en grave peligro la independencia nacional de España", in *Nuestra Bandera*, no. 29, August 1948, pp. 597–601, 615.
26. Santiago Carrillo, *Demain l'Espagne* (Paris, 1974), p. 100; Líster, *¡Basta!*, pp. 123–4; Carrillo, 'Sobre las experiencias de dos años de lucha', in *Nuestra Bandera*, no. 31, November–December 1948, pp. 824–39.
27. Dolores Ibárruri, *Informe al Comité Central al 5° Congreso del P.C. de España* (Paris, 1955), pp. 10, 20, 70–91.
28. Ibid., pp. 8, 11, 16–17, 81–5, 116.
29. Ibid., pp. 71, 99–104.
30. Santiago Carrillo, *Informe sobre problemas de organización y los estatutos del Partido* (n.p., n.d.); Fernando Claudín, *Documentos de una divergencia comunista* (Barcelona, 1978), pp. ii [hereafter *Documentos*].
31. Semprún, *Autobiografía*, pp. 36–7, 216–17; Claudín, *Documentos*, p. iii.
32. Santiago Carrillo, "Sobre el ingreso de España en la ONU: una victoria de la política de paz", in *Nuestra Bandera*, no. 15, 1956, pp. 11–33.
33. Semprún, *Autobiografía*, pp. 217–24; María Eugenia Yagüe, *Santiago Carrillo* (Madrid, 1976), pp. 52–3.
34. Claudín's investigations resulted in his book *La crisis del movimiento comunista: de la komintern al kominform* (Paris, 1970). See also Claudín, *Documentos*, p. iii.
35. Partido Comunista de España, *Declaración por la reconciliación nacional, por una solución democrática y pacífica del problema español* (Paris, 1956), pp. 3, 5, 29–31, 37–40; Santiago Carrillo, *La situación en la dirección del partido y los problemas del reforzamiento del mismo* (Paris, 1956), pp. 23–4; Semprún, *Autobiografía*, p. 38.
36. Dolores Ibárruri, *Por la reconciliación de los españoles hacia la democratización de España* (Paris, 1956), pp. 39–42, 83–9, 94–7.
37. Carrillo, *La situación en la dirección*, pp. 16–17, 25–31, 68–9, 87; Semprún, *Autobiografía*, pp. 222–4; Hermet, *Los comunistas*, pp. 54–7.
38. García was regarded, if only retrospectively, as a KGB agent by several senior PCE members. Cf. Semprún, *Autobiografía*, p. 38, whose views were echoed by several central committee members in conversation with the author. See also Claudín, *Documentos*, pp. iv–v.
39. Federico Sánchez, "Informe al VI° Congreso del PCE" in *Nuestra Bandera*,

no. 25, March 1960, pp. 63–74; Semprún, *Autobiografía*, pp. 204–5.
40. Sánchez Montero's optimism was not entirely subjective. In February 1957, the PCE had successfully organised a widespread boycott of public transport in Madrid; cf. Semprún, *Autobiografía*, p. 243. For Sánchez Montero's report, see Vicente Sainz (his pseudonym), "Informe sobre la lucha de masas y la jornada nacional de demostración pacífica", in *Nuestra Bandera*, no. 18, October 1957, pp. 3–17.
41. Santiago Carrillo, "Algunas cuestiones en torno a la jornada de 5 de mayo", in *Nuestra Bandera*, no. 21, July 1958, pp. 15–24.
42. Luis Ramírez, *Nuestros primeros veinticinco años* (Paris, 1964), pp. 169–71; Claudín, *Las divergencias*, pp. 21–7; Semprún, *Autobiografía*, pp. 44, 79–80.
43. Semprún, *Autobiografía*, pp. 7–9; Líster, *¡Basta!*, pp. 187–9.
44. Federico Sánchez, *Informe al VI° Congreso*, passim; Eduardo García, "La organización de las masas", in *Nuestra Bandera*, no. 27, July 1960; *Estatutos del PCE aprobados en su VI Congreso* (n.p., n.d.), pp. 13–14; VI Congreso del PCE, *Programa del PCE* (n.p., n.d.), p. 17.
45. The best account of the Maoist fractions is in Antonio Sala and Eduardo Durán, *Crítica de la izquierda autoritaria en Cataluña* (Paris, 1975). See also Ier Congreso del PCE (M–L), *Informe del Comité Central* (Madrid, 1973).
46. Claudín, *Documentos*, passim; Semprún, *Autobiografía*, passim; *Nuestra Bandera*, No. 40, January 1965.
47. Conversations of the author with Francesc Vicens and Fernando Claudín.
48. Interview with López Raimundo in *Cambio 16*, 8 January 1978; Claudín, *Las divergencias*, pp. 112–20.
49. Conversation of the author with Rossana Rossanda and Jorge Semprún. Palmiro Togliatti, *Promemoria sulle questioni del movimento operaio internazionale e della sua unità*, special number of *Rinascita*, 5 September 1964.
50. Semprún, *Autobiografía*, pp. 280–1.
51. "Sobre el reemplazamiento del camarada Jruschov", *Mundo Obrero*, no. 18, 15 October 1964; Santiago Carrillo, *Informe sobre el XXII Congreso del PCUS* (n.p., n.d.), pp. 15–18, 32–5; Fernando Claudín, "La crisis del Partido Comunista de España", in *Cuadernos de Ruedo Ibérico*, no. 26/27, August/November 1970, pp. 52–3 [hereafter "La crisis"].
52. Santiago Carrillo, "China a través del caos maoista", in *Nuestra Bandera*, no. 53, 1er trimestre de 1967, pp. 91–100.
53. Claudín, "La crisis", pp. 54–8; Santiago Carrillo, *Nuevos enfoques a problemas de hoy* (Paris, 1967), pp. 140–59.
54. Santiago Alvarez, "La renovación en Checoslovaquia", in *Mundo Obrero*, no. 11, 1[a] quincena de Mayo de 1968; Santiago Carrillo, "La lucha por el socialismo hoy", in *Nuestra Bandera*, supplement to no. 58, June 1968, pp. 32, 38–40.
55. *Mundo Obrero*, no. 22, 2[a] quincena de Diciembre de 1968, p. 4.
56. K. S. Karol, "La déchirure des partis comunistes européens", in *Le Monde*, 23 October 1970; Alfonso Carlos Comín, "Liquidate the Heritage of Patristic Marxism", in *Power and Opposition in Post-Revolutionary Societies* (London, 1979), pp. 150–52.
57. *Mundo Obrero*, no. 16, September 1968, p. 1.

58. On Gómez's career, see Agustín Gómez, "En manos de la brigada social", in *Nuestra Bandera*, no. 30, April 1961. *Mundo Obrero*, no. 18, 2ª quincena de Octubre de 1968; no. 22, 2ª quincena de Diciembre de 1968.
59. *Mundo Obrero*, no. 17, 7 October 1969; no. 22, 20 December 1969; no. 1, 8 January 1970; Líster, *¡Basta!*, pp. 68–73; Claudín, "La crisis" pp. 66–70.
60. *Mundo Obrero* (Líster tendency), no. 1, September 1970; Líster, *¡Basta!*, pp. 36–54, 100–3; *Nuestra Bandera*, no. 65, 3er trimestre de 1970, pp. 3–24; Claudín, "La crisis", pp. 74–5. The other four men expelled, Celestino Uriarte, Jesús Saiz, José Barzana and Luis Balaguer, were all prominent figures in the section of the PCE resident in the Soviet Union.
61. Ignacio Gallego, *El partido de masas que necesitamos* (Paris, 1971), p. 42 [hereafter *El partido*].
62. Claudín, "La crisis", p. 81.
63. Fernando Claudín, "Dos concepciones de 'la vía española al socialism'", *Cuadernos de Ruedo Ibérico, Horizonte español 1966* (Paris, 1966), pp. 59–100; Claudín, "La crisis", pp. 79, 82; Ier Congreso del PCE (M–L), *Informe del Comité Central*, pp. 30–6; *La Voz Comunista* (Portavoz de la Oposición de Izquierdas del PCE), no. 4, 15 January 1974.
64. Carrillo's report to the September 1970 *pleno ampliado* was published as *Libertad y socialismo* (Paris, 1971), q.v. pp. 56–66.
65. *Nuestra Bandera*, no. 62, October–November 1969, pp. 22–5; Gallego, *El partido*, pp. 7–9.
66. For the crisis of the dictatorship and the transition to democracy, see Raymond Carr and Juan Pablo Fusi, *Spain: Dictatorship to Democracy* (London, 1979), pp. 189–227, and Paul Preston, "La crisis política del régimen franquista" and "La oposición antifranquista", in Paul Preston (ed.) *España en crisis: evolución y decadencia del régimen de Franco* (Madrid and Mexico, 1978), pp. 11–26, 254–63.
67. Cf. Preston, *España en crisis*, pp. 217–54.

4 Eurocommunism and the French Communist Party*

JEAN ELLEINSTEIN

What is Eurocommunism? It is a spectre haunting the communist parties in the West, the State Department, the Kremlin and some academics. Why is it still only a spectre? Eurocommunism is, in fact, an expression created by journalists. This in itself does not constitute a crime, but is merely the result of a common practice which you all know well, but which sometimes gives rise to debatable expressions. That this particular expression is debatable is due to the following reason. There is no communist party in power in any West European country, and none of them participates directly in government. Even in Italy, where the communists occupy important positions in the regional councils and belong to the governmental coalition, it is impossible to say that they take a direct part in power. It is therefore impossible to define in precise terms the nature of Eurocommunism.

From this point of view there is a fundamental difference between China, for example, and the countries of Western Europe, which constitute the geographical basis of Eurocommunism. In China, the communist party has been in power for almost 30 years, and thus the relations between the CPSU and the CCP are complemented, and one could even say dominated, by inter-state relations between the Soviet Union and China. In fact, the Sino-Soviet conflict is due much more to state interests, to the clash between two nations and two big powers, than to ideological disagreements over the nature of socialism or the link between socialism and democracy.

* A lecture delivered at St Antony's College, Oxford, on 5 June 1978.

Eurocommunism is a historical phenomenon of crucial importance, as it corresponds to a need to create something totally new, rather than simply to continue the existence of communism as it was formed almost 60 years ago. I believe we could define this new element on three essential levels. These three criteria, representing Eurocommunism – if the word really means anything at all – are as follows: first, a radically new concept of the relationship between democracy and socialism; secondly, the absolute independence of communist parties in the West *vis-à-vis* the CPSU; and thirdly, a major democratisation of the internal functioning of these communist parties. As you may know, the IX Congress of the Spanish Communist Party did introduce some relatively important changes in its internal structure. But in spite of these changes, I feel that in many ways we are still very far from the end of this process.

We are facing here, undoubtedly, a new conception of communism. It has been alleged that the term "Eurocommunism" has a propagandist, instrumental, electoral meaning only. In my view it has a real meaning, which must be related to the three points I have already mentioned: namely, the new relationship between democracy and socialism; independence from the Soviet Union; and an internal democratic functioning of the communist parties.

What is the position of the French Communist Party on this problem? What are the problems the party still has to solve, and how is it likely to tackle them in the foreseeable future?

The crucial task the French Communist Party is facing, as well as all other communist parties, and in particular those exercising a real political and social influence in their respective countries, is the definition of a new road to socialism, which will also be democratic.

I shall try to describe the problems raised by this new road to socialism.

Why is it of such importance? Because the communist parties have been shaped by their origins in the Communist International (the Comintern) since 1919. The Comintern's main idea, which is embodied in the Twenty-one Conditions which the communist parties had to accept when they joined, was embraced by the French Communist Party in December 1920, when it was constituted at Tours. This main idea was that the revolution had to be violent, brutal and rapid, that it had to develop through a series of cataclysms, of which civil war was the apogee and the apotheosis.

This basic strategy of the communist parties implied a resolute struggle against those whom they defined as the most dangerous allies of the bourgeoisie, namely, against the socialist and social-democratic parties. It also meant the legitimisation of the use of violence, considered not as an accident of history, but as a necessary imperative of historical development. The model was that of the Russian Revolution, as it was created, I would almost say frozen, in 1917–18. In this framework, any appeal to political democracy was rejected because it was seen as bourgeois. From Lenin's point of view, although it was possible to admit that some forms of democracy were necessary, these forms were essentially seen as a product of history, which one had to suffer rather than enjoy, and which could be used rather than revered. Trotsky was later to call them a transitional mechanism.

As you well know – and I am not going to elaborate on this point, which falls outside the scope of our discussion today – this conception of political democracy had serious consequences for Soviet Russia itself, and was, in my opinion, the origin of Stalinism. When there is an omnipotent state, without any checks or balances, where there is a total lack of democratic life and of civic liberties, this must inevitably lead to what the Soviet Union went through in the Stalinist period. But it is not my purpose to discuss this aspect of the problem, although it is of fundamental interest to us, but to analyse the consequences of this policy in the history of Western communist parties.

I believe this view of democracy was the reason why Western communist parties ran into so many difficulties after 1922–3. At the end of the First World War, a truly revolutionary situation prevailed in Western Europe, and indeed, some extremely important revolutionary movements occurred in Germany and in Hungary. This revolutionary situation – in the Soviet sense of the term – was quickly eliminated by history itself. From 1922–3 violent revolution was not possible any more, and a totally new historical phase began. Thus, what Lenin thought to be the law, and the model to be imposed on other countries as well, was in fact only the exception. The history of Western Europe since 1922 was to demonstrate categorically to what extent the Soviet model of revolution, based on the concept of the conquest of power and the dictatorial road to socialism, was fundamentally erroneous and unsuitable for the realities of Western European countries.

So much so, that this policy led to the victory of fascism in Germany. I would not claim that the German Communist Party was solely responsible for Hitler's triumph. The responsibility of the German Social Democratic Party was at least as great. Yet the German Communist Party was to blame to a large extent for Hitler's success. In Italy, too, not only did the same policy help fascism triumph, but it also contributed towards its consolidation during the 1920s and the 1930s.

It may be said that the only important historical event in the history of the working class movements of Spain and France at that period was the constitution of the Popular Front. This development was, in fact, in total contrast to the Soviet revolutionary model. This contrast, however, is limited to the purely pragmatic and practical level. The French communists, for example, defined the situation as involving a choice between democracy and fascism, not between communism and fascism. But they never analysed the historical experience of the Popular Front as an original and possible mode of transition to socialism in a Western developed country. They went only half-way, even on a practical level, and they never dared to elaborate a theory on the basis of this historical experience. They were opposed in particular to the idea of including nationalisations in the programme of the Popular Front. In Maurice Thorez's view in 1935, nationalisations amounted to reformism. According to an expression of Engels, nationalisations would merely throw dust in the workers' eyes, as they did not involve any real progress toward socialism. The position of French communists remained unchanged up to 1946. In 1945, immediately after the Second World War, the communists participated in the government, as a continuation of the policy of national unity initiated during the resistance to Nazism. But they justified their participation on national grounds only. They did not join the government in order to transform society, because they thought it was impossible to find a new way of doing this which would be different from the Soviet model. They accepted nationalisations solely for national reasons, that is, in order to punish those who collaborated with the Nazis during the occupation. But to consider nationalisations as a means to reduce the power of capitalist companies was seen as tantamount to dangerous reformism, as the articles in the *Cahiers du Communisme* of 1945 and 1946 clearly show.

It was not until November 1946 that Maurice Thorez, in an interview in *The Times*, redefined the communist attitude, stating that the road to communism in France could be different from that of Russian communists, that democracy could somehow become the instrument of the transition to socialism, and that nationalisations might constitute one step towards the transformation of the economic and social structures of French society, thus creating the conditions for a peaceful passage to socialism.

I must say that this idea of Thorez did not prosper at the time, and was abandoned by the French Communist Party which adapted its position to the Cold War, and to the Soviet criticism of it in September 1947, at the conference which founded the Information Bureau of Communist and Workers' Parties, the famous Cominform. Thorez, or rather Duclos and Fajon, the PCF's delegates, as Thorez was not present, were severely criticised by the Yugoslav delegation and then by the Soviet representatives Zhdanov and Malenkov. The result was a complete historical stalemate, and one may almost say that France's communists turned back to the line fixed by the Congress of Tours. They again spoke in terms of the socialist revolution in an abstract way, stressing Soviet successes and exalting Soviet realities. The Soviet model remained the sole model for them.

Not until 1964 did the French Communist Party begin questioning its own values, and then only very timidly, without any attempt to work out a theoretical basis, and ask certain questions. This questioning was a result of the party's decision to abandon the thesis that the transition from capitalism to socialism should be realised by a single party. In his book *The Democratic Challenge*, published in 1974, Georges Marchais rejected the one-party thesis, but he gave the examples of Czechoslovakia and the DDR to illustrate the possibility of building socialism in a multi-party system. This, of course, was hardly convincing.

The PCF's XXII Congress, held in February 1976, was meant to initiate a major transformation of the theory and the policies of the French Communist Party in this domain. Not only did it proclaim the possibility, but indeed the necessity of a democratic road towards democratic socialism. This included universal suffrage and civil liberties, conceived as a basic element of the class struggle. Moreover, these were to be maintained in the framework of the socialist regime itself, in contrast with existing societies which claim to be socialist. I use this expression in order to avoid the discussion over the nature of the USSR. Not that I do not recognise the importance of such a discussion, but as we are not concerned with this question today I would be cautious and define these societies as claiming to be socialist.

Democracy, conceived both as a means and an aim of socialism – to repeat the formula used by Marchais at the XXII Congress – was truly original and new, theoretically as well as politically. Although Marchais did not elaborate on these matters, this was the beginning of a new policy, and this policy could be called Eurocommunist, if what we mean by Eurocommunism is a new type of relationship between democracy and socialism, which has no equivalent either in societies claiming to be socialist, or in communist theory itself. It is true that this point is not very clear in Marx's writings, as he never expressed his views on the subject. Anyhow, this was clearly in contrast to what Lenin wrote on the problem.

Yet this major innovation by the XXII Congress remained ambiguous and insufficient. Why is that? Well, this new approach to a fundamental problem of Western societies was not accompanied by an analysis and a debate, essential for the study of the theoretical and political implications of the new idea. This is, in my opinion, the crux of the present debate in the French Communist Party. When democracy is considered to be both the means and the aim of socialism, it is impossible not to be critical of those societies calling themselves socialist. Not only did they not establish political democracy, but, in most cases, such as that of Czechoslovakia, they even destroyed existing political democracy. These past experiences require a theoretical review of the whole history of the communist movement throughout the world, and in particular in the countries lying east of the Elbe.

For the Western communist parties, such a review would mean bringing Marxist theory up to date in a serious and profound way, as well as unambiguous criticism of the traces left by history in this theory since the end of the nineteenth century.

I agree that for Marx, the dictatorship of the proletariat was a fundamental theoretical concept, an essential pillar of his theory. But we must understand that this could not become a dogma, for the simple reason that Marxist thought cannot accept any dogma, on principle and by definition. Otherwise Marxism is transformed into a religion, and the communist parties become a Church. This may indeed happen, and I do not say it has never happened. But I believe that one should have the political and intellectual courage to call things by their name. Thus, if Marxism is transformed into a dogma, and becomes a religion, and if the communist party becomes a Church, it may well admit the validity of dogmas. But as it is in no way based on religion, the communist party cannot maintain dogmas.

Take the Catholic Church, for example. I suppose some aspects of Christian life have barely changed over the last fifteen centuries, because certain dogmas of the Church have persisted throughout. I think that the belief in God has not changed throughout these centuries. Either one believes in God, or one does not. I agree it may not be as simple as that, but what I mean is that belief in God is a dogma, and if one does not believe in God and in Christ, one cannot consider oneself to be a Christian. But Marxism is absolutely different. There is nothing in Marx's theory which is not open to study, analysis and criticism from the point of view of Marxist methodology itself. I believe this is in the straight line of Marx's own thinking. When asked how he would define his thought (this was part of a game he played with his daughters), Marx himself answered, "Doubting everything". Such was Marx's profound thinking. There were some more dubious sentences in Marx's game with his daughters. When he was asked how he would define man, he replied, "Through his power"; "And woman?" – "Through her weakness". Here it is perhaps more difficult to define his thought as critical.

It is impossible to reduce Marx's thinking to any dogma. To me it seems totally false to do so, and this can only be the outcome of a theological conception of Marxism. This theological approach to Marxism is opposed to Marx's own thinking, even if it became predominant in the communist movement, and in communist parties, where it too often still prevails. It does not correspond to Marx's thinking. Nor does the concept of the dictatorship of the proletariat.

Nevertheless, it is not enough simply to reject this concept, and it is impossible to stop at this point. Althusser is right to insist that one cannot throw out the baby with the bath-water. I am totally opposed to Althusser's conclusions, but I do agree with him that it is not enough merely to reject the concept of the dictatorship of the proletariat, or to get rid of it: what is needed is to formulate a new theory of the state and of revolution in our time, without which there is no way of bringing Marxist thought up to date. Marxist thought has virtually abdicated the political and social spheres of contemporary society. What is left is merely a pragmatic vision, namely, the communist parties' political activity, based on political realities, which is no longer linked to any theory. This, to some extent, was the main handicap of German social democracy in the period before 1914. It was conducting a reformist policy, but it refused to recognise it as such. When Bernstein defined the social-democratic policy as reformist, justifying this by the lack of any viable alternative, the reply was: "Shut up, you are spoiling the merchandise by demonstrating we are reformists!" This was Kautsky's reply to Bernstein. It was only Rosa Luxemburg who attempted to go beyond this purely negative answer, and to define a new conception of the relationship between reform and revolution. She was preoccupied by this problem to such an extent that she entitled her book *Reform or Revolution*. Personally, this is not the title I would have chosen for the book. I would have preferred "Reform *and* Revolution". With the methodological and conceptual tools of the period, Rosa Luxemburg pointed to the real problems created by the political practice of German social democracy. This practice was purely reformist, but the social democrats refused to make a theory of this practice, because this would have obliged them to go beyond Marx's thinking in this domain. This would have made them question the theory in several spheres, and they were not prepared to do so, as the theological aspects of Marxism had already struck profound roots.

The development of these theological tendencies is not surprising. I believe it was the result of the need to spread and propagate Marxism. No doctrine, not even Marxist thought, could strike deep historical roots and break through the narrow framework of our university system, without some amount of vulgarisation and pedagogy, and these may result in formalism and dogmatisation. We are always obliged to schematise, and I think the transmission of Marx's thought to millions of people, in very different countries, of a very different cultural level, must bring about substantial changes, and even a kind of dogmatisation of which Stalin was undoubtedly an exponent of genius. I do not mean it as a joke. It was precisely Stalin's genius to be able to present Marx's theory using terminology adapted to the cultural level of Russia of his epoch. This is why he easily defeated his opponents, who were so different from him, being mostly intellectuals such as Trotsky, who was profoundly civilised, but unable to address the moujiks and Russian peasantry in terms which they could understand.

It is therefore true to say that the XXII Congress of the French Communist Party put its finger on the most essential need of our time: namely, a complete renovation of Marx's thought. This clearly implies criticism of Lenin's thinking on a variety of subjects. Not only does this reappraisal make it imperative that the concept of the dictatorship of the proletariat should be abandoned, but also, if one is to be consistent, to reject the term Leninism, traditionally attached to that of Marxism, as the Spanish Communist Party has done. This does not necessitate the abandonment of Lenin's thinking, but rather that it should be reintegrated into Marxist thought on the same merits as Rosa Luxemburg's and Gramsci's. I also believe that the thinking of these two is more relevant to the needs of Marxism in the West than Lenin's. The latter should be relativised in the framework of the renovation of Marxism. We need this renovation and *aggiornamento* of Marxism if the communist parties are to constitute a real vanguard and to give a clear answer to the basic questions raised by the evolution of Western societies, which have nothing in common with Russian society in 1917 or with Chinese society in 1945 or 1950. I believe we should clearly and openly state what we are talking about.

This is the major difficulty the French Communist Party is facing. The party is afraid of the void. I feel I can say that Georges Marchais is standing on the edge of an abyss, and when he looks at this abyss, he asks, "What are we doing? We may lose our identity, and we may also lose our soul! We cannot allow ourselves to do this: we may even become social democrats, if we allow a full theoretical and political debate on the relationship between democracy and socialism." But there is no return. The relationship between reform and revolution must be reviewed. Thus we may commit the most abominable sin in the eyes of traditional Marxist thinkers, as we conclude that the revolution cannot be either brutal, violent or rapid, and, as Gramsci has already put it, we are not dealing any more with mobile warfare, but with trench warfare. Revolution can therefore only be democratic, and because it is democratic it can only be peaceful; as it is to be democratic, it can only be legal; and as it is democratic, it cannot help being gradual. There is no other alternative for Western communists, but to admit explicitly that their plan for revolution consists of a succession of reforms.

One should make absolutely clear what one means by the term reform, as it is ambiguous. We are not concerned with *ad hoc* reforms which do not make any real difference, though they may improve the workers' lot here and there. We do not want reforms such as those advocated by Chancellor Schmidt, for example. Such reforms constitute a policy of class collaboration, which has nothing to do with a real revolutionary policy, even according to my definition of the term. It must be clearly stated that the communist parties in the West do not want this kind of reforms. What we mean by reforms is structural reforms, which will gradually transform the whole social and political structure, over a relatively long period, and throughout an uninterrupted historical process. This is where we rediscover the idea of the uninterrupted or permanent revolution, which Marx elaborated in *The Class Struggles in France*, and which seems to me to be the fundamental theme of the dialectical relationship between reform and revolution. Yet this naturally is very different from what the communist parties said in the 1920s or even in 1950 and 1960, or even what some of them still say today.

It is necessary to face these problems, and not to be afraid to drawn the necessary conclusions. This is the only way to solve the problems the communist parties are facing. Otherwise we may find ourselves in the situation of the French Communist Party today – and I do not want to deal with other communist parties, as each party is acting on a different terrain – which is no longer what it used to be, but is not yet what it should be. The party is losing ground in some fields and gaining none in others. This situation is made even worse by the fact that the communist party has to compete both electorally and politically with a socialist party invigorated and transformed by historical causes which may be debatable but which are none the less real. In these conditions the communist party finds it even more difficult to accept the necessary transformation.

These are the problems Eurocommunism has created for the French Communist Party (PCF). The PCF is, to a certain degree, a Eurocommunist party. The resolutions passed by the XXII Congress are clearly on these lines. These resolutions contain a certain amount of criticism of the Soviet Union and of similar countries. The Congress specifically referred to the question of socialist democracy; and criticism, on this point as well as on others, continues to be made by the PCF. But here again, the party does not realise the implications of its own line. It hesitates to analyse Soviet realities for what they are; it refrains from analysing class relations, social problems and the role of bureaucracy in the Soviet Union. It hesitates to follow the argument through. Therefore any criticism of Soviet policies is made from a specific angle rather than on the basis of a general principle. Here again, the party stops short, and there is a risk of regression in this field as in all others.

On the one hand, the PCF has destroyed the old myth, on the basis of which communist parties were formed, namely, that a terrestrial paradise was being built in Russia, and it has rejected the idea of an unconditional loyalty to the Soviet Union. On the other hand, the party proclaims its quasi-unconditional solidarity with the Soviet Union in the struggle against imperialism. It particularly avoids criticising those aspects of Soviet foreign policy which may themselves be characterised as imperialistic, such as its African policies. The party does not make a systematic analysis of Soviet realities, with all their economic, social and political contradictions. On this second question too, the PCF is surely Eurocommunist, but it is not so in the full sense, and its position remains half-hearted.

Finally, there is the third question of the party's internal functioning. Here we have not yet seen even a real beginning. In reality, the PCF is still refusing to democratise internally.

I am not suggesting the creation of tendencies and fractions. On the contrary, I think that fractions often tend to crystallise around personalities and thus block discussion. What is important, what is crucial, is that the party should allow an internal debate, and that the leadership should encourage not only a vertical but also a horizontal exchange of ideas, without which no real internal democracy is possible. If I cannot communicate my ideas to people in Marseille, Avignon, or Aix-en-Provence and vice-versa, there is no horizontal circulation of ideas, and there is no public debate. In other words, there is no internal democracy in the party.

I have the right to address my party cell. If I am lucky, my cell will support my ideas. They will then move on to the Section. If I am lucky again, and if the Section too espouses my ideas, they will now be discussed by the Federation. If they are to go before the party's national congress, my ideas must first be adopted by the Federation. While this is not absolutely impossible, it still is very far from being the daily practice of communist parties, or at least, of the PCF.

This is obviously the greatest question communist parties will eventually have to tackle. I must be very frank about this, and I have already publicly declared that in its attempt to avoid discussing this problem, the present leadership of the PCF is using dubious arguments. These arguments are based on regulations which are not part of the party statutes, and which are not written.

According to the party statutes, it is forbidden to form internal fractions. For my part, I have never intended to form a fraction. I have published articles, but this does not constitute fractional activity. There is nothing in the statutes of the PCF to forbid publication of articles in a non-communist paper, in particular in such a distinguished one as *Le Monde*. There is nothing, absolutely nothing, in the statutes to forbid it.

I have also signed a paper, together with members of other federations of the party. At the moment, 1250 people have already signed this paper. They are not exclusively intellectuals. There are among them dockers, factory workers and railwaymen too. Well, this does not constitute a political platform. The proof is that I have signed this declaration together with my friend Althusser, with whom I disagree on practically everything except on the need to democratise the communist party. And the leadership response is: "This has really become an unprincipled conspiracy: these people collaborate even though they do not agree on anything." This is obviously not true. We do agree on something fundamental, and the fact that we disagree on the rest proves that it has nothing to do with a political platform. It is just a circumstantial text dealing with a specific problem which I have considered and still consider to be important, as do the 1250 people who have already signed the paper.

This problem illustrates the whole problem of internal democracy in the communist party. I shall of course be criticised for what I am saying, along with all the others who raise these problems in public. But I believe that this is one of the crucial tests of Eurocommunism: namely, whether the communist parties will be sufficiently transformed, so as to be able to eliminate, not democratic centralism in itself, but the Stalinist practices which accompanied this princople. The party's unwritten regulations, which Gaston Plissonier referred to in a long interview published in *L'Humanité*, are mechanisms created in the Stalinist era, which began to be introduced in communist parties from 1924.

As I have already said, these are unwritten regulations. They are indeed so disgraceful that they have never been written into the statutes. Moreover, if you search in the statutes of the PCF, you will not discover any of these unwritten regulations. They exist only in the political practice of the party leadership.

I believe we have now reached the historical stage, when it is no longer possible to retain these regulations. This is not a short-term debate. The party will be obliged to introduce important changes in the coming years. Otherwise the communist parties, and in particular the PCF, cannot become Eurocommunist. If these changes are not introduced, it will become impossible to maintain the theses of the XXII Congress, which, if taken to their logical conclusions, lead to a new definition of the relationship between reform and revolution; they imply a new definition of Leninism; they necessitate a more serious and more scientific analysis of Soviet reality and that of other countries claiming to be socialist. These theses lead to a transformation of the internal functioning of the communist parties. Some communist parties, moved by the logic of events, are openly discussing these problems. Thus, the Spanish Communist Party has recently introduced important changes, which are not merely formal. I am not saying that these changes are sufficient, but they have been passed, and I would be pleased to see them adopted by the PCF. The PCF would be much more Eurocommunist today if it could adopt a form of organisation and statutes like those of the Spanish Communist Party. I would like to emphasise that this is not enough, but it would nevertheless constitute a big step forward. The Italian Communist Party is also undergoing important changes, which have not yet come to an end. A lot more is bound to change, because the Italian Communist Party itself is confronted with historical problems of considerable magnitude, and which are totally new. The Italian party has to formulate a series of new concepts, based on its own historical experience, and thus to try to update both its political practice and political theory.

To sum up, it seems to me that this is a new era in the history of the communist movement in Western Europe. This new era is only starting. We can just hear its baby-talk. The communist parties still have a long way to go along this new road, and they should not be afraid to carry on once they have taken the first steps. True, history is made by human beings. Nothing is predetermined, nothing is compulsory, even though sometimes everything is necessary. I am neither a pious optimist, nor an absolute pessimist. I am not saying communist parties in the West will become authentically Eurocommunist. What I am saying is that they will have to develop on these lines, if they really want to provide a proper answer to the problems which Western societies are facing, and if they want to play a major role in the new conditions created by history itself at the end of the twentieth century.

Where communist parties are strong and influential, their transformation is of decisive importance for the evolution of Western societies. I shall not despair, therefore, in my expectation that these changes and this transformation can be brought about in the coming years, even if this road may be difficult and hazardous, as it is a new road, that of Eurocommunism.

Translated by Isaac Aviv

5 The French Communist Party under the Fifth Republic: a Political Party or an Ideological Community?*

ISAAC AVIV

I THE TRADITONAL PARTY

In the *International Herald Tribune* of Friday, 11 November 1977, Norman Jacobs wrote on the collapse of the efforts to achieve a programmatic union of the French left:

> Clearly French communism is suffering from a credibility problem, and it seems safe to predict that its commitment to democracy will continue to evoke skepticism until the party starts acting like a normal political formation and stops acting like a crusade which possesses a monopoly of all truth and virtue.

This criticism of the French Communist Party (PCF) has been repeated many times during the last decade, whenever a debate took place on the position this party occupies in the French political system, or on the role of its ideology versus its political activity.

According to some observers this is a revolutionary party, the aim of which is to establish in France a dictatorship of a minority, in order to modify the country's economic and social structure. This, they claim, is part of a universal project, elaborated by

*This chapter was given as a paper to a seminar at St Antony's College, Oxford, on 16 January 1978.

the Soviet leadership, in line with its Marxist–Leninist ideology.

Annie Kriegel, a former member of the PCF, adopts this view in her book *Les Communistes français*:

> Everyone knows that "the elimination of the power of the monopolies" and "the establishment of a true democracy" are communist slogans implying, respectively, the liquidation of the present regime, and the creation of a new one, similar to those of the people's democracies in Eastern Europe in their first stages.[1]

This view is contested by others, who emphasise the fact that the French communists have never tried to realise the revolution. They argue that the last 40 years have witnessed a slow but constant process by which a dynamic and revolutionary party has become a reformist and conservative organisation.

This view is held, among others, by Georges Lavau, according to whom the PCF has become a special kind of a social democratic party, and has been integrated into the French political system, resembling any other French political party.[2]

It is almost unnecessary to say that the communists themselves deny the validity of these definitions, and keep insisting that they are both revolutionary and democratic at the same time. They argue that there is no contradiction between these two aspects of their ideology, and that there was no need for them at any point of their history to make a crucial decision between their revolutionary ideology and parliamentary democracy.[3]

The gap between these interpretations has not been bridged, and even recent scholarship into the nature of communism has followed the lines mentioned above,[4] not least because of the rise of what looked like an independent tendency within the PCF, called "Eurocommunism". This tendency implies the victory of an open, Westernised attitude to politics over what remained of the Stalinist past. Its main emphasis is on close collaboration with the socialists.

The policy of collaboration with the socialists is not an innovation of the 1970s. It constituted an important element of the party policy in the 1930s and 1940s, throughout the period of the Popular Front, the Resistance and participation in the first post-war governments. Moreover, this line became an integral part of the communist ideology in France in the party's XVII and XVIII Congresses, in 1964 and 1967 respectively.

Each of the contrasting interpretations of the party's nature and behaviour mentioned above tends to underline a specific aspect of the party's personality. But at the same time all of them arouse new series of questions: If the communist party is a reformist social democratic organisation, as seen by Lavau, what is the point in defining itself as revolutionary? Why does it adopt such an extreme position, which is controversial not only within the French nation in general, but also within the French left?

On the other hand, if the PCF is a revolutionary party, according to Kriegel's view, why is its activity limited to propaganda, demonstrations, electoral campaigns and the organisation of popular festivals of the *Humanité* kind? Why was the party so hesitant during the political and social crises of 1936 and 1968, when it could have tried to live up to its alleged revolutionary aims?

This question of whether or not the PCF is a revolutionary party is linked with the party's position within the French political scene, and with the debate aroused by its international attachment: Why does a French party insist on its relationship with a foreign political system, i.e. the Soviet one? And how can one explain the longevity of such a "foreign" party, as its adversaries like to name it, for more than half a century? How has it managed to retain the loyalty of at least one-fifth of the French electorate, even during the Cold War, when its links with the Soviet Union, France's avowed ideological and political enemy, were never denied?[5]

To sum up, why does the PCF define an aim which it has never tried to realise, and why does it concentrate on aims which it has defined as secondary, such as the immediate economic demands of the workers? And how can we explain the interesting fact that this gap between aspirations and realisations has never seriously done any lasting damage to the PCF's electoral strength?

In our opinion it is precisely this gap that constitutes the source of the PCF's vitality. Does this mean to say that the communist party simply manipulates its members, as some of its analysts maintain?[6] Even if one tended to accept the manipulation theory, one would still have to explain to what end the PCF's leaders manipulate their followers, and why the latter are amenable to the leaders' manipulation. There is, in our view, little point in manipulating people if the communists have never tried to seize political power in France.

Nevertheless, there is no doubt that the ideology as well as the organisation and the political and social activity of the PCF contain a series of internal contradictions, especially between its "revolutionary" aspects and its "reformist" ones.

As we have already said, the continuity of the PCF indicates that not only have these contradictions not caused any major harm to the party, but also that in themselves they reflect the basic needs of those who follow the PCF. Moreover, what appears to us, the outsiders, as contradictions, may be perceived as a coherent system by the party member.

We shall therefore not try to argue that these internal contradictions do not exist, or that they are unimportant. We shall instead concentrate on the following question: what is the source of strength of such an ideology, and who are the people for whom this ideology, with its internal contradictions, is the only framework of political action and social integration?

In contrast with most political parties, which aspire mainly to achieve political power and influence, while maintaining a loosely defined ideological platform, the PCF has always seemed to be more concerned with its ideology than with the effectiveness of its political activity. Moreover, the communist-controlled trade union organisation, the CGT, has systematically refrained from challenging the present structure of French industry, subordinating structural changes to the distant aim of the socialist revolution.[7] The party is frequently engaged in disputes which give the impression that it really prefers an ideological victory over its rivals or even friends, rather than an immediate political achievement.[8] What is still more surprising is that this phenomenon, as well as the contradictions we have mentioned, which would have destroyed other political parties, have not stopped hundreds of thousands of workers, intellectuals and other people from joining the PCF or from voting for the party in elections.

It is clear from what we have said that it could not be the party's success in realising its ideology that constituted the main criterion for those people to join the party. But the communists claim that they are the only ones to base their political action on a clear ideology, which they describe as the most "progressive" and the most "scientific" one in France. And in his book on the history of the PCF, Jacques Fauvet writes that if there is such a thing as an organisation in the service of a doctrine, the PCF is its best example.[9]

It seems to us therefore that any serious discussion of the PCF must begin with a study of its ideology.

Every ideology consists of various attitudes and aspects, which we would like to define as myths, the myth being a cultural structure, carrying an internal meaning and emotional connotations.[10]

The essential myth of the PCF is that of the French working-class. In this myth, the workers are conceived as an exploited class, whose destiny it is to redeem itself through the creation of a new kind of society.

Another myth, that of "Revolution", i.e. a radical change of the structure of society, is considered an essential element in the liberation of the working class. The French nation is itself a cornerstone in the thinking of the communist party, as it is seen as the historical avant-garde of rationalism and democracy since 1789. There is also the myth of "proletarian internationalism", embodied traditionally in the international communist movement and in the Soviet Union, the ultimate proof for the PCF of the viability of a working class state.[11]

What characterises this combination of myths is that all of them derive from historical French left-wing traditions, of revolution and the revolutionary avant-garde, of Jacobin internationalism and patriotism. At the same time the same combination turns the social hierarchy constructed around these myths, i.e. the predominance of the French bourgeois culture and bourgeois politics, upside-down. Through the particular optic of the PCF it is the French working class which is defined as the authentic heir of the rationalistic and scientific traditions of the French culture of the eighteenth century, and therefore it is the working class, together with its "allies" (meaning in communist terminology people or social groups accepting the communist analysis of French society and history), which incarnates the whole of the French nation.[12] The "bourgeoisie", in contrast, has been governing thanks to the usurpation of the revolutionary achievements of 1789, 1830, 1848 and 1871, in collaboration with international capitalism.[13] It is therefore under the leadership of the PCF, which holds the key to the understanding of "History", that the working class will assume its legitimate role and thus enable France to come back to her true self.

This particular synthesis of revolution and nationalism is the result of a major shift in the communist ideology, achieved from 1934 on under the leadership of Maurice Thorez, and in line with the new policy adopted by the Comintern, relinquishing its anti-patriotic and anti-collaborationist ideology, recommending co-operation with the socialists and even with bourgeois parties in the framework of an anti-fascist front. It is only through this combination of myths that the PCF stopped being a small ideological sect and achieved a major transfer of working-class votes and allegiance from the socialist party to itself: in the 1936 elections the PCF obtained 15 per cent of the votes in comparison with 8 per cent in 1932, and in 1946, 25 per cent of the electorate supported the party. The SFIO was losing ground: the socialists had 21 per cent of the vote in 1932, and 20 per cent in 1936, but never repeated this performance after 1945 until the 1970s.[14]

The main attraction this new communist line had for the French working class was that it enabled working people to regain their self-esteem vis-à-vis the established social order, which not only limited their chances of improving their lot as individuals, but also condemned them as a group to a marginal position in their own society.[15] Thus the communist party legitimised the needs and the hopes of the hopes of the working class, and was able to offer its members "something more than just political organization, something resembling a social family, a reference group, giving a real meaning to their daily life and to their existence".[16]

The communist ideology, based on these "patriotic", "revolutionary" and "internationalist" myths, succeeded in confirming and redefining the identity of French working people, especially those among them who are more educated and therefore also motivated by an ambition for social and political promotion, and who therefore joined the communist party. Activity within the PCF gives these people emotional and intellectual satisfaction as well as a better chance of pursuing a political career in the party and through it within the existing institutions, such as parliament, municipalities, etc.

The PCF ran into serious problems in the 1939–41 period, when its patriotic and internationalist myths clashed. But even this episode did not diminish the basic loyalty of the working class to the communist party, and the Soviet Union, as a "working-class state", continued to be considered as an essential guarantor of the interests of the French working class. There was no real drop in the support the communist party enjoyed among working people during the Cold War period (1947–56), in spite of the fact that this loyalty was keeping both the communists and large sectors of the working class in political isolation.[17] The monolithic and rather simple nature of this loyalty was presumably important for the maintenance of the ideological structure offered by the PCF to its members and supporters. The party adopted an "internationalist" and "revolutionary" line, but it did not actually try to make a revolution, nor did it abandon its patriotic myth, which it claimed it was serving best by its anti-American line, as well as through opposition to the bourgeois–socialist government.

No wonder, then, that the "revaluation of national values", carried out by Thorez in 1936, also brought about the rehabilitation of the Republic as such. The latter, especially after 1945, was incorporated into communist ideology. As for the Fourth Republic the PCF had the justifiable feeling that it was one of its main sponsors, as the communists collaborated in drafting its constitutions and participated in its first governments.

Nevertheless, during most of the Fourth Republic, the PCF remained in political isolation. The Cold War cut it off from a real participation in power. Its ideology needed a balance between its various components. If "the working class", i.e. the PCF, had wished to implement its self-styled role as "the people's vanguard", it would have had to do so through revolution. But neither the working class nor the PCF wanted bloodshed, and the "revaluation of national values" paradoxically meant the integration of the working class into the social and political system as it was. Thus the revolutionary myth could be limited to ideology and propaganda especially through the emotional identification with the Soviet Union, "the homeland of world revolution". This identification with the USSR was serving once again, as in the 1920s and 1930s, as a compensation for the PCF's lack of a real revolutionary drive.

It was through communist ideology, then, that the protest and resentment of the French working class could be articulated and even sublimated, as this protest could serve as a reassertion of the communists' identification with the cultural and political traditions of the French left. Thus the marginal position of the PCF throughout the Fourth Republic, coupled with a conditional support of the regime was a comfortable stance for the party: an attempt to seize power would have meant a revolutionary struggle and probably civil war and the bloody suppression of the communists. Participation in a socialist–bourgeois-led government, on the other hand, would have alienated the working class, which would have felt betrayed. In this context, the support of the Soviet Union and of sister-parties, especially from countries which had already undergone revolution, became a compensating and stabilising factor. This explains why the communists did not lose their influence among the working people in the 1950s in spite of the party's political isolation. This was, indeed, a very delicate balance, and the party had to face a series of threats, both from right-wing communists, who accused the party of preferring isolation to political effectiveness, and from left-wing members, accusing the PCF of not being revolutionary enough. Both tendencies were dealt with as "deviations", and their advocates were expelled from the party.[18]

The PCF's immobilism was thus a factor of emotional stability and of solidarity amongst its members. Its monolithic organisation of the party, based on the principle of "democratic centralism" turned the party into a solid, working-class community. The preservation of this community thus became more important than the need to influence the political system and decision-making. The communists became ideologically conservative, in the sense that they refused to consider major ideological changes; and socially conformist, underlining the importance of the family, and only very reluctantly promoting members of ethnic minorities in their ranks.[19] But in spite of their conservatism, the communists still frightened the French middle class by their verbal radicalism. This hostility of the outside world towards the communists was in itself a stabilising force when it collided with communist ideology, and convinced the PCF of the rightness of its criticism of the system.

2 THE COMING OF THE FIFTH REPUBLIC

The birth of the Fifth Republic and Gaullist ideology in 1958 dealt a shattering blow to communist ideology, to its system of myths and to its working-class following. The Fourth Republic, hostile though it generally was towards the communists (except for two short periods: when it was established, and then just before it was toppled in 1958), did not contest the legitimacy of the PCF's links with the working class or the stability of the community the party had carefully constructed around its self-confirming myths.

The ambition of General de Gaulle to incarnate the whole of the French nation at the expense of political parties and the drafting of the new constitution threatened the party's positions within the working class proper. In the 1958 parliamentary elections the PCF lost a million and a half of its voters, as well as about 100,000 of its members. Its parliamentary representation was reduced to ten.[20]

The myth of "proletarian internationalism" suffered serious blows at precisely the same period. From 1960 onwards there was a steady deterioration in the relations between the two communist giants, the USSR and China, which encouraged the emergence of left-wing opposition to the PCF's pro-Soviet line, especially among intellectuals, whose support the party needed for ideological legitimisation. At the same time a "right-wing deviation" re-emerged, stressing the difference between Gaullism and American imperialism, and the virtues of the former in comparison with the latter.[21]

But the four-year crisis (1958–62) did not end with a collapse of the party and the absorption of the working class by the regime. In 1962 the party stabilised and adopted a new policy, similar to that of the Popular Front, and to that which it pursued during the Resistance and when it participated in government. This new line consisted in gradually increasing political collaboration with the socialist party which also found itself in the opposition to the Gaullist government, and at the same time a new emphasis on the values of democracy and of "the peaceful transition to socialism".

The old "Republican" line of the PCF in the 1930s and 1940s meant an attempt by the communists to consolidate a wide front to defend the Republic against fascism, and was consequently of a tactical character. The policy adopted by the PCF from 1962 on was an initiative taken by the communist party to incorporate the working-class community it had constructed within the broader framework of the French left.

The main factor facilitating the success of the new communist enterprise was, paradoxically, the stabilisation and the prosperity brought about by the Gaullist regime. The political stability, the economic achievements and technological efficiency characterising the Fifth Republic did not modify the basic values or the social structure of French society. The 1962 elections showed that an important sector of the French electorate, traditionally linked with the PCF, but which had deserted in 1958, had slowly moved back to its traditional position and voted for the PCF. This comeback inspired the PCF with such confidence that the party allowed itself to renew its ideology and to modify its system of myths.

We shall be dealing here with the central myths characterising communist ideology, those of the mission of the French working class and of its relationship with the French nation as a whole, as well as those of revolution and proletarian internationalism, and we shall thus try to explain the new balance between the PCF's separatist myths and its integrationist ones.

3 THE WORKING CLASS

There is no major innovation in the communist definition of the French working class in the 1960s. The communists underline in each of their articles on the subject, as well as in their public statements and in party congresses, the virtues of the working class which distinguish it from other social groups: it is mainly composed of miners, factory workers, masons, public transport workers and employees in the public services, as well as agricultural workers, all of who are defined as "creators of value";[22] the workers are still oppressed by the bourgeoisie as they were a hundred years ago;[23] they have to fight a constant battle against their alleged oppressors;[24] the workers occupy an essential place in the framework of the French nation, not only because they are the only "productive force", but also because they are the main factor of progress and modernisation since their industrial activity and wage claims make the capitalists introduce technological innovations, so as not to lose their profits.[25] The PCF sees the workers as continuing to assume a leading role in the "struggle" against the Gaullist economy, which they call "state monopoly capitalism", the other "non-monopolistic social groups", such as students and technicians, being of middle-class origin, and therefore less resolute in their anti-Gaullist attitudes.[26] This leading role can be assumed by the working class alone, because, unlike these other social groups, it has a clearer vision of politics and history through its Marxist–Leninist ideology, and it is politically organised and represented by the PCF.[27] Moreover, supported by statistical evidence, the communists can rightly claim that both the working class and "its allies", i.e. employees and technicians, were growing in numbers throughout the 1950s and 1960s.[28]

At the same time, the communists now recognised for the first time the existence of "non-monopolistic" and anti-Gaullist groups other than the working class, and accepted them as legitimate and independent partners.[29] Moreover, the PCF not only admitted that these groups exist sociologically but the party collaborated to an ever-increasing degree with the political organisation which it considered to be representative of these groups, as well as of some sectors of the working class, i.e. the socialist party (SFIO). The two parties concluded electoral alliances in 1962 and in 1967, and the communists supported the socialists' candidate in the 1965 presidential elections, François Mitterrand.

It was in this atmosphere of growing mutual acceptance and ideological legitimisation that the XVII Congress of the PCF introduced a major ideological change in its concept of the transition to socialism. Not only did the party insist on the peaceful nature of this process, but also:

> The French Communist Party has rejected the idea that it is necessary that only one party should lead the road to socialism. This idea, upheld by Stalin, was an erroneous generalization of the specific circumstances in which the October Revolution occurred. . . . The merit of this thesis, submitted to our Congress, is that it has lifted a serious obstacle on the road to unity. From now on the argument of the one party system can no more be used as an impediment to collaboration between the two parties (the PCF and the SFIO).[30]

But how could the party reconcile its repeated confirmation of the uniqueness of the working class with the ideological legitimisation of other social strata? How could the party define the working class as the only real productive social force and at the same time declare that this proposition does not necessarily have to undermine collaboration between socialists and communists towards the signing of a Common Programme, which the communists demanded as the climax of a long process of mutual ideological and psychological acceptance?[31]

The communists tried to eliminate these potential sources of tension by creating a new kind of ideological balance, characterising their self-confirming myths in the 1960s, in contrast with the preceding period: the party concluded electoral alliances with the socialists, with the aim of enhancing the union of the left, but at the same time called for "mass action" outside parliament.[32] This attitude reflected the communist resolution to engage in a policy of growing dialogue with the political and religious bodies of opinion outside the party and its working-class community,[33] and at the same time the communist desire to present the PCF as the true initiator of dialogue itself.

"Action, Union, Combat": these are the three major mottos characterising communist political activity in the 1960s. The self-confirming myths grow into mobilising myths, and the static balance between the "revolutionary" and "separatist" myths on the one hand, and the "democratic" and "collaborative" myths on the other hand, characterising the PCF during the 1950s and early 1960s, becomes a source of new dynamism.

It is this dynamism which encouraged Waldeck Rochet, the party's enterprising general secretary, nominated in 1964 after the death of Maurice Thorez, to move closer to the socialists. While in the 1964 party congress he still called for the "united action of all working class and democratic forces", the XVIII Congress, held in January 1967, adopted a new motto, fixing the PCF's new aim as the complete unification of the French working class, and thereby, of the two "working-class parties":

> We think that it should be possible, after a series of frank and serious discussions, not only to reduce the ideological differences which still separate the Communists from the Socialists, but also to reach agreement on essential questions. This will constitute a great move towards the unity of the working class, which is one of our fundamental objectives. . . . Our party, having defined the right political line, benefiting from the unlimited devotion of its members, more united than ever, will not spare any efforts to accomplish the following major aim: the unification of the working class, the alliance of the social

> groups victimized by the big monopolies, the coming together of all democratic forces to fight for democracy, social progress and peace.[34]

Maurice Thorez's "revaluation of national values" of 1936 implied the renewed identification of the communists with the basic patriotic values, while insisting that the working class alone incarnated them. It was clear, therefore, that Thorez's collaboration with other political forces was partial and tactical. Waldeck Rochet tried to turn this collaboration with the socialists into something more permanent, as he was not convinced that socialism could be achieved through one party's action alone, even the communist party.

4 "PEUPLE FRANÇAIS – PEUPLE ROI"[35]

The PCF's national values did not undergo any major changes in the 1960s. The party maintained its historical distinction between what it called the "patriotic" values of the left, and the "nationalistic" of the right, described as prejudicial to national interests.

At the Party's XVII and XVIII Congresses, Gaullism was still presented as an economic system plundering the working class and the other non-monopolistic social groups in the interest of the monopolies. Waldeck Rochet claimed on both occasions that the regime was gradually destroying democratic liberties by concentrating increasing powers in the hands of the President. At the same time integration in the Common Market was denounced as disadvantageous to France's national interests and sovereignty. On the other hand, the communists were satisfied with de Gaulle's rapprochement with the Soviet Union and with France's withdrawal from NATO in 1966. But they still defined the regime as economically dependent on the international monopolies, and politically as based on de Gaulle's "personal power".[36]

The PCF's utmost hostility was directed at Gaullist ideology, based on the principle of collaboration between individuals and, within society, between social classes. This, the Gaullists believe, can be achieved through the democratisation of capitalism and the disappearance of class conflicts through economic prosperity, extending to all social classes. This result the regime hoped to achieve by what it called "the association between capital and labour".

Communist hostility towards Gaullist ideology was born of the 1958 trauma, when so many communist voters and party members succumbed to the attraction of this ideology, hoping they could eventually escape their social and economic conditions through this kind of industrial democracy. The PCF called these people "dupes", in view of the vagueness of this Gaullist slogan,[37] emphasising the regime's technocratic and autocratic aspects.

Gaullism was presented as an authoritarian regime, established by the upper bourgeoisie to protect its interests. At the same time this bourgeoisie was described as a declining class, which therefore has to resort to anti-democratic methods to cover up its moral decadence.[38]

In the communist view, the bourgeoisie is about to be replaced by the working class, described as "progressive" and increasingly well organised, whose role it is to save society and culture from decay. The "bourgeoisie" is recognised as the social class that has created the "progressive" materialist and rationalist traditions in eighteenth-century France, but has abandoned these traditions since then, as they stopped serving bourgeois interests, being too "democratic" in character.[39] It is therefore the PCF's aim to take up the patriotic and democratic traditions of 1789 and to imbue them with new life.[40]

There is no major change, then, either in the party's analysis of French society and the existing regime, or in the concept of the historic role of the working class. The new element is the alternative which the party proposes to the working class and to its potential allies.

The traditional communist attitude was to cling to the ideologically defined strategy of the socialist revolution, without trying to implement it, but at the same time underlining the specific identity of the working class and of "its" communist vanguard *vis-à-vis* all the social groups, including those middle-class and even working-class sectors represented by the socialist party. On other occasions the communists used to freeze their "revolutionary" ideology when they wished to implement a "Popular Front" policy, presented as tactical, and therefore in no evident contradiction with the revolutionary myth.

The PCF of the 1960s chose a line reminiscent of the Popular

Front. Maurice Thorez's "revaluation of national values" became a myth in itself,[41] and a series of meetings and articles commemorated the thirtieth anniversary of the Popular Front, as a mobilising factor towards "the union of all democratic forces".[42]

The real innovation in the PCF's line lay in its decision to raise this collaborative line from the tactical to the strategic level. The alliance with the socialists became in the 1960s a central theme of the PCF's ideology and its aim was defined as "True Democracy" or "Advanced Democracy".[43] The party developed from an immobile pseudo-revolutionary organisation, whose radical rhetoric served mainly to assert the identity of a socially marginal group, into a realistic political party, aspiring to influence the nation's decision-making in a direct way. In order to obtain some kind of an agreement with the socialists before the 1967 elections, the PCF even agreed to drop its demand that France should withdraw from the Common Market.

The growing collaboration with the socialists and the dialogue with the Catholics legitimised Western democracy, parliamentarism and political pluralism in the eyes of party members.[44] All these elements became in the communist credo aspects of socialist–communist cooperation, and were seen as a necessary stage in France's development. Socialism itself was postponed indefinitely, while the main aim became the united action of left-wing parties. Pierre Juquin, the party's ideologist wrote in 1964:

> "We cannot separate our dreams from reality. We must be realistic if we want to realize our hopes. And this world will go on being cruel and unjust as long as we are unable to construct our imaginary kingdom. . . . But our France will be created only by mass action. This is why we must achieve unity: first the unity of the working class, then that of the people as a whole. First we must achieve a Common Democratic Programme, realizable now. In the future we may go further.
>
> The French people, when it is united, is a royal people,
> A people of real greatness,
> A people with a future.[45]

To sum up, the communists extended the myth of the nation to include social classes and political parties other than the working class and the communist party. The PCF granted legitimacy to the

Socialists, collaborated with them and became legitimised by them and through them by large sectors of the population. The PCF faced left-wing criticism throughout the 1960s for having abandoned its radical line, and for having adopted "the peaceful road to socialism" as its main ideological theme.[46] But the party still considered itself as the only real revolutionary force in France, and hit back at its critics, mainly intellectuals, rather than workers, the latter remaining loyal to the party. It is interesting to note that the percentage of manual workers among both the PCF membership and electorate actually increased in the 1960s. In 1967, 60 per cent of party membership consist of manual workers, and there was also a continuous growth in the weight of employees, in the public as well as in the private sectors. Together with manual workers they constituted 80 per cent of party membership, as compared with 65 per cent in 1950. In that year only 52 per cent of party membership consisted of manual workers. On the other hand, the percentage of professionals and peasants declined. Paradoxically, the policy of dialogue motivated the party to reduce artificially the number of workers among the delegates to its XVII and XVIII Congresses, in order to give more representation to other social groups, such as professionals and intellectuals. At the top of the hierarchy, i.e. the political bureau, most of the members were again of working-class origin.[47]

5 REVOLUTION AND PROLETARIAN INTERNATIONALISM

All through the 1960s the communist party defined itself as a revolutionary party, and still insisted on the need for the dictatorship of the proletariat, following the revolution. But at the same time the communists emphasised that the dictatorship was only a transitory phase, and that it was wholly democratic, and moreover, that they believed in a "peaceful transition to socialism", which the advanced level of development of French society and economy made possible.[48]

These modifications were particularly significant in the light of the threat by Maoist and Trotskyite groups to the revolutionary monopoly of the PCF. These groups became active among students and intellectuals, and attacked the communists as traitors to the revolution and therefore to the working class. The communists reacted sharply, defining these elements as adventurers, verbal revolutionaries of bourgeois origin, and as objective allies of the right-wing government.[49]

The shift of emphasis from separatist attitudes to a more co-operative orientation was also reflected in the development of the myth of "proletarian internationalism" and in the relations between the PCF and the Soviet Union.

On the occasion of the 50th anniversary of the October Revolution, Waldeck Rochet said that "it is the eternal glory of Russian proletariat and of its Communist Party to have realised the ideals of scientific socialism".[50] The communists insisted on their attachment to the Soviet Union and to the International Communist Movement, and maintained open and secret contacts with both.[51]

But at the same time, the French communists suggested that there was a variety of roads to socialism, and that therefore all communist parties, whether in power or in opposition, were independent and equal. As early as 1963 Waldeck Rochet declared that "there are no 'dominating' nor 'subordinate' parties, nor 'major' parties or 'minor' parties; all Communist Parties are responsible for the fate of the communist movement, and are equal members of the great world revolutionary community".[52]

Moreover, the PCF allowed itself for the first time to criticise those aspects of Soviet society, which might threaten its own image as a democratic party in France, especially concerning the freedom of speech and conscience. Thus *L'Humanité* published on 16 February 1966 a strong attack by the communist poet, Louis Aragon, on the trial of the two Soviet dissident writers, Sinyavsky and Daniel.

6 CONCLUSIONS

We have discussed in detail the changes in the four central communist myths, as these are the main elements of the self-confirming ideology of the working-class community which the PCF has created. The party keeps intact its internal organisation based on the principle of "democratic centralism", but the changes in the ideology enable the party to act within the political sphere proper.

But this is a gradual development rather than a sudden change. In 1968 the party experienced a double crisis: first that of May, when the students rebelled against an archaic university system, the workers went on general strike and Gaullism was on the verge of total collapse. The PCF refused to seize power, even with the collaboration of the socialists. Then came the invasion of Czechoslovakia in August, when the communists denounced the Soviet bloc's military intervention, but accepted "normalisation", i.e. the stabilisation of Soviet control in Czechoslovakia as well as the Brezhnev doctrine of limited sovereignty of Eastern European countries in relation to the USSR. The PCF did not normally like to precipitate processes, as this could arouse internal conflicts and endanger the party's unity. The PCF always preferred to adopt a cautious and gradual approach to politics, especially in crucial moments such as the spring and summer of 1968. This attitude was disapproved by the socialists, and in 1969 the two parties supported rival candidates during the presidental elections. The two candidates, Jacques Duclos and Gaston Defferre, obtained less than 27 per cent of the votes between the two of them, and the two parties had to resume their uneasy alliance.

The PCF and Mitterrand's new socialist party signed a Common Programme for the left in 1972, a major achievement for the communists, who had demanded such a programme for a long time. Never had the two parties gone so far on the road to united action. The left scored a growing number of votes in the parliamentary elections of 1974, when the candidate of the left, François Mitterrand, obtained almost half the votes cast. These successes enabled the PCF to liberalise its ideology even further, and in recent years it has frequently voiced its objection to the way dissidents are treated in the Soviet Union. Moreover, in 1976 the Party's XXII Congress definitively rejected the principle of the dictatorship of the proletariat, thus firmly establishing its new Eurocommunist line. For the first time in the history of the Fifth Republic the left had a chance to win the 1978 legislative elections if the communists and the socialists had been able to overcome their differences in time.

This, however, did not happen. Instead, the negotiations between the two parties broke down on 23 September 1977 over the question of nationalisations which the communists wanted to take further than the socialists would agree. The communists directed their electoral propaganda at the poorest strata of the French electorate, and the left lost the floating vote of the undecided centre. Both the communists and the socialists did make some advances in the March elections, but despite the optimistic opinion polls, the centre–right coalition was left with a parliamentary majority of 90.

In the weeks following the defeat of the left, relations between the two main partners of the left were characterised by mutual recrimination and bitter criticism.

The communists accused socialist voters of having undermined the chances of the left by refraining from giving support to communist candidates in the second round of balloting, when these candidates were opposed by right-wing ones. The socialists, on the other hand, criticised the communists for their systematic attack on the socialist leadership launched by the PCF in September 1977 and sustained throughout the electoral campaign. The socialists argued that this communist campaign was designed to emphasise the PCF's would-be sincerity vis-à-vis their marginal electorate and thus help the party regain its position as the first organisation of the left, which it had been losing to the PS for some time.

Interestingly enough, the controversy then spread into the upper ranks of the PCF itself. Although the party's Central Committee approved the report presented by the General Secretary, Georges Marchais, on his conduct during the electoral campaign,[53] two important intellectuals, both members of the PCF, openly criticised the leadership. These were Louis Althusser, France's most important Marxist philosopher, who called for a democratisation of party structures and organisation, and Jean Elleinstein, the theoretician of Eurocommunism, who referred to the Soviet Union as the anti-model of a socialist society and came out in support of a free debate within the party on its past history and future prospects.[54]

In *Le Monde* of 30 April–2 May 1978 the dissident communist writer, Jorge Semprún, analysed the situation as a crisis within the PCF. According to him, the crisis was engendered by the PCF's self-imposed isolation from society, characterised by an ideological commitment to old-fashioned ways of thinking which the PCF was reluctant to abandon. Although the party had repudiated much of the Stalinist ideology, it still had a Stalinist leadership and a

Stalinist structure. The PCF still wanted to dominate the left and to reduce the socialists to the role of minor partners in the coalition, and it preferred to lose the elections altogether rather than let the socialist party lead the victorious left.

Semprún's attack on the PCF became even more bitter when he denounced what he saw as the "incredible" unanimous support the party's Central Committee gave to Georges Marchais on his conduct. He considered this as an attempt to prevent a real debate on the questions raised by the electoral defeat, and as a lost opportunity for self-criticism, necessary for the party's regeneration and opening up to French society and its problems. Semprún predicted a prolonged crisis in the party, resulting from the choice it had made, and the title he chose for the article in *Le Monde* – "The death-knell of Eurocommunism" – reflected his approach to and analysis of the PCF's conduct during the previous eight months.[55]

Did the communists reverse their collaborative line on orders from Moscow, who wanted de Gaulle to survive in 1968, and Mitterrand to be prevented from reaching power in 1978, as some critics of the PCF maintain? This interpretation seems to us an over-simplification of the PCF's conduct: we must not forget that in 1965 and in 1974 the party did support Mitterrand against the express wishes of the USSR and that it collaborated with the socialists in the 1973 parliamentary elections.

We believe that these shifts in the communist party's policies reflect traditional dilemmas of the PCF itself rather than a direct influence by external factors. None of these basic dilemmas is ever articulated as such by the PCF or its followers, but they are implicit in communist ideology and political attitudes. We would define them as follows:

> Does the working class constitute the incarnation of the nation at present, or will it become the nation only in the distant future, when the communist party seizes power?
>
> Is French culture usurped by the bourgeoisie and does the working class therefore still have to conquer it? or does the working class, under the guidance of the PCF, already express the French national and philosophical traditions, and has only to wait until the others acknowledge its dominant role?
>
> Is the working class revolutionary by the nature of its

struggle for political power, or is it enough for it to get organised within the communist party in order to be acknowledged as such?

The basic dilemma is therefore whether the French working class and the communist party have to undertake a political action in order to realise its revolutionary ideology; or is it sufficient to identify with such an ideology and with "the homeland of revolution" and thus lay a permanently self-confirming claim to social and political predominance?

These dilemmas can be solved only at a very high cost: the PCF can either attempt revolution and risk bloody suppression, or admit it is never going to act, and condemn itself and its working-class following to permanent marginality. Even a peaceful collaboration in power tends to tempt the communists less than the socialists, as the exercise of power in unfavourable conditions may alienate their working-class supporters, if, for example, they have to agree to austerity measures to solve the economic crisis.

This does not mean that the PCF was not efficient when it was in power in the period 1944–7, or that it did not comply when it had to leave the government in 1947. But the party definitely prefers to preserve its ideological integrity, if necessary outside the government, even if it is not hostile to it, when it cannot realise its own programme and fulfil its promises to its members.

The PCF is first and foremost an ideological community rather than a conventional party, and the question of political effectiveness raised by the *International Herald Tribune* is therefore meaningless in this context. The core of the PCF's ideology is its ambiguous attitude to French society and government. The party's continuity and its working-class support reflect the basic ambiguity of the working class's feelings toward the existing society in France, against which it protests through the PCF's ideology, but the history and culture of which it shares and venerates.[56]

NOTES

1. Annie Kriegel, *Les Communistes français* (Paris, 1968), p. 210.
2. G. Lavau, "Le Parti communiste dans le systeme politique français", *Cahiers de la Fondation Nationale des Sciences Politiques*, no. 175, vol. 1: *Le Communisme en France* (Paris, 1969), pp. 7–82.
3. M. Thorez, *Oeuvres Choisies* (Paris, 1965), vol. 3, p. 182; Publication de

l'Institut Maurice Thorez, *La Marche de la France au Socialisme* (Paris, 1966), pp. 34ff., 77.

4. See R. Tiersky, *Le Mouvement communiste en France, 1920–1972* (Paris, 1973), pp. 309–46; and K. R. Libbey, "The French Communist Party in the 1960s: an ideological profile", *Journal of Contemporary History*, XI (1976), pp. 145–65. Both writers accept either of the interpretations mentioned above.
5. J. Touchard, "Introduction à l'idéologie du Parti communiste français", *Le Communisme en France* (see n.2), p. 91; R. Tiersky, op. cit., p. 154.
6. A. Kriegel, op. cit., pp. 220–6.
7. C. Durand, "La signification politique de l'action syndicale", *Revue Française de Sociologie*, IV, no. 3 (July–September 1968), pp. 320–37.
8. How else can we describe the party's conduct in May 1968 and now again, in 1978? See pp. 96–8.
9. J. Fauvet, *Histoire du Parti communiste français, 1920–1976* (Paris, 1977), pp. 594–5.
10. We are using the term "myth" as implying a cultural structure serving for the consolidation of the identity of a given social group, in this case, the French working class. See G. Sorel, *Réflexions sur la Violence* (Paris, 1946), pp. 117, 182.
11. See, for example, W. Rochet, "Cinquante ans après le tournant décisif d'Octobre 1917", *Cahiers du Communisme*, October–November 1967, p. 20.
12. See W. Rochet's speech in the Palais des Sports on 10 June 1968, where he quotes from the *Communist Manifesto*: "Les travailleurs aspirent . . . à devenir eux-mêmes la nation."
13. Cf. G. Mury, "Serge Malet et la troisième révolution industrielle", *Cahiers du Communisme,* May 1959, p. 478; P. Juquin, "La France démocratique de demain", *Cahiers du Communisme*, April 1964, p. 37.
14. R. Tiersky, op. cit., pp. 50, 116; J. Ranger, "Le vote communiste en France depuis 1945", *Le Communisme en France* (see n.2), p. 212.
15. On the marginality of the working class see: G. Lasserre, "Le monde ouvrier dans la société francaise", in A. Siegfried *et al.*, *Aspects de las Société francaise* (Paris, 1954), pp. 117–22; J. I. Guglielmi and M. Perrot, *Salaires et revendications sociales en France, 1944–1952* (Paris, 1953). Both writers describe the decline of real wages at that period. See also R. Hamilton, *Affluence and the French Worker in the Fourth Republic* (Princeton, NJ, 1967), on the rising expectations of the workers; and more recently P. Bénéton, "Quelques considérations sur la mobilité sociale en France", *Revue Française de Sociologie*, XVI (1975), pp. 517–38.
16. F. Goguel and A. Grosser, *La Politique en France* (Paris, 1975), p. 103.
17. J. Ranger, op. cit., p. 212; F. Goguel and A. Grosser, op. cit., p. 99; A. Werth, *France, 1940–1955* (London, 1956), pp. 436–7.
18. J. Touchard, "De l'affaire Lecoeur à l'affaire Hervé", *Revue Française de Science Politique*, April–June 1956, pp. 389–98; J. Ranger, "L'évolution du PCF: organisation et débats idéologiques", *Revue Française de Science Politique*, December 1963, pp. 951–65.
19. For Communist conservatism see A. Kriegel, op. cit., pp. 132–4; for an

earlier period see F. Delpla, "Les communistes français et la sexualité (1932–1938)", *Le Mouvement Social*, April–June 1975, pp. 121–52.

20. "Le référendum et les élections de 1958"*Cahiers de la Fondation Nationale des Sciences Politiques*, no. 109 (Paris, 1960), pp. 138ff.
21. On the Servin–Casanova affair see J. Fauvet, op. cit., pp. 489–94.
22. M. Thorez, "Notion de classe et rôle historique de la classe ouvrière", *Cahiers du Communisme*, April 1963, p. 6; A. Barjonet, "La classe ouvrière française: nouveaux problèmes", *Èconomie et Politique*, November–December 1962, pp. 168–9; Institut Thorez, *La Marche de la France au Socialisme*, p. 101.
23. A. L. Barjonet, op. cit., pp. 176–7; G. Frischmann, "Où en est la conscience de classes", *Cahiers du Communisme*, April 1963, p. 27.
24. Frischmann, ibid.
25. P. Juquin, "La France demócratique de demain", *Cahiers du Communisme*, April 1964, p. 39.
26. P. Juquin, "Les monopoles capitalistes contre la nation" (editorial article), *Cahiers du Communisme*, July–August 1963, p. 10.
27. G. Marchais, "Un parti toujours plus fort, pour mieux servir les interets du peuple", *Cahiers du Communisme*, February–March 1967, pp. 273–4.
28. M. Thorez, "Notion de classe", op. cit. The number of manual workers in France grew from about 6,500,000 in 1954 to over 7,000,000 in 1962, to 7,505,752 in 1968 and to 8,207,165 in 1975. The only working-class groups whose numbers have diminished are those of apprentices and miners, sailors and fishermen. The rise in the number of employees is even more conspicuous: from 2,068,000 in 1954 to 3,840,000 in 1975; L. Thevenot, "Les categories sociales en 1975: l'extension du salariat", *Economie et Statistique*, no. 91 (July–August 1977), pp. 3–32. Thevenot minimises the differences between technicians and manual workers: both are economically dependent, and in 1970 40 per cent of the technicians in France were of working-class origin. In 1973, their average wage was within the working-class range of salaries (2640 francs per month), and their numbers are also growing: 193,000 in 1954, 530,716 in 1968, 758,890 in 1975, Ibid., p. 25.
29. Barjonet, op. cit., p. 169; Institut Thorez, *La Marche de la France au Socialisme*, pp. 104–20.
30. Waldeck Rochet, in his speech to the party congress. Supplement to *L'Humanité*, 15 May 1964, pp. 52–3.
31. A third of the editorial articles of *France Nouvelle*, the weekly of the PCF's Central Committee, between 1964 and 1972, is dedicated to the prospective Common Programme.
32. W. Rochet, op. cit., pp. 3, 29, 50; Institut Thorez, *La Marche de la France au Socialisme*, pp. 76, 91–2; W. Rochet, speech to the XVIII Congress, *Cahiers du Communisme*, February–March 1967, pp. 54, 63, 66.
33. The main protagonist of an open dialogue with Catholics and Socialists, as well as of an internal dialogue between "humanists" and "scientific materialists" within the PCF, is the Communist philosopher Roger Garaudy, who was stressing throughout the 1960s what Marxism has in common with the major European trends of thought. See, for example, R.

Garaudy, *De l'Anathème au Dialogue: un Marxiste s'adresse au Conseil* (Paris, 1965), and the interesting debate on ideological questions in the meeting of the PCF's Central Committee in Argenteuil, near Paris, on 11–13 March 1966, *Cahiers du Communisme*, May–June 1966.

34. W. Rochet, speech to the XVIII Congress, p. 91.
35. P. Juquin, "La démocratie socialiste", *Cahiers du Communisme*, December 1964, p. 62.
36. W. Rochet, Speech to the XVII party congress, *Cahiers du Communisme*, June–July 1964, pp. 3–29, as well as his speech to the XVIII congress, op. cit., pp. 34–44.
37. Ibid., p. 38.
38. G. Cogniot, "L'idéologie du Gaullisme", *Cahiers du Communisme*, May 1963, pp. 10–11; P. Juquin, "Le P.C. et la grandeur française", *Cahiers du Communisme*, February 1964, p. 72; Institut Thorez, *La Marche de la France au Socialisme*, pp. 37–9.
39. See M. Thorez's interview, granted to a Canadian journalist, in *L'Humanité*, 26 February 1964; P. Juquin, "La France démocratique de demain", op. cit., pp. 36–7.
40. Ibid., pp. 40–1; Institut Thorez, *La Marche de la France au Socialisme*, pp. 32–51.
41. The whole of the April–May 1965 issue of the *Cahiers du Communisme*, the PCF's ideological and theoretical journal, is dedicated to the subject: "Maurice Thorez, le communisme et notre temps". See especially articles of W. Rochet, pp. 5–12; G. Marchais, pp. 53–62; and V. Joannès, pp. 97–104.
42. J. Duclos, "Le VIIe Congrès de l'Internationale Communiste", *Cahiers du Communisme*, October 1965, pp. 42–55; W. Rochet, "L'anniversaire du Front populaire et la lutte actuelle pour l'union des forces de gauche", *Cahiers du Communisme*, September 1966, pp. 5–9.
43. W. Rochet, speech to the XVII Congress, pp. 29–58; speech to the XVIII Congress, pp. 16–69.
44. C. Vallin, "Rôle et nécessité des partis politiques", *Cahiers du Communisme*, January–February 1963, pp. 84–102; Institut Thorez, *La Marche de la France au Socialisme*, pp. 83–95. When the Socialist–Communist Common Programme was finally signed in 1972, the communists accepted not only a "democratic multi-party system" (a term designating traditionally only Left-wing parties), but also the principle of alternation in power, i.e. the possibility that the "democratic" parties would have to give up power if defeated in the polls.
45. P. Juquin, "La démocratie socialiste", p. 62.
46. R. Johnson, *The French Communist Party versus the Students* (New Haven, Conn.,1972), pp. 54–66.
47. G. Rossi-Landin, "Le Parti communiste français: structures, composition, moyens d'action", *Le Communisme en France*, p. 191; A. Kriegel, op. cit., pp. 148–65.
48. W. Rochet, speech to the XVII Congress, pp. 49–52.
49. R. Leroy, "La bataille idéologique", *Cahiers du Communisme*, February 1968, p. 118.

50. W. Rochet, "Cinquante ans après le tournant décisif d'Octobre 1917", *Cahiers du Communisme*, October–November 1967, p. 20; see also W. Rochet, *Qu'est-ce qu'un rèvolutionnaire dans la France de notre temps?* (Paris, 1967), pp. 7–10.
51. Waldeck Rochet played an important role during the Czech crisis in the spring of 1968, when he mediated between the Soviets and the Czechs. See "Procès-verbal de l'entretien Waldeck Rochet–Alexandre Dubćek (19/20 July 1968)", reproduced in *Politique Aujourd'hui*, a journal edited by dissident Communists, in its issue of May 1970, pp. 27–41.
52. W. Rochet, "Problèmes de la guerre et de la paix", speech to the Central Committee, delivered in Ivry, near Paris, on 8 May 1963, *Cahiers du Communisme*, June 1963, p. 152.
53. On the declaration of the PCF's political bureau on the Socialists' responsibility for the electoral defeat, see *Le Monde*, 9–10 April 1978.
54. On Althusser's and Elleinstein's criticism of the PCF, see *Le Monde*, 6 April and 13–15 April 1978.
55. J. Semprún, "Le glas de l'eurocommunisme", *Le Monde*, 30 April–2 May 1978.
56. We are, of course, aware of the fact that only about 50 per cent of those who vote for the PCF are manual workers, and that only one-third of the French working class votes for the party. Nevertheless, one should remember that this is the only French party which defines itself as a working-class party, and which promotes workers to political responsibility. The workers tend to recognise this fact: all public opinion polls prove that the majority of French workers and employees, while not actually joining the PCF or even voting for the party, tend to judge the PCF much more favourably than any other social groups in France. See M. Fichelet *et al.*; "L'image du PCF d'après les sondages de'l IFOP", *Le Communisme en France*, pp. 255–79; A. Lancelot and P. Weill, "L'attitude des Français à l'égard du PCF en février 1968, d'après une enquête de la SOFRES", ibid., pp. 281–303; SOFRES, *Image du Parti communiste* (Paris, July 1971); J. Elleinstein, *Le P.C.* (Paris, 1976), p. 141.

6 The "Eurocommunist" Perspective: the Contribution of the Italian Communist Party*

DEMOCRACY AND SOCIALISM IN THE ITALIAN COMMUNIST TRADITION

GIUSEPPE VACCA

1 COMPARATIVE INTERPRETATIONS

Does "Eurocommunism" exist or not? What is "Eurocommunism"? To similar questions, often asked of them, the leaders of the Italian Communist Party (PCI) usually reply more or less in the following terms. An idea exists of the characteristics of socialism that are both desirable and possible in Western Europe and, more generally, in advanced capitalist countries; and there exists also a consolidated parliamentary experience which is common, by now, to a number of communist parties. These are, in the first place, the Italian, Spanish and French Communist Parties, which base their action for socialism on common principles which unite old and new values of "political democracy": the defence of all individual and collective freedoms; the guarantee of plurality and autonomy for organisations of a political, economic or cultural character; the method of alternation between government and opposition in the management of the State; the necessity to develop institutions for workers' control and to create a framework for democratic programming of the economy; representative

* A revised and expanded version of a lecture at St Antony's College, Oxford, on 29 May 1978.

democracy as the general form of the State and as the method for the formation of government trends. As can be seen, these are positions of principle, which espouse "political democracy" as a "value in itself" (Berlinguer). They are expressed in common documents, signed by these parties at the end of the bilateral meetings held over the last three years.[1]

However, if we limit ourselves to the assertions contained in such documents and consider only the chronicle of activities which have generated them we shall merely skim the surface, and obtain a deceptive or at least a limited reading of the subject. The conviction is being generated, who knows quite why at the moment, that the major communist parties of the capitalist area have at last rediscovered the values of parliamentary democracy. Only in the 1970s, in Western Europe, have they taken note of the historical peculiarities of this area of the world and have decided to distance themselves from the Soviet Union in a definitive way. Only now does their pledge to work for the establishment of a socialist society (different from those which, up to now, have been created by communist parties in power) become credible. The essential difference from those communist parties in power lies in the pledge to maintain intact, in a socialist society, the principles and institutions of parliamentary democracy. The reasons for such a difference are summed up in the need to follow the democratic political traditions of Western Europe.[2]

Viewed in this way it becomes obvious that we are dealing simply with a tactical adjustment by the European communist parties, to a new situation in which, for the first time in many years, the opportunity to govern is offered to them. Not wishing to miss out, they are striving to accelerate an ideological revision, already overdue, which dissolves the old inhibitions of Leninist derivation and moves instead in favour of parliamentary democracy.[3]

I find this interpretation both inexact and unsatisfactory. First, it leaves room for the impression that this is a question of a conversion – complete indeed, but belated and sudden – undergone by these communist parties, to the values of parliamentary democracy, which therefore has a superficial and instrumental character. Second, if this was the only question, those critics who (for example in Italy) maintain that we are seeing a long overdue acceptance of Kautsky's arguments, and therefore a progressive and now accelerated conversion of these parties into social-democratic parties, would be right.[4] Third, it is incorrect to say that only now are the West European communist parties making the values of parliamentary democracy their own, in order, *inter alia*, to offer the prospect of a passage to socialism by a different way, and with particular characteristics, in comparison with the experience of October and the Soviet "model". The support of the French or Italian Communist Parties for the values of parliamentary democracy is not recent; it was already at the basis of the experience of the Popular Front in France in the 1930s, and then at the turning-point of the Communist International in its VII Congress (1935).[5] Fourth, the common commitment of these parties to build a socialist society "on the foundation of political democracy" does not consist just of a belated conversion to parliamentary democracy as the only model possible for the State. We are dealing with a much more complex phenomenon, which I will seek to examine thoroughly in this essay, within the limits of the experience of the PCI.

Considering the positions of the PCI, recognised by all as the forerunners of "Eurocommunism", I would like to underline the fact that their intention is to outline "*a new idea of socialism*".[6] Therefore, at least in intention, this is an ambitious project, which is not limited to observing the historical peculiarities of Western Europe and deriving from these peculiarities, the need to follow different ways to power and in the construction of a socialist society. We are not concerned with the establishment of a democratic socialism in Western Europe which would cooperate tranquilly with the authoritarian socialism that exists in Eastern Europe. If this was the case, "Eurocommunism" would be vitiated by a restricted Eurocentric view, and also it would result in a belated arrival at classic social-democratic positions. To give the lie to this, it is enough to recall that the propositions included in the joint declarations of the PCI with the Spanish and French Communist Parties are found in the same punctilious and solemn manner in a joint declaration of the PCI with the Japanese Communist Party. So "Eurocommunism", as far as the PCI is concerned, suggests that a more complex scheme of motives and objectives must be taken into account. According to the PCI, the crisis of the 1970s, in the most advanced capitalist countries, can be met in a socialist fashion *only if* very different economic and political arrangements are created, not only different from those in existence but different also from those that prevail in Eastern Europe. We are well aware of the likely repercussions of this on the realities of East European countries, fostering changes in them too marked by "political democracy". Indeed, this objective is also included in the outlook of "Eurocommunism". It is thus evident that the PCI wishes to create a new model of socialism, both complete and expansive; a socialism which "will establish a higher phase of democracy and liberty; democracy realised in the fullest way".[7]

Really the "Eurocommunism" of the PCI implies a complex elaboration characterised by particular positions within the entire range of problems in the international workers' and socialist movement, and I cannot illustrate it completely here. I will limit myself to isolating some aspects of it, drawing attention to two principal themes: first, the analysis of the crisis of the 1970s, from which the PCI has concluded that there are now new possibilities for transformation of a socialist type in Western Europe; second, the PCI's considered view of the relationship between democracy and socialism.

There is a precise connection between these two aspects of the PCI position: the theme of "political democracy" becomes a priority for the international communist movement precisely because the crisis of the 1970s renews the immediate relevance of socialism in Europe. The tasks which this lays upon the PCI are centred on the subject of "political democracy": first, because democratic institutions in advanced capitalist countries are also threatened by the crisis; second, because without the defence and development of democracy it is unthinkable that the working classes will become leaders in Europe and will be capable of changing the place and role of Europe in international trade and world politics (and it is on this level that the principal moves are played for a positive solution to the international economic and political crisis); third, because the transformations of a socialist type, which are called for in Europe, take the form of a much more democratic economic and political order than that in existence; fourth, because only from this point of view is it possible to work for unity between communist, socialist and social-democratic parties, without which there is no possibility for socialist transformations in Europe; fifth, because in countries with a high level of capitalist development transformations of a socialist type are the work of a *plurality* of social and political *subjects*, which cannot otherwise be unified; finally, because the subject also indicates concisely the direction in which, according to the PCI, irrevocable transformations of an economic and political character must be stimulated and promoted in countries of "realised socialism".

In such a frame of reference the subject of "political democracy" cannot be reduced to a simple acceptance of the representative State, according to the forms of liberal-democratic traditions. It has much more complex significance, which will not be difficult to outline by reviewing the long and sophisticated development of the PCI's views on the subject.

2 THE PCI'S ANALYSIS OF THE CRISIS OF THE 1970s

Before doing this, it seems essential to consider the PCI's analysis of the international crisis. Commenting on the brief speech made by Berlinguer in Moscow on 27 February 1976 on the occasion of the XXV Congress of the CPSU, some observers stressed how, while upholding the arguments of "Eurocommunism" before the highest assize of international communism, in the midst of lively polemic and in an obviously hostile environment, Berlinguer "did not limit himself to keeping his distance" from Moscow, "but placed the autonomy of the Western Communist parties in the wider picture of the capitalist crisis which places socialism on the agenda, forcing the communists to leave their immobility and pass from a war of position to a war of movement".[8] On the other hand, the joint declarations of the Italian and Spanish Communist Parties do not fail to place "Eurocommunism" in the wider picture of that "new internationalism", which the Italian communists have been claiming since 1956, and which the crisis of the 1970s makes both topical and necessary.[9] This is stated precisely:

> It is a question of being able to take account of all the new opportunities, to secure for all the countries of Western Europe the capacity to offer their own original contribution to the construction of an international society founded on respect for the right of each single people to choose freely the road to its own future, on the elimination of imbalances, on justice, pro-

> gress, development and peace. A new West European political strategy, founded on friendly and co-operative relationships, on the basis of equality, with all the countries of the world, beginning with the United States and the Soviet Union, and on new relations with developing countries, can ensure an irreplaceable contribution to the realisation of these objectives.[10]

It is probably in the statement made by Berlinguer to the Central Committee in December 1974, in preparation for the XIV Congress of the PCI, that the most complete exposition of the Italian communists' analysis of the international crisis can be read. Above all, in it the reasons and mechanisms of a political and economic character can be seen. Berlinguer affirms that it is a question of

> A profound crisis of a new type, due to the concurrence of great processes of historical import, namely: the change in power relationships between imperialist and socialist countries; the entry and growing weight in the world arena of peoples and States earlier subjected to colonial domination; and the explosion of intrinsic contradictions which are inherent in the economic and social mechanisms that have characterised the post-war development of the most progressive capitalist countries. In this picture the salient fact is the great historical process of advancement and liberation amongst peoples and countries once colonial and dependent: a process that today conditions the history of the world. . . . The ascent of new peoples and countries sharpens the crisis and shakes the foundations of the models of capitalist development (that is, the "Western" models of production and life), all based on the search for maximum profit, on the dissipation of resources in distorted consumption and on wastage: a type of development made possible precisely because of the existence of great resources available at the lowest prices, and by the exploitation of peoples subject to the imperialist yoke, as well as the exploitation of the working class and working masses in those same capitalist countries.[11]

The decisive economic element of the crisis lies in the *upsetting of terms of trade* between countries exporting raw materials and those producing industrial goods. This has new dimensions and a significance that is great enough to put *the entire order of relations between development and backwardness on a world scale* in crisis. This system of relations must therefore be changed, if emergence from the crisis is desired. It is necessary, therefore, to put a stop to the growing incidence of *inequalities in development* and their disastrous effects. In his speech to the XIV Congress (March 1972), Berlinguer adopted the platform proposed by Boumedienne at the recent summit of oil-producing countries in Algiers. He justified support of this by the need to alter the system of exchange between developed countries and the "Third World", in anticipation of "a Western Europe that would be capable of 'affirming its own political identity'", and in order to adopt "temporary measures to allow the industrialised countries to overcome their crisis".[12]

The stressing of these elements, at the break-up of a 30-year-old economic and political order, brings into the open some very significant aspects of the Italian communists' analysis of the crisis. First, in industrialised countries a policy of economic expansion based on Keynesian mechanisms of control of the cycle (the maintenance of effective demand through the stimulation of individual consumption) is no longer possible. In fact, in the changed picture of international economic and political relations, those mechanisms help to bring about an inflationary process that is no longer controllable:

> The rates of inflation growth have been exceeding for some years those which were considered 'normal' in times when, after 1929, the policy of the maintenance of demand was adopted by which it was sought to avoid the dangers of the cyclical crisis of capitalism or to contain their range.

Second, the crisis of Keynesian policies has brought about a real economic war between industrialised countries, the strongest of which, the United States, have sought to unload the effects of inflation on their partners. Thus the basis of a 30-year reconciliation of interests between these countries, which had made possible a phase of great expansion in the international capitalist system, entered into crisis. The expansion had taken place under the guidance of the United States and in a pattern of increasingly unequal development, which was above all to the advantage of the strongest partner, at least until the end of the 1960s; but in a framework of mutual convenience, which had secured the consensus of all the partners to this type of development, set up by the United States. This had allowed for the creation and persistence of a new international monetary system, characterised by the hegemony of the dollar. It is not by chance that the dollar-based system appears now to be irrevocably shattered, while all the industrialised countries seem to have resorted chaotically to the same means of dealing with the crisis ("import less and export more"); and in reality they aggravate it.[13]

On the other hand, the re-launching of Keynesian policies appears to be hampered, within industrialised countries, by the fact that "the dominant capitalist classes clash with the resistance and struggle of the working class and other social strata".[14]

> This new factor [said Berlinguer in a Report to the XIV Congress], while restraining the fall in employment and incomes of workers in a more or less considerable measure, makes it more difficult to use mechanisms adopted in the past to overcome crises by discharging all the costs onto the working masses.[15]

All these tendencies drive the strongest imperialist countries to look for solutions to their own crises which augment the inequalities in development. And this profoundly and irreversibly undermines the international economic and political order that has prevailed in the West in the 30 years since the Second World War.[16] On the other hand,

> in the immediate present [this] makes a democratic programme for the economy in individual capitalist countries and international co-operation an urgent task, following a line which is not yet that of socialism, but which already steps outside the logic of capitalism and moves in the direction of socialism.[17]

In the meeting held in Leghorn on 11 July 1975, together with Santiago Carrillo, on the eve of the common Declaration of the Italian and Spanish Communist Parties, which constituted the official act for the birth of "Eurocommunism", Berlinguer effectively synthesised these lines of analysis of "a new type of crisis in capitalist countries", focussing on its particular incidence in Europe and the opportunities which, on the other hand, it offers here for action by the communist party and the whole workers' movement:

> The crisis which has hit all the European capitalist countries – and continues to worsen – is not a passing fact, it is not a parenthesis that can be closed so that all will return as it was before. Instead, it is a question of a profound crisis of a new type, which pervades all aspects of economic and social life. Within the schemes and forms in which European capitalist societies have been organised and developed in the last ten years, there are no prospects other than those of economic decline, social chaos, disorder in civil life, degradation in moral life, sterility in cultural and intellectual life, and ever more serious encroachments on democracy. . .
>
> To insist on going any further, in the face of a world that is changing and asks to be changed, and in particular in the face of the emergence of countries and peoples of the Third World, to insist on the old schemes and models on which European capitalist society has rested up to now, means condemning Europe to the definitive loss of all its functions of progress in the world: leading it to the abdication of the role assigned to it by its long history of achievements which signalled the advance of all human civilisation.[18]

Therefore the basis of "Eurocommunism" lies above all in the possibility of passing to a different order in economic and political relations, and to a real form of "international cooperation" between the industrialised countries of Western Europe and the countries exporting raw materials economically integrated with them. This calls for transformations of a socialist type in Europe. These appear possible today partly because new social groups are entering into the field criticising the capitalist system and struggling against it, and partly because tendencies are becoming visible towards a profound revision of the objectives and lines hitherto followed by social democracy. The possibility arises of establishing close links and proposing common objectives both inside European countries, and as regards Europe's international position.

In his speech at the XXV Congress of the CPSU just cited Berlinguer stated:

> In present conditions a series of positive phenomena are revealed: the criticism of the distortions and failures of capitalism acquires a mass character, even among non-proletarian social strata; aspirations grow for a new order of society moving in the direction of socialism; the struggles of workers become more powerful and at the same time fuller and more unified. In this picture the fact is also stressed that in socialist and social-democratic parties a movement to the left is being registered and that, in some countries, the obstacles to agreement with the communists are coming down. Also of great interest are the anti-capitalist and anti-imperialist moves which are developing in movements with a Christian inspiration.
>
> In this way, new possibilities open up to advance the dialogue and convergence between the various workers' and popular forces, both inside single countries and on a West European scale and this both for immediate objectives and to explore and travel together new roads to the building of a new society.[19]

To pursue an objective "we are bound once again not only to reflect on previous socialist experiences but to search for new roads to socialism in West European countries". In fact, neither the ways followed by countries of "realised socialism", nor those of social democracy seem useful in facing these tasks. As Berlinguer said in a speech to the conference of European communist and workers' parties (30 June 1976):

> Which roads, which socialism? The roads followed by social democracy, while realising certain improvements in the conditions of life of workers in this or that country, have not shown themselves capable of effectively overcoming capitalism. On the other hand, the models of socialist society followed in East European countries do not answer to the particular conditions and trends of the great working and popular masses of Western countries.[20]

The roads of "Eurocommunism" have not yet been traced. Nevertheless some aspects of it can be gleaned from the nature of the transformations that the crisis puts at the top of the agenda, from the peculiarities of their protagonists, from the need to follow new political roads: these are the only roads which allow for the liberation of all the energies necessary to confront such a task and to unite them, with full respect for their diversity and characteristics.

3 "POLITICAL DEMOCRACY" AS A "VALUE IN ITSELF"

In this analysis of the crisis and in this vision of the topicality of socialism, "political democracy" becomes the central element of the "Eurocommunist" perspective. The mass character of the processes of transformation necessary in Europe, and the historically differentiated and evolved attitude of the protagonists, are the facts which reaffirm political democracy as the only form congenial to socialist transformation, according to the teaching of the greatest Marxist thinkers in the West European tradition. Hence acceptance of it as a matter of principle, beyond historical peculiarities and the concrete ways in which both a given transition to socialism could mature and its democratic political foundation could be built in practice. Berlinguer had occasion to stress this, perhaps for the first time in such explicit terms, when, commenting on the Portuguese events of March 1975, he openly criticised some "putschist" attitudes of the Portuguese Communist Party. Here for the first time some characteristic traits of the Italian experience are defended by the PCI, no longer in the name of its own autonomy and national peculiarities, but because they establish positions of principle and of general validity. They concern precisely *the inseparable unity between socialist transformation and political democracy*.

During the course of the XIV Congress of the PCI, the Portuguese Communist Party shared with the militarists in power the refusal of democratic rights to the Catholic Party, following the supposed implication of some of its leaders in a supposed attempt at a reactionary coup. This Berlinguer took as a cue to stress, in the conclusion to the Congress, some PCI positions on the theme of democracy and socialism. The most relevant points of his speech are the following. First, there is the affirmation that as regards political democracy there are, "positions of principle . . . from which our party cannot deviate whether it is working in Italy, or evaluating events in other countries". Second, the conviction that political freedoms constitute an achievement which has to be defended against authoritarian temptations or degenerations of *any type of State power*, is confirmed.[21]

These statements correspond to a very precise conception of the revolutionary process, which Berlinguer does not fail to express, at the end of a brief excursus on the principal stages and particular characteristics of the experience of the PCI from the war of liberation onwards:

> The revolutionary forces definitely change the course of events when – avoiding the opposite errors of "tailism" and vanguardism, of opportunism and extreme radical sectarianism, which make them equally subordinate – they know how to find their place in the centre of the stream of progress and know how to associate the most varied forces with their struggle. Every advance, each real social, political and civil progression, has always been the fruit of an alliance of diverse forces, not homogeneous but heterogeneous, both socially and ideally.
>
> But this is not only the enunciation of a strategy that is uniquely ours. It is, for us, and we think this must become so for everyone, a general vision of the ways in which Italian society can develop, political relations can develop, together with contacts between individuals and therefore in moral life itself . . . . *This is what the revolutionary process is for us*.[22]

To combat the possible impression that this is simply a surreptitious recovery of a mechanistic idea of the historical process and an evolutionist smoothing over of the idea of revolution, we must examine in concrete terms how the PCI's political behaviour has been informed by such principles and evaluate the results attained by it in 30 years of struggle. This is certainly not the place for such an analysis. I would like to pause, instead, on the particular idea of the State, which is present in this approach to political democracy as "a value in itself". This is the real point of difference between the Italian communist tradition of ideas and political behaviour and those of other communist parties. And it is this which determines every difference in the idea of the transition to socialism. The differentiation originated long ago: it goes back to the times and political ideas of the Third International, with which the PCI disagreed over this theme from the 1920s, a theme crucial to any political formation. We must therefore return to Gramsci, who is at the source of the difference. We shall then follow the development of the party until 1956. In fact, at the time of the VIII Congress, the present positions of the PCI were already largely shaped and their peculiarities will become clear in the light of the whole thinking of the party on the theme of the State and in its evolution on the theme of the transition to socialism.

4 THE "CLASS NATURE" OF THE STATE IN GRAMSCI'S INTERPRETATION: THE STARTING POINT OF THE ITALIAN COMMUNIST TRADITION

At the origins of the communist movement, as has been noted, was the theory that the October Revolution represented the experimental verification of a definite idea of history, of the State and of revolution. Out of this came the need to draw from it a set of rules of behaviour and to make the new proletarian revolutionary organisations, regrouped in the Third International, behave accordingly. The axis of this construction is the idea of the socialist revolution as a *replacement* of the parliamentary State by a Soviet State, resulting from a "final clash" between "bourgeois democracy" and "proletarian democracy". This was based on an idea of the "class nature" of the State, which deserves some consideration. Consider, for example, the formulations of the *Programme* approved by the VI Congress of the Communist International, which on this point can be considered symbolic of the entire train of events of the International and is still basic today in the ideas that the enormous majority of the communist movement follow. There it is stated:

> Bourgeois democracy, with its formal equality of citizens before the law, is built on the glaring economic inequality of classes. Bourgeois democracy does not tamper with the monopoly of the capitalist class and the largest landowners in the decisive means of production. On the contrary, it strengthens that monopoly and so converts, for the exploited class and above all the proletariat, formal equality before the law, democratic rights and liberties – which in any case are in practice systematically curtailed – into a legal fiction, a means of deceiving and enslaving the masses.[23]

The assessment of the institutions of parliamentary democracy as a web of "legal fiction" and a "means to deceive and oppress the masses", treats the State as no more than a group of apparatuses which the dominant classes use to impose their own corporate interests, that is, their own political will, on all other classes and on all citizens in a unilateral and oppressive way. The "class nature" of the State is therefore *external* to its "machinery"; it rests instead in the character of *interests* and *will* which certain social groups, adopting those devices as their own *instrument*, impose exclusively against the interests and will of the subordinate classes and all the exploited. The latter suffer this state of affairs with violence and deceit.

Gramsci's position is very different. I would like in this case too to limit myself to a brief exposition, choosing some passages from the *Prison Notebooks*, to my mind the best examples, in which there is an outline of the Marxist theory of the State which is entirely his own, which Gramsci himself called an idea of the State "according to the productive function of classes". We can see the way in which he posed the problem of the "class nature" of the State. Gramsci states in a note dedicated to reflection on the peculiar features of the formation of the national State in Italy:

> Although it is certain that for the fundamental productive classes (capitalist bourgeoisie and modern proletariat) the State is only conceivable as the concrete form of a specific economic world, of a specific system of production, this does not mean that the relationship of means to end can be easily determined or takes the form of a simple schema, apparent at first sight. It is true that conquest of power and achievement of a new productive world are inseparable, and that propaganda for one of them is also propaganda for the other, and that in reality it is solely in this that the unity of the dominant class – at once economic and political – resides. But the complex problem arises of the relation of internal forces in the country in question, of the relation of international forces, of the country's geo-political position.[24]

Gramsci does not speak of the "class nature" of the State in a simplified way; nor does he follow the crude definitions of the Marxist tradition, which exhaust the theory of the State by defining it as an *expression* of the interests of the dominant class, not allowing therefore for a concrete analysis of various State forms, which in practice are those which count. To elaborate a Marxist idea of the State, we must first distinguish those concepts which define the mode of production, and which allow us to establish the nature of classes and their relationships, in contrast to those concepts which allow for a concrete class analysis. This latter comes from the recognition of the classes' political history, from their form of consciousness, from their modes of organisation. It is this dynamic, concretely defining the forces in the field, which allows us to determine the particular forms of the State, which is the principal objective of Marxist political theory.

Therefore, if at the basis there is a correspondence between economic forms and political forms; if the State is composed of institutions which allow the dominant class to become united; if the politically dominant class is always the class which dominates relations of production; all of these are still not enough to determine the concrete forms of the State. The peculiarities of these come definitively from the ways in which relationships between the dominant and the dominated are realised, and which change the equilibrium of power.

It therefore happens, according to Gramsci, that a certain State form acquires particular characteristics because, while being born on the basis of a given mode of production and corresponding to the interests of the fundamental productive classes, nevertheless the initiative for its formation has been taken by particular sections of a possible dominant bloc, which does not correspond to the fundamental economic part of it. In the formation of the modern bourgeois States, in general, the essential impulse came from the capitalist bourgeoisie, which took the initiative and determined the State form. But there are cases, like the Italian Risorgimento, when:

> the impetus of progress is not tightly linked to a vast local economic development which is artificially limited and repressed, but is instead the reflection of international developments which transmit their ideological currents to the periphery – currents born on the basis of the productive development of the more advanced countries – then the group which is the bearer of the new ideas is not the economic group but the intellectual stratum, and the conception of the State advocated

by them changes aspect: it is conceived as something in itself, as a rational absolute.[25]

Therefore the relationship between the State and the economically dominant class is neither linear nor simple. It does not say anything concrete about the State if the dominant class is conceived as an anthropomorphic subject endowed with consciousness and defined by its corporate interests, abstracted from the particular form of the State; or if the latter is conceived as the instrument for promoting those interests, but one which is always the same and therefore, if necessary, also useful for imposing the interests of another class, when the first is eliminated or defeated. On the other hand, the concrete form of the State springs from the way in which the fundamental classes succeed in organising the entire web of relations between governors and governed; and this particular whole establishes the State in flesh and bone. Gramsci states in another fundamental passage in the *Notebooks*:

> The State is seen as the organ of one particular group, destined to create favourable conditions for the latter's maximum expansion. But the development and expansion of the particular group are conceived of, and presented, as being the motive force of a universal expansion, of a development of all the "national" energies. In other words, the dominant group is coordinated concretely with the general interests of the subordinate groups, and the life of the State is conceived as a continuous process of formation and superseding of unstable equilibria (on the juridical plane) between the interests of the fundamental group and those of the subordinate groups – equilibria in which the interests of the dominant group prevail, but only up to a certain point, that is, stopping short of narrowly corporate economic interests.[26]

There is, in short, no State without hegemony. It is the concrete forms of hegemony which determine the degrees and various modes of coercion. This concept of a hegemony, which permits the fundamental class to realise its historic ends, goes beyond narrow-minded corporate economic interests, concretely reconnecting State forms to methods of "compromise" between governors and governed.

From the socialist perspective therefore, it is a question of critically examining and transforming the way of being of entire social groups and large cultural constellations, which embody the different forms of "compromise" between antagonistic classes, giving life to "knowledge", procedures and apparatuses which they articulate in concrete terms. In the functioning State, the class foundation of a given domination is always found transcribed in the knowledge, practices and relationships which shape the relationship. It can be criticised and superseded in fact only through the weaving of a complex form of relations between leaders and led, the principal inspiration for which, according to Gramsci, is in the ultimate idea of the extinction of the State.[27]

As can be seen, we are on a very different plane from that of the Third International. If the relationship between the State and the dominant class always needs to be specified by the concrete ways in which governors and governed are arranged, political contradictions cover the entire web of institutions and relationships of hegemony, and are not reducible to a crude opposition between bourgeois democracy and proletarian democracy. There is no doubt that the working class must elaborate its own form of the State. But this cannot be considered already given on the basis of forms which define its antagonism with capital and with the bourgeois State, and which determine its political constitution as a class. The formation of a socialist State can be nothing other than a *differentiated process*, determined by the various ways in which the working class and its allies break the web of existing relations between governors and governed, producing a new and comprehensive organisation of classes and social groups. Furthermore

> it must be clearly understood that the division between rulers and ruled – though in the last analysis it has its origins in a division between social groups – is in fact, things being as they are, also to be found within the group itself, even where it is a socially homogeneous one. In a certain sense it may be said that this division is created by the division of labour.[28]

Therefore the elaboration of a new State is a much more complex affair than the *substitution* of a system of Soviets in place of parliamentary democracy.

5 EAST AND WEST IN THE ANALYSES OF GRAMSCI AND TOGLIATTI: POSSIBILITIES OF AN "ANTI-FASCIST REVOLUTION" IN ITALY (1925–9)

Only with the appearance of the "Eurocommunist" phenomenon has this radical theoretical distinction between the PCI positions and those of the Soviet-inspired communist movement been openly declared. Only now is it completely unfolded on the political plane. As elaborated by the party this distinction is the fruit of an uneven evolution, which is not derived from theoretical premises of a general character, but from political experience and growing historical differentiation. In the beginning this developed around the "search for forms of *transition* or *approach* to the proletarian revolution".[29]

From the III Congress of the Communist International this was the central theme for the entire communist movement. After the first two congresses, which were engaged above all in defining the characteristics that nascent communist parties should assume, from 1921 the Communist International registered the defeats of the European proletariat and the start of a revival in the capitalist economy. It took note of the fact that the conquest of power and the world-wide proletarian revolution were no longer within reach. Therefore, the "united front" tactics and the slogan "worker and peasant government" (different in content and objectives from the "dictatorship of the proletariat") were elaborated. Thanks to this, communist parties should have been able to place themselves in a position of "going to the masses", conquering the majority of the working class and fulfilling the principal task in a new historical phase: to "accumulate" forces to ensure the victory of the proletariat at the next rising of a new "revolutionary wave".

Already, in *"Left-wing" Communism*, Lenin had offered an invitation to the communist parties to make a careful consideration of the differences between East and West, in the light of these objectives. Arguing with communists of the left, amongst whom was the entire group of PCd'I* leaders, he called to the fact that in

*The Italian Party was known as the *Partito comunista d'Italia* (PCd'I) until 1943; when the name was changed to *Partito comunista italiano* (PCI) (translator's note).

Western Europe, as distinct from the Soviet Union, "almost all workers are organised"; the influence of the parliamentary system on the great masses and on the working class itself was enormous, and the working class was characterised by forms of consciousness and profoundly consolidated organisations, such as the trades unions.

The recognition of the differences between East and West was the point of departure of Gramsci's research around 1923–4. These were the years of his residence in Moscow and Vienna, as representative of the PCd'I in the Communist International. And they were also the years in which he centred his attention on a fact that was decisive for the entire history and evolution of the PCI: the coming of fascism. Italy is the only country in Europe in which the post-war crisis was rapidly brought to an end by the defeat of the workers' movement and the ruin of the old liberal State. To Gramsci and Togliatti it soon became clear that fascism confronted the working class with a process of reactionary transformation in the State.[30] On the one hand, this gave a special character to the search for "forms of approach" to the proletarian revolution, because very soon the new party found itself working in illegal conditions and in a State in which all democratic freedoms were suppressed. On the other hand, it established a rich laboratory for investigation into the tendencies at the root of the authoritarian transformations present in all the countries of old liberal Europe. In fact, in the analysis which Gramsci and Togliatti soon sketched out, fascism was certainly characterised above all by Italian peculiarities (characteristics of the recent national unification, fragility of the liberal State, peculiarities of the workers' movement, etc.); but it was also a national response of the upper bourgeoisie to problems that were presented in various ways in the whole of Europe.

In this setting, from 1924 Gramsci put his analyses and initiative into shape, aiming at giving a solid national platform to the new party by recognising the "forms of approach to the proletarian revolution", and in gathering around himself a new leading group which took the helm of the party at the III Congress at Lyon in 1926.

Writing from Vienna to Togliatti, Scoccimarro, Leonetti and other former colleagues on *Ordine Nuovo*, 21 March 1924, Gramsci asked,

> Is it possible to believe that we shall pass directly from fascism to the dictatorship of the proletariat? Which intermediate phases are possible and likely? I think that in the crisis which the country will undergo, that party will gain the upper hand which has best understood this necessary transition process, and thus impressed its seriousness on the broad masses.[31]

Although taking its cue from the presence of fascism in power in Italy, this way of putting the question broaches a much broader reflection on the peculiarities of a socialist revolution in the West. In fact, little more than a month before, on 9 February, in a letter to Togliatti, Gramsci had shown that for a European communist party the essential fact to be considered was that:

> the outcome, which in Russia was direct and drove the masses onto the streets for a revolutionary uprising, in Central and Western Europe is complicated by all these political superstructures, created by the greater development of capitalism. This makes the action of the masses slower and more prudent, and therefore requires of the revolutionary party a strategy and tactics altogether more complex and long-term than those which were necessary for the Bolsheviks in the period between March and November 1917.[32]

Two years later, in a report to the Central Committee on 2 August 1926, he stressed that:

> in the advanced capitalist countries the ruling class possesses political and organisational reserves which it did not possess, for instance, in Russia. . . . This means that even the most serious economic crises do not have immediate repercussions in the political sphere. Politics always lags behind economics, far behind. The State apparatus is far more resistant than is often possible to believe; and it succeeds, at moments of crisis, in organising greater forces loyal to the régime than the depth of the crisis might lead one to suppose.[33]

In the *Notebooks*, lastly, in a fundamental passage in his reflections on the necessity for the tactics of the proletarian revolution in the West to assume the methods of a "war of position", he observed:

> In Russia, the State was everything, civil society was primordial and gelatinous; in the West there was a proper relation between State and civil society, and when the State trembled a sturdy structure of civil society was at once revealed. The State was only an outer ditch, behind which there stood a powerful system of fortresses and earthworks: more or less numerous from one State to the next, it goes without saying – but this precisely necessitated an accurate reconnaissance of each individual country.[34]

From this standpoint, assuming an early end to the "relative stabilisation" of capitalism and "a new phase in the development of the capitalist crisis", in August 1926 Gramsci noted the inadequacy of the "united front" tactics and claimed that it was necessary to adopt intermediate slogans of a political character and general validity, differentiated in such a way as to comply with different national situations:

> For all the capitalist countries a fundamental problem is posed – the problem of the transition from the united front tactic, understood in a general sense, to a specific tactic, which confronts the concrete problems of national life and operates on the basis of the popular forces as they are historically determined.[35]

Assuming the leadership of the party after Gramsci's arrest, and following Gramsci's reflections, Togliatti continued to seek a creative development of the united front tactics. In Italy, in particular, the proletariat was presented with the problems of struggling, in different ways, with both capitalism and fascism. In the *Directive for Political Action of the PCd'I*, June 1928, Togliatti stated:

> This problem can be formulated, in a precise way, thus: is it possible that the first wave of a mass anti-fascist movement could carry with it the installation of the dictatorship of the proletariat; or is it foreseeable that there would be a period in which, in the open struggle of the masses against fascism, the non-communist anti-fascist forces could succeed in leading the masses or a part of them, and succeed in seriously opposing the

> proletarian and communist leadership of the movement? We believe the second hypothesis is also possible.[36]

Therefore, he maintained that the party should proceed according to a "double perspective". The prospect of a proletarian revolution could be open only from an intermediate phase, in which the political objective of the proletariat, if it was to assume leadership of the anti-fascist struggle and thereby give it the character of a struggle against the capitalist system, had to be that of a new democratic form of the State. In June 1927, Togliatti affirmed that the possibility could not be excluded that "in order not to be separated from the masses", "in the moment of revolutionary action the Party may have to adopt" the slogan of the Constituent Assembly.[37]

The lesson of fascism therefore pushed the PCd'I to a very different position from that of the International and other communist parties in the confrontation with "bourgeois democracy". As Togliatti observed in June 1927:

> Democratic freedoms were, in the period of the liberal revolutions, a condition for the extension and reinforcement of the economic and political power of the bourgeoisie. . . . With the war and after it, when the crisis of the ruin of capitalist society opens, and the bourgeoisie has to defend its power by means of dictatorship, democratic freedoms become a stumbling-block and are liquidated by the bourgeoisie itself, in its own interests; all the more promptly in so far as its resources and its capacity for resistance on a purely economic level, are limited, and the attack of the proletariat directly threatens the whole of capitalist society.[38]

In general, the "relative stabilisation" carries with it a diffuse tendency towards authoritarian reorganisation of the capitalist State. It draws its premise from the defeat of the proletarian revolution in the first years of the 1920s and feeds on the organisation of a permanent offensive against the levels of life and employment of the working masses, authoritarian compression and, if necessary, annihilation of the political autonomy of the working class. In such a context, the struggle for democratic freedom assumes an anti-capitalist character. It becomes the essential task of the working class and an integral part of the struggle for socialism. As Togliatti put it in a report to the Italian Commission of the Executive of the Communist International on 20 February 1928:

> We do not believe that capitalist stabilisation is possible in a democratic régime. Stabilisation carries with it the necessity to reduce wages and the bridling of worker resistance, it ends in the suppression of such trades-union and political freedoms as have already been won. It is not possible to resolve these problems with democratic solutions. A possibility for stabilisation does not exist in a democratic picture. This is why the struggle for democratic freedoms acquires a revolutionary character.[39]

In the Italian situation this meant that the socialist revolution would assume particular forms: it would take on the character of an "anti-fascist revolution".[40]

6 THE SPREAD OF FASCISM IN EUROPE AND THE TOGLIATTIAN HYPOTHESIS OF A "NEW TYPE OF DEMOCRACY" (1934–6)

The difference between this line of enquiry and the guidelines of the Communist International was not slow to show itself and explode in open conflict. At the X Plenum of the Executive of the International, in July 1929, Manuilsky attacked the slogan "Republican Assembly on the base of worker and peasant committees", followed by the PCd'I after the Lyon Congress to indicate the methods and objectives of the "anti-fascist revolution" and its character as a "popular revolution". "There's no doubt that the policy of our party as Manuilsky proposes", replied Togliatti, "means changing everything that we did at the Third Congress of the Party".[41] But, in the conditions of life of the Communist International and the situation of the Italian communists, Togliatti could do nothing other than capitulate, accepting the renunciation of his own line and his own enquiry, and wait for better times. In fact, he concluded the clash with Manuilsky with the following words:

> If the Comintern says that it is not right [to pose the problems in which are hinted at in the slogan "republican assembly"], we cannot then do so any longer; each one of us will think of these things and no longer speak of them; saying only that the anti-fascist revolution will be a proletarian revolution. But each one of us thinks that it is not certain that we will have the leadership right from the beginning and we think we may conquer it only in the course of the struggle.[42]

The promising enquiry begun by the Italian communists on the crux of relations between democracy and socialism was thus interrupted. It is necessary to wait until 1934 for it to re-emerge, through the experience of the French Popular Front, together with the theme of the specificity of transition in the West. But only in the VII Congress of the International, a year later, did it in some way become legitimate. Here, in Dimitrov's statement, there is a complex reconsideration of "bourgeois democracy" and an indication of the necessity for a positive relationship of the working class with it.

Many years later, in 1959, evaluating this Congress, Togliatti said that with it "the communists took the flag of democracy into their hands", and added:

> the line was no longer tactical, but strategic. . . . Around the problem of government and the State, the participation of communists in a power that was not the dictatorship of the proletariat, was acknowledged, declared to be right and to be something that should be pressed for. . .
>
> The communists wanted to participate in power to destroy fascism and save democracy. They said openly, however, that the democratic order could not be salvaged and developed unless it acquired a new content, which had to be given to it by the support of the popular masses and political and economic reforms which cut the roots of reaction and fascism.

Togliatti stressed that "the idea of a new type of democracy arose in this way".[43]

For the real truth on this crucial point, Dimitrov's statement is not in fact clear. With regard to prospects for transition, which a popular front government could also open up, he affirmed:

> We say openly to the masses: this government *cannot* lead you to *definitive salvation*. It is not capable of beating the domination of the exploiters and therefore cannot definitively eliminate the danger of a fascist counter-revolution. It is therefore necessary *to prepare for the socialist revolution! Soviet power* alone and uniquely can lead to salvation! . . .
>
> If our parties know how to use the possibilities of establishing a united front government in a Bolshevik way, the struggle for its affirmation and permanence in power with the aim of *the revolutionary preparation of the masses*, we will have *the best political justification* for our line on the formation of a united front government.[44]

The attitude of the Communist International towards political democracy remains totally instrumental: in the framework of a democratic régime and a united front government, the proletariat *takes the opportunity* to impose, "in a Bolshevik way", "Soviet power". In reality, this still did not outline a hypothesis for socialist transformation different from that tried in Russia, despite the failures of the Bolshevik model in the West, which had already taken place in the early 1920s.

On the other hand, it is not by chance that the VII Congress limited itself to presenting its own politics as a tactical turn.[45] In reality, the Communist International, right up to its dissolution in 1943, never succeeded in defining any relationship between democracy and socialism which did not reduce the first to an instrument of the second. Neither did it follow the policies of the united front and popular front with conviction nor develop them with any result. However, it is right to state, as is done in the *Elements for a Programmatic Declaration*, approved by the VIII PCI Congress in 1956, that simply from the strategy of popular fronts "an elaboration of the idea of a new type of democracy, which was neither the dictatorship of the proletariat, nor a Soviet régime, but a different form of power, began to be reached". This concept is not found complete in the entire history of the Communist International. Nevertheless, Palmiro Togliatti did set out on that road and followed it to good purpose far enough to formulate such hypotheses.

Togliatti's opportunity came with the development of the Spanish situation after the 1936 Republic. This was an example of a democratic Republic in which the working class, struggling against fascism, placed itself at the head of an immense reserve of exploited masses, which were roused to the struggle by the imminent danger of fascism. Winning thus the leadership of the country, the working class was capable of shifting the relationship of forces progressively to its advantage and of imposing profound changes in society and production, giving life to "a new type of democratic Republic". This republic could have been distinguished by the permanence of the working class in the leadership of the State, in such a way as to guarantee its evolution towards transformations of a democratic and socialist type. In the fundamental essay written in 1936, *On the Peculiarities of the Spanish Revolution*, Togliatti traced the features of this new political form of transition on the basis of a concrete political experience:

> The democratic Republic created in Spain does not resemble a bourgeois democratic Republic of the common type. It is created in the fire of a civil war in which part of the leadership goes to the working class; it is created in a moment when in one sixth of the globe socialism has already won and in a series of capitalist countries conservative bourgeois democracy has been destroyed by fascism. The characteristic trait of this new democratic Republic consists in the fact that in it fascism, raised against the people, was crushed by the people with arms in their hands: in consequence there is no longer any place, in this Republic, for this enemy of the people. . . . Secondly, in this Republic the material basis for fascism is destroyed. Already now, lands and enterprises belonging to those who supported the fascist revolt have been confiscated and given over for the use of the people. Already now, in connection with the war situation, the Spanish government is forced to introduce controls over the economic apparatus in the interests of the defence of the Republic, and the more the rebels persist in waging war against the regular government, the further the government has to go in disciplining the whole economic life of the country. Thirdly, this new type of democracy cannot, in the case of a victory for the people, be other than the enemy of every conservative spirit. It possesses all the conditions which allow for further development. It offers a guarantee for all further economic and political achievements by Spanish workers.[46]

Thus Togliatti arrived at:

> a definition of the character of a new democratic State, in which the working class and its parties participate in power, but which does not correspond in any way to the State which was organised when the working class took power in Russia in 1917.[47]

A new experience of proletarian power had emerged, which gave life to a new hypothesis of the transitional State, different from that of the dictatorship of the proletariat. The embryo was born of a new political conception, which would soon inspire the conduct of Italian communists in the war for liberation and in the collaboration in the building of the new State: the theory of *progressive democracy*.

7 "PROGRESSIVE DEMOCRACY": THE STATE FORM OF SOCIALIST TRANSFORMATION IN THE WEST (1944–7)

The essential traits of this conception were defined when the Italian communists, having taken the lead in the war for liberation and having made the *svolta di Salerno*, assumed a decisive role in the political direction of the country.

The political form which they intended to stamp on Italy, once fascism was overcome, was that of a democratic Republic of a new type, characterised by the permanent hegemony of parties "which had a basis among the people and a democratic and national programme".[48] The programmatic contents of progressive democracy are shown in synthesis in the text of a report and proposals presented by Togliatti at the first sub-committee for the elaboration of a new constitution:

> (a) the need for an economic plan, on the basis of which the State would be able to intervene in order to co-ordinate and direct the productive activity of individuals and the whole nation; (b) the constitutional recognition of forms of ownership of the means of production other than private; more precisely, co-operative and state ownership. . . ; (c) the need for those firms to be nationalised which through their character as public or monopoly ser-

vices should be divorced from private initiative; (d) the need for the organisation of factory councils as organs for the exercise of control over production, on the part of all categories of workers, in the interests of the collective; (e) the necessity that the right of ownership which on the one hand is guaranteed the protection of the law, should be limited on the other by social interests; and lastly (f) the need for the distribution of land in our country to be profoundly changed, in such a way as to limit large properties and defend small and medium-sized properties, and particularly the family farm.[49]

Once having gathered such programmatic contents in the Constitution, Togliatti interpreted the reality of the country as characterised by:

> a profound revolutionary process, which, however, through the common orientation of the progressive forces, developes without abandoning the terrain of democratic legality. By democracy that is, by accepting the principle of the free expression of the majority, we are forced to realise those changes in our social structure which are mature both in the reality of things and in the consciousness of the mass of workers. Due to this we now all, or almost all, speak, not of pure and simple democracy, but of a 'progressive democracy', and the value of this definition is found precisely in the fact that it recognises and affirms this tendency towards a profound upheaval carried through with legality.[50]

The criteria for evaluating the originality and effective orientation of this new form of the State cannot be only those of legal formality nor purely institutional:

> When dealing with guaranteed rights of a prevailingly political nature, the guarantee can be found either in an organisation of the State which makes abuse by the governors impossible or at least limited, or in institutions of particular jurisdictional application; but the guarantee for an effective translation into practice of new rights of a social character [collected in the Constitution] cannot be found other than in the particular direction of the economic activity of the whole country.[51]

The political foundation of progressive democracy lies then in the possibility that it may embody the line of economic development and structural transformation of society and the State, of which the working class is the most consistent upholder. The particular character of this new form of democratic republic is determined by the working class's admittance to and permanence in, the leadership of the country, and by the establishment and maintenance in it of the necessary conditions for "the organisation of the working class as a leading class".

> It is not necessary to hide, and it was never hidden [recalled Togliatti in 1951], that this evolution went in the direction of socialism, because such has been the real and most important question in Italy since the time when capitalism reached that stage of imperialist maturity.[52]

Therefore, *progressive democracy is characterised as a form of intermediate or transitional State*, through economic and social transformations which are promoted by it and, through the new power bloc which determines its course, open a new road of advance towards socialism.

This was required and made possible, at one and the same time, by a profoundly new international framework and by the need to follow ways different from the Soviet Union in the struggle for socialism in Western Europe. Togliatti said in fact:

> The action of the working class is at a point where, in order for it to develop, new paths must be followed, paths which have not been cleared in the past. Tracing these paths, foreseeing the way in which they can be developed and cleared with a sure step, is what the leadership of the Marxist party must succeed in doing today. It is not possible to repeat the plans and formulae of the past: it is necessary to know how to create something new, through political action and organisation adapted to national and international conditions in which the struggle for democracy and socialism develops in the whole world. . . . The international experience tells us that in the present conditions of the class struggle in the entire world, the vanguard working class and working masses can find, in order to arrive at socialism . . . new paths, different from those for example, that have

been followed by the working class and workers of the Soviet Union.[53]

Thus the search for what was already called (1945–7) "the Italian road to socialism", was placed in a European context characterised by the unfolding of new and diverse forms of transition to socialism, on the morrow of the victorious war against fascism and nazism. Togliatti did not fail to stress such processes, outlining a full picture of new State forms which were developing in Europe in those years and which for the most part took the name of "people's democracy".[54]

But with the arrival of the Cold War, the creation of the Cominform and the split between the Soviet Union and Yugoslavia, these new developments came to an end, or were at least brought to a brisk halt. It was precisely on those new realities of "people's democracy" that the Cominform imposed "the Soviet model from outside and above",[55] arguing that "people's democracy" performed basically the same functions as the "dictatorship of the proletariat". The Italian communists also followed this line and set aside the search for their national road to socialism. As Berlinguer put it in a self-criticism in the name of the party in December 1974:

> We must ask ourselves if our response to events in Eastern Europe has not sinned through ambiguity, if it has not taken too little account of the need to reply to the questions, the preoccupations and the sincere fears of many democrats; we must affirm (not only in our own behaviour, as in substance happens, but also in explicit theoretical elaboration) that we remain persuaded of a necessary diversity in roads to socialism, and that we should have searched for, and continued to follow, original roads, different from those of East European experience.[56]

In any case, with the condemnation of Yugoslavia and the Italian elections of 1948, the enquiry set in motion by the experience of "people's democracy" and "progressive democracy"

> was cut short and everything was resolved with the scholastic formula that people's democracy was nothing more than a 'synonym' of the proletarian dictatorship which had been real-

> ised in the Soviet Union. The greatest historical issue put to the workers' movement in our times was in this way reduced almost to a problem of terminology: the issue of the search for new roads of advance towards socialism, of the elaboration of new forms of progressive democratic power and, in relation to that, of the organisation of a socialist economy with new methods, recommended and imposed by new objective and subjective conditions.[57]

8 THE REVIVAL OF 1956; AN OUTLINE FOR DEMOCRATIC AND SOCIALIST TRANSITION

This situation was changed with the maturing of new international equilibria and with the crisis of the Cold War. The XX Congress of the CPSU could thus promote, in 1956, a profound revision of the positions of the communist movement.

Why did Togliatti judge it "the most important Congress of the Communist Party of the Soviet Union since the death of Lenin?"[58] With the formulation of the policy of peaceful coexistence, the proclamation of the non-inevitability of war, the affirmation of the necessary diversity of roads for the advance to socialism and the sanctioning of possible democratic forms of transition, the Congress was the prelude to a new phase of initiative for communist and revolutionary forces. It opened the way for a fuller development of their unity and impelled communists to examine thoroughly their knowledge of, and bring out the value of, the diverse situations in which they worked.

> The importance of the XX Congress [said Togliatti at the end of February 1956] lies above all in its having posed, affirmed and stressed the new elements of the present-day situation; in not only having registered but justly evaluated what is new in the world today and in having known how to draw the principal conclusions to be derived from it.[59]

First among these was that the world revolutionary process could receive an exceptional impulse from the new and extraordinarily wide unity which the working class and popular masses in Europe, in particular, could reach.[60]

It was possible and necessary, at this point, to develop completely the conception of "national roads" to socialism: in its applicability to the Italian situation, in our case, but also in its foundations, both in general and in principle. Here then, in his speech to the VIII Congress of the PCI, at the end of 1956, Togliatti outlines a full picture of the principles which, in his view, underlie the general conception of democratic and socialist transformation:

> The need to destroy the capitalist order and create a socialist order does not come out of the decisions or ability or strength of a political party. Nor does it come out of the strength of a class trades union movement. It comes out of the development and contrasts of the real and subjective forces from which present-day society is woven. It is this development and these contrasts which make the passage to socialism historically necessary, so that one can say that socialism matures objectively in the midst of capitalism itself. It is therefore evident that the conditions and forms of maturing must differ from one place to another and from one moment in history to another. Not only the strength but the very structure of the capitalist regime is different. Forces of production have reached different levels in different countries; relations of production are differently ordered, within a general picture, which is broadly uniform in places where capitalism is the dominant factor. There is no uniformity in the relations between city and countryside, which change according to the way in which the bourgeois revolution was conducted; nor in the weight and nature of the groups of small and medium independent producers; nor in cultural traditions. This diversity contributes to determining the structure of States, the nature of leadership groups and the conditions and forms of the class struggle. Also, the transformations that are common to all the capitalist world, such as today the growing domination of great monopoly groups, are not carried out everywhere in the same way, nor lead everywhere to the same practical consequences, and do not give rise to equivalent problems everywhere.
>
> The diversity in ways of advance to socialism springs from history, the economy, the development of the workers' movement and is often found in the spontaneous processes of this

> movement. The political leadership of the working class is presented with the task of being aware of this and passing this awareness on to at least the vanguard of the proletariat; therefore not breaking away from those political guidelines and methods of work which, in their diversity from one country to another, are the only things that can possibly ensure the fundamental unity and success of the whole movement.[61]

The reminder of the decisive role of conflicts, on an objective plane, and of the initiative of the masses, on a subjective plane, both in the imposition of socialist transformation and in the definition of characteristics of the new society, is rich with resonance and significance. Above all, it argues against any mechanistic and voluntaristic imitation of the Bolshevik experience. Secondly, it contains the most well-founded rejection of a conception of socialism in which the active subject of the transformation is the party, identified in a totalitarian way with the State apparatus, according to the Soviet model. Thirdly, it requires a democratic foundation as much in the development of the revolutionary process, as in the definition of socialist society. In fact, the protagonists of the process are necessarily *differentiated*. This process is articulated through the full expression of their *differences* and their *autonomy*. The unification of classes and social groups which gives life to the process is by nature *political*. Such it remains also during the building of socialist society.

The political peculiarity of the new society lies therefore in the growing *self-government of the masses*. From now onwards, in the language of the Italian communists, the transition to socialism and the construction of the new society are designated preferably as *a process of democratic and socialist transformation*. And by this they mean to stress not just *the continuity of the two phases* of social transformation, but rather, the inseparable interlacing of the *two forms* of the process: the political, of a peculiar democratic character, and the economic, to which the concept of socialism more properly pertains.

We are here concerned with a full recovery of the classic conception, in West European Marxist thought, of the characteristics of socialism "at the highest points" of its development, and of a further enrichment of this thought.

This does not diminish the need also to outline the features of the road of advance to socialism which it is intended to follow on the institutional plane. Indeed, such a *mise au point* appears all the more urgent, the more the new political concepts take impetus from the conviction that the conditions for democratic and socialist transformation of our country and, more generally, of Western Europe, are more mature. At the VIII Congress the *Elements for a Programmatic Declaration* were set out, defining the characteristics of the new State, for which the Italian communists and working classes were struggling.

In this document, fundamental to the history of the PCI, basic to all subsequent developments in its policies, up to the present day, it is solemnly affirmed that

> the historic task of proceeding to the establishment of socialism by a new road, other than that by which the dictatorship of the proletariat was realised in other countries, lies before the working class and Italian people.

How was the task of a democratic advance towards socialism posed in Italy? In what relationship did democratic transformations and those of a socialist type stand? More specifically, what *form of State* was considered adequate to the objective, and in what relationship, within this, did democracy and socialism stand?

The PCI considered the Constitution of the Italian Republic and the institutions that it provided for, as the adequate political basis for socialist transformation of the country. This was because, in the words of the *Programmatic Declaration*

> the Republican Constitution, even though distinguishable from Constitutions of a socialist type both in its social content and because it does not provide for a directly articulated democracy on the basis of production, does however concretely recognise the rights of workers to enter into the leadership of the State, and proposes some conditions that could, where realised, favour this entry and allow for a notable start for national society on the road to its transformation in a socialist sense.

The democratic republic outlined in the Italian Constitution is characterised above all by a political regime of a parliamentary type. With regard to this, the *Programmatic Declaration* stated precisely that:

> the parliamentary regime, respect for the principle of the freely expressed majority, the method defined by the Constitution to ensure that the majority is formed in a free and democratic way is not only compatible with the fulfilment of profound social reforms and with the construction of a socialist society, but also facilitates and ensures, in present-day conditions, the contact and collaboration of other social and political forces, the coming of a new ruling class, in the midst of which the working class is the decisive force.

Further:

> Parliament can and must exercise an active function, both for the transformation of the country in a democratic and socialist sense, and in the new socialist society; with the condition that beside it, forms of direct democracy can and must develop to ensure further developments and the superiority of socialist democracy.

Here there is, it seems to me, a theoretical innovation of importance. Not only does the PCI not think that socialism is a model of society characterised by the replacement of parliamentary democracy by Soviet democracy. Not only does it leave behind the conception of the socialist revolution as an opposition of proletarian democracy to bourgeois democracy. It also affirms that, in the conditions in which the struggle for socialism developed in Italy and in so far as political characteristics of a future socialist society can be foreseen and fostered, this latter would also be characterised by a representative system of a parliamentary type, however profoundly corrected by the development and extension of new democratic institutions, enacted to determine the progressive promotion of self-government by the masses.

At this point, I think, one can affirm that the PCI has by now outlined *a new form of democracy*; in its view the one most suitable for the promotion of socialist transformation in Italy, one which is certainly not a democracy of a Soviet type, but nor is it a parliamentary democracy in a true sense. Incorporated in an original democratic web, rich with new institutions of a democracy of the producers, of direct democracy and a democracy "of the base", the Parliament, differing from the representative systems of a liberal-democratic type, can really become the place for the formation of a complex political synthesis, in which the progressively united body of citizen-producers is recognised, and through which the entire economic process is managed in a democratic way and socialisation is progressively promoted.

In such an outlook, "there exists no principle which excludes the plurality of parties in the country and in power during the construction of a socialist society, and the free confrontation between different ideologies".

Although the new interlacing of democracy and socialism, stated in these terms, is worked out on the basis of the Italian experience, its structure already seems, in the *Programmatic Declaration*, to fit wider problems and processes of a European character.

To conclude, let us read any of the documents which enunciate the principles of "Eurocommunism"; for example, Berlinguer's speech at the Conference of European Communist and Workers' Parties (30 June 1976):

> In Italy, where the working class and our party have been and are protagonists in the struggle for the achievement, the defence and the development of democracy, we struggle for a socialist society which has at its base the recognition of the value of personal and collective freedoms and their guarantee: of principles of a secular and non-ideological character of the State and its democratic structure; of the plurality of parties and the possibility of alternating the government majority; of the autonomy of trade unions, religious freedom, freedom of speech, culture, art and science. In the economic field it is a question of ensuring a high level of productive development through democratic planning which hinges on the existence and positive function of various forms of initiative and management whether public or private, all turned towards the satisfaction of the great needs of men and the national collective.

It is hardly necessary to point out the linear concordance of these statements with the contents and objectives of that "new type of democracy" which was already claimed by the PCI in 1945–7 for the reconstruction of the country; and which not only the PCI but also other democratic political forces, during the war of liberation and in the phase of the Constituent Assembly, called "progressive democracy". Thus, it seems to me, such a passage says nothing more than that which, from 1956, the PCI had already pointed out and affirmed on the subject of "political democracy" and its necessary foundation in the transition to socialism in a West European country.

Therefore, it is not by chance that, while in recent years new shifts in workers' parties and the working masses in Europe were taking place, the PCI has found itself the most active promoter of the convergence towards a common inspiration in the way of understanding and socialism, above all among communist parties. Nor is it surprising that such a convergence is outlined around an ensemble of positions and principles which have been the basis of PCI policies for some time. Berlinguer, again, describes the process thus when, in the same speech in Berlin, he dwells on the "Eurocommunist" phenomenon in the following manner:

> It is very significant that some other Communist Parties and Workers' Parties in Western Europe have reached, through their own autonomous research, analogous ideas about the road to follow to reach socialism and about the characteristics of the socialist society to be built in their countries. This convergence and these common traits have been expressed recently in the declarations that we have agreed upon with comrades of the Spanish, French and British Communist Parties. And it is these ideas and this new type of enquiry that some call "Eurocommunism".[62]

Finally, I hope that this summary and extensive recapitulation of the development of the PCI's views on the relationship between democracy and socialism will help to clarify the particular significance of the subject of "political democracy" in the definition of "Eurocommunism", and to avoid misunderstandings, at least of the position of the PCI.

Translated by Alyson Price

NOTES

1. Such documents can be read in the Appendix to the volume by Enrico Berlinguer, *La politica internazionale dei comunisti italiani* (Rome, 1976).
2. For example, it is this interpretation of "Eurocommunism", it seems to me that Jean Elleinstein gives. See his conversation with Bernardo Valli, in the volume edited by them, *Gli eurocomunisti* (Milan, 1976), pp. 60ff.
3. Thus comments Bernardo Valli on the "Eurocommunist" phenomenon, ibid., pp. 11–12.
4. Cf. Massimo L. Salvadori, *Kautsky e la rivoluzione socialista, 1880–1938* (Milan, 1976), the Introduction. And again Massimo L. Salvadori, *Eurocomunismo e socialismo sovietico* (Turin, 1978).
5. Regarding the PCI, allow me to cite my own *Saggio su Togliatti e la tradizione comunista italiana* (Bari, 1974), chapter IV. Regarding the French Communist Party, the judgement of Elleinstein is valuable in *Gli eurocomunisti*, pp. 66–7; and in general Giorgio Caredda, *Il fronte populare in Francia: 1934–1938* (Turin, 1977).
6. The expression is used by Berlinguer in the speech to the Central Committee, 13 May 1976. Cf. E. Berlinguer, *La politica internazionale*, p. 120.
7. Ibid., p. 132.
8. Bernardo Valli, *Gli eurocomunisti*, p. 153. But one can also look at Berlinguer, Carrillo, Marchais, *La via europea al socialismo*, edited by Ignazio Delogu (Rome, 1976), p. ix.
9. As is noted, in 1956 Togliatti revived the demand for a "polycentric" articulation of the international communist and workers' movement. This was accompanied by a new vision of the protagonists in the liberation struggle and of possible forms of unity among them, in obvious disagreement with the Soviet idea, and with the role that it attributed to the positions and interests of the "socialist camp". Also on this crucial point of PCI politics and Togliatti's elaboration allow me to refer again to my *Saggio su Togliatti*, ch. VII. The expression "new internationalism" is more recent and was coined by Giancarlo Pajetta.
10. Berlinguer, *La politica internazionale*, p. 191.
11. Berlinguer, *La "questione comunista"* (Rome, 1975), pp. 824–5, 828, 831–2.
12. Berlinguer, *La politica internazionale*, p. 12.
13. Berlinguer, *La "questione comunista"*, p. 825.
14. Ibid., p. 826.
15. Berlinguer, *La politica internazionale*, p. 6.
16. Introducing his collection on the *Politica internazionale*, Berlinguer writes:

> Every day that passes, and in all fields, the West European crisis gets worse. The causes of this process of regression are many and have old roots; but there is one cause that is perhaps the essential one, at least among the recent causes: with the devaluation of the dollar carried out in 1971 by the United States, and shortly after with the outbreak of the oil crisis, those spurts towards expansion of productivity and consumption and towards political and economic expansion lost their propulsive

energy; those which – under the protection of and thanks to the support of the United States – had revitalised, for more than twenty years, the mechanisms for accumulation and for the market of old Europe and with the liberalisation of trade, had managed, in some measure, to give it a unified continental market. For some time, on the economic level, both in individual countries and on a community level, there has been no real development, no real collaboration, but rather a tariff and monetary war, while general inflation puts every equilibrium (and every advantage) reached in prices, exchange and monetary value at risk. (p. xi)

In his report to the XIV Congress, noting the same events, he commented:

> thus there is a further exacerbation of the struggle and economic competition between the principal capitalist countries, particularly between the United States on one side, and Western Europe and Japan on the other, but also between European capitalist countries. The United States seek to regain, by all means possible, part of the ground lost in these years to old and new competitors: with speculative manoeuvres by great companies (and not only the oil companies), with a growing intrusiveness of capital, with technological blackmail, with the brain drain. (*La "questione comunista"*, p. 826)

17. Berlinguer, *La "questione comunista"*, pp. 827–8.
18. Berlinguer, *La politica internazionale*, p. 74.
19. Ibid., p. 113. Some months later, talking to young communists in Milan, Berlinguer returned more thoroughly to the argument.

> In the capitalist West the roads tried up to now [of transformation in a socialist sense] are those of social-democracy. . . . Not one of these social-democratic experiments has led to an effective overthrow of capitalism, nor to an effective overcoming of that decisive aspect of contemporary capitalism established by the dominion of great economic and financial concentrations. It is also true that in some countries where the social-democratic parties have been in power for decades, there are all the typical signs of a fundamental crisis in the "neo-capitalist" societies, of the social arrangements created by so-called "mature" capitalism. This goes to show that the experiments have remained inside the capitalist system.
>
> Precisely because this is the obvious reality, today within the ranks of social-democrat parties there is rethinking, critical assessment and investigation . . . of ways to go forward other than using the experiments already tried, to go beyond the schemes so far followed. . . . This opens possibilities for dialogue, for meetings between communists and forces gathered in social-democratic parties . . . not towards solutions that have already been defeated, but towards others, which could be victorious, that is, capable of effectively overcoming the capitalism of the developed countries of Western Europe. (Ibid., pp. 142–3)

20. Ibid., p. 170.

21. Ibid., pp. 29 and 33.
22. Ibid., pp. 35–6.
23. In Jane Degras (ed.), *The Communist International 1919–1943, Documents* (London, 1971), vol. II, p. 493.
24. Antonio Gramsci, *Selections from the Prison Notebooks*, edited and translated by Quintin Hoare and Geoffrey Nowell Smith (London, 1979), p. 116.
25. Ibid., pp. 116–17.
26. Ibid., p. 182.
27. The way in which Gramsci takes this ultimate idea as a regulating principle of socialism, is set out concisely in a celebrated passage in the *Prison Notebooks*. Deprived of any utopian connotations, the principle of "extinction of the State" shows itself to be decisive for an intimate connection between democracy and socialism, and appears as an operable criterion capable of intervening in the concrete politics of a revolutionary movement of socialist inspiration. In Gramsci's words:

    > There really do exist rulers and ruled, leaders and led. The entire science and art of politics are based on this primordial and (given certain general conditions) irreducible fact.

    Therefore the recognition of "relationships of strength" condenses in a certain way all political science in progress and establishes the basis for political art. That is, on the concrete political plane, it will have to be considered how one can lead most effectively (given certain ends); hence how the leaders may best be prepared. But for the working class:

    > In the formation of leaders, one premiss is fundamental: is it the intention that there should always be rulers and ruled or is the objective to create the conditions in which this division is no longer necessary? In other words, is the initial premiss the perpetual division of the human race, or the belief that this division is only an historical fact, corresponding to certain conditions? (ibid., p. 144).

28. Ibid., p. 144.
29. This is the classic formulation of Lenin's *"Left-wing" Communism*. Cf. Lenin, *Collected Works*, vol. 31 (London, 1966), p. 92.
30. At the end of October 1922, Togliatti sent a report to the Communist International, in which were outlined the original features of the analysis of fascism which was increasingly characteristic of the position of the Italian communists in the internal debate in the communist movement until 1929. It was, on the explicit admission of Togliatti, largely inspired by Gramsci. Cf. Palmiro Togliatti, *Rapporto sul fascismo per il IV Congressor dell' Internazionale*, in *Opere*, edited by Ernesto Ragionieri, vol. I (Rome, 1967), pp. 423–45.
31. This appears in Antonio Gramsci, *Selections from Political Writings 1921–1926*, translated and edited by Quintin Hoare (London, 1978), p. 221.
32. Ibid., pp. 199–200.
33. Ibid., p. 408.

34. Gramsci, *Selections from the Prison Notebooks*, p. 238.
35. Gramsci, *Selections from Political Writings*, p. 410.
36. Togliatti, *Opere*, vol. II (Rome, 1972), pp. 404–5.
37. Ibid., pp. 224–5.
38. Ibid., pp. 223–4.
39. Ibid., p. 363.
40. Ibid., pp. 224–6.
41. Togliatti, *Intervento alla commissione italiana del X Esecutivo allargato dell'Internazionale comunista* (July 1929), in *Opere*, vol. II, p. 798.
42. Ibid., p. 794.
43. Palmiro Togliatti, *Alcuni problemi della storia dell' Internazionale comunista*, now in *Problemi del movimento operaio internazionale 1956–1961* (Rome, 1962), pp. 327 and 328.
44. Georgi Dimitrov, *L'offensiva del fascismo e i compiti dell'IC nella lotta per l'unità della classe operaia contro il fascismo*, in Franco De Felice, *Fascismo Democrazia Fronte popolare* (Bari, 1973), p. 154.
45. Ibid., pp. 71ff.
46. Ibid., pp. 532–3.
47. Togliatti, *La via italiana al socialismo*, Report to the Central Committee of 24 June 1956, now in *Problemi del movimento operaio internazionale 1956–1961*, pp. 132–3.
48. Togliatti, *La politica di unità nazionale dei comunista*. Report to the cadres of the Neapolitan communist organisation (11 April 1944), now in *La politica di Salerno*, edited by Aurelio Lepre (Rome, 1969), p. 36.
49. Togliatti, *Discorsi alla Costituenta* (Rome, 1958), pp. 40–1.
50. Ibid., p. 42.
51. Ibid., p. 40.
52. Togliatti, *Appunti e schema per una storia del partito comunista* (1951), now in *Momenti della storia d'Italia* (Rome, 1963), p. 159.
53. Togliatti, *La nostra lotta per la democrazia e per il socialismo* (January 1947), now in *Critica Marxista*, nos 4–5 (1964), p. 191.
54. Ibid., pp. 191–2.
55. Berlinguer, *La "questione comunista"*, p. 943.
56. Ibid.
57. Togliatti, *Viaggio in Yugoslavia* (February 1964), now in *Togliatti editorialista*, edited by Alessandro Natta (Rome, 1971), p. 254.
58. Togliatti, *Il XX Congresso del PCUS*, speech to the Central Committee, 13 February 1956, now in *Problemi del movimento operaio internazionale 1956–1961*, p. 28.
59. Ibid., p. 29.
60. Ibid., pp. 208–9:

> The West European working class has its own word to say in the fight for peace and socialism. And it must speak, restoring its unity in the struggle for democracy and against the power of the great monopolies; establishing valid agreements and alliances not only with the impoverished peasant masses, but with the middle class of the city and countryside, made up of brain-workers, technicians, teachers, a whole

part of the population that the leading capitalist groups today tend to reduce to a pure executive and passive instrument of their will. Thus opens the possibility for a united movement, which can interest all parties and organisations, whether of social-democratic tendency or of Catholic inspiration, which do not wish to submit to the domination of the great monopolies, nor intend to accept passively the end of democratic regimes and the rush towards atomic catastrophe.

61. Togliatti, speech to the VIII Congress of the PCI (December 1956), now in *Nella pace e nella democrazia verso il socialismo* (Rome, 1966), pp. 39–40.
62. Berlinguer, *La politica internazionale*, p. 171.

7 The PCI's Taste of Power

CHRISTOPHER SETON-WATSON

In June 1975, on the day after the regional elections in which the Italian Communist Party (PCI) polled 33.4 per cent of the votes, its General Secretary, Enrico Berlinguer, declared that "Italy can no longer be governed without us". The morale of the ruling Christian Democratic Party (DC), whose lead over the PCI had dropped to 1.9 per cent, received a stunning blow, and the PCI seemed to have reached the threshold of power. A year later, after a parliamentary election in which the PCI increased its percentage of the vote to 34.5 (but the DC increased its lead to 4.2 per cent), Berlinguer repeated his assertion. He repeated it yet again in his report to his party's XV Congress in Rome in March 1979 and during the campaign leading up to the parliamentary election of 3 June. This chapter is concerned with the PCI's experience of the threshold of power, and the light which that experience has thrown on its nature, power and aspirations.

In the parliament elected in June 1976, it would have been numerically possible to find a majority for a new version of the centre–left (DC–Socialist) coalition which had ruled Italy since 1962. But the Italian Socialist Party (PSI) declined the invitation except on condition that the PCI be given some kind of formal association with the government, a condition which the DC refused. Giulio Andreotti therefore formed a minority DC government dependent for its survival on the PCI's abstention. This arrangement could only be temporary, and in April 1977 Berlinguer declared that "the present anomalous and precarious situation must be replaced by a firmer agreement". In July representatives of the six parties of the "constitutional arc",[1] in which the PCI was now included, reached agreement on a seven-point common programme dealing with the most urgent political problems of the day. Parliament approved it and Andreotti pledged his government to carry it out. At the end of 1977 the PCI increased its pressure again. In March 1978, largely through the efforts of the DC's president, Aldo Moro, a five-party parliamentary majority[2] was formed with the DC and the PCI its dominant partners. Andreotti carried on with a reshuffled minority government. In January 1979 the PCI withdrew its support, so precipitating the crisis which ended in the early dissolution of parliament and the election of 3 June.

After March 1978 Berlinguer claimed that the PCI had finally achieved the legitimacy denied to it during its 30 years of opposition, and had ended the DC's monopoly of political decision-making. This achievement took many visible forms. In July 1976 the Chamber of Deputies elected a communist president, and the PCI obtained the chairmanship of six parliamentary committees. In the following months it secured its share of governmental patronage in appointing its nominees to the Constitutional Court, the Supreme Judicial Council, the national radio–TV organisation, and the boards of many public corporations. A practice of regular consultation grew up between the leaders of the majority parties, and Berlinguer established close personal relations with Moro, and to a lesser extent, after Moro's tragic death, with Andreotti. In the presidential election of July 1978, a veteran communist leader, Giorgio Amendola, proved a popular, though not the victorious, candidate. The PCI has also since 1975 held power in six of Italy's twenty regions, and enjoyed consociational forms of power-sharing with the DC in many others. Most of Italy's major cities now have communist mayors.

Nevertheless after June 1976 the PCI soon became painfully aware that it had abandoned the role of opposition without securing the full rewards of power. Born as a party of revolution in 1921, it had enjoyed only one brief experience of power between 1944 and 1947, and the transition from a party of opposition (which at times looked in danger of becoming permanent) to a party of government caused perplexity. In 1976–7 there were protests in the central committee, widely reported in the press, against propping up a government drawn from a corrupt and discredited bourgeois party. Berlinguer felt it necessary to reassure his rank and file that "we are still communists", and to announce that the PCI must be both "a party of government and a party of struggle". This formula accurately described, but scarcely solved, the PCI's basic dilemma.

The PCI's success in reaching the threshold of power in 1976 was founded on the growing credibility of its triple claim to be national, democratic and honest. As early as 1944 Palmiro Togliatti had announced his party's intention to become a national, no longer a class, party. Today only about 50 per cent of its 1,800,000 members belong to the working class. The PCI has been described, with some exaggeration, as "the natural party of Italian intellectuals", and in recent years it has been successful in recruiting from the professional and managerial classes.

From its determination to be a national party has followed its policy of conciliation towards the forces of Catholicism. It was the PCI's votes in the Constituent Assembly in 1947 which ensured the incorporation in the republican constitution of the concordat of 1929, by which Mussolini had conceded to the Church a privileged position in Italian society. Since then the PCI has striven to avoid "religious war" by playing down issues which might divide Church and State. It was the socialists and radicals, not the communists, who initiated the campaigns for the legalisation of divorce and abortion. Togliatti preached that the reforms which Italy so urgently needed could be achieved only through a broad national consensus. Berlinguer was making the same point in 1973, in the light of the Chilean tragedy, when he outlined his vision of an "historic compromise" between the forces of socialism and Catholicism. Allende, he argued, had failed to win that consensus and alienated Catholicism, an error which the PCI would never make. In more recent years Berlinguer has publicy reaffirmed his conviction that there is no incompatibility between the active practice of the Catholic faith and active membership of the PCI.

Since 1975 the PCI has been calling for an emergency government of national unity. This is the logical application of Berlinguer's assertion that even 51 per cent of the votes would be insufficient for the PCI to take power, even in coalition with the socialists. Unlike Marchais, he has displayed an almost masochistic desire to share the unpopular responsibilities of power. It was he who in January 1977 prescribed a programme of *austerità*, including wage restraint, the reduction of public expenditure and an emphasis on increasing industrial productivity. Since then the

PCI has used all its influence with the trades unions to carry out that policy, and to put the national interest above "corporatist" or narrow class interests.

In the international context the PCI has demonstrated its national character by successive declarations of independence from the Soviet Union. It was the most critical among Western European communist parties of the invasion of Czechoslovakia in 1968. Since then its determination to pursue an Italian road to socialism, and its rejection of external interference, has been reaffirmed by Berlinguer and his colleagues on many occasions, sometimes in the presence of Soviet leaders.[3] As a symbol of its independence, the PCI at its last Congress removed from its statutes the obligation of all members to study and be guided by the principles of Marxism–Leninism, and revised the list of those historic figures from which it draws inspiration: after the names of Marx, Engels and Lenin now appear those of Antonio Labriola,[4] Gramsci and Togliatti. The party's daily newspaper, *L'Unità*, criticises Soviet persecution of dissent, and its publishing house, Editori Riuniti, publishes the works of such authors as Roy Medvedev. Unlike Marchais, Berlinguer has since 1975 accepted the desirability of Italy remaining in NATO: first, because Italy's withdrawal would be a destabilising act and so not conducive to the maintenance of peace; and second, because NATO's protection precludes Soviet interference (in the style of 1968) with the pursuit of the Italian road to socialism. In November 1977 the party's senators subscribed to a five-party declaration on foreign policy which was ratified by the *direzione* three months later. Unlike Marchais, Berlinguer favoured direct elections to the European Parliament and was himself elected on 10 June 1979. In his congress speech of 31 March he defined his party's policy as follows:

> Italian communists, while rejecting any uncritical or rhetorical vision of Europe, have fully understood the importance assumed by the European Community today. . . . The development of the process of integration must be seen as a condition of the true independence and the internal economic development of the Community's member states. . . . We Italian communists believe we can play a particular and unique role in the new European Parliament.

The PCI's claim to be democratic has been elaborated in successive well-known declarations, some made jointly with the French and Spanish Communist Parties. It stands committed to the retention in a "socialist" Italy of a plurality of parties, civil, religious, cultural and trades union liberties, and a mixed economy. Berlinguer has gone further than Marchais or Carrillo in promising, in the event of attaining power, to abide by the rules of the democratic game and resign after an adverse verdict of the electorate. Such promises can of course be tested only by performance in power, and a majority of Italians are still not ready to risk putting those promises to the test. While both the Soviet and East European models have been rejected by the PCI as inapplicable to Italy, the Italian model remains undefined. In a major speech at Genoa in September 1978 Berlinguer spoke in vague terms of the need to find "a third way" between northern social democracy and the "actual socialism" (*socialismo reale*) of the east. But his treatment of the two was ill-balanced: while he harshly criticised social democracy for "failing to escape from the logic of capitalism", he declared that the PCI will never deny or renounce "the value for the whole working class world of the work of Lenin and the October Revolution, the greatest event of the twentieth century".

Doubt is often cast upon the PCI's democratic credentials by pointing to its retention of the practice of democratic centralism. The issue has recently been much debated both within and outside the party. Some of its intellectuals have argued that, just as there are many variations of socialism, so there may be many variations of democratic centralism, of which Lenin's was only one. The chief justification for its retention is that without it the PCI would lapse into the debilitating fractionalism which has plagued other Italian parties. At the Rome Party Congress Berlinguer made the following statement:

> It is necessary to develop ever more fully the free circulation of ideas; all comrades must exercise ever more effectively their right to participate to the full in the life of the organisations to which they belong, and to contribute to the comprehensive elaboration of the party's policy and its execution.

It is indisputable that the PCI is more tolerant of argument and debate than, for instance, the French Communist Party. It is not necessary for internal criticism of the party's line to be published in the bourgeois press, as was the case in France after the left's electoral defeat in March 1978. In Italy remarkable latitude has been given to communist historians and autobiographers in publishing conflicting interpretations of the PCI's past. It is also the case that those non-communists who agreed to be elected on the PCI's list as "Independents of the left" have, after election, been accorded real independence.[5]

In recent years the PCI has become the most ardent supporter of law and order in defence of the republican constitution. Its record during the Moro tragedy was impeccable. Indeed its intransigence in refusing to negotiate with the terrorists may well have been decisive in maintaining the resolve of the sorely tried Christian Democratic leadership. When student violence erupted in March 1977 in Bologna, the showpiece of communist local government, its mayor, Renato Zangheri, praised the action of the police in breaking up the demonstrations and so earned the opprobrium of the ultra-left. The PCI has shown no inhibition in supporting the most drastic anti-terrorist legislation, and in the referendum of June 1978 it fought resolutely against the abrogation of the very same law which it had opposed as too repressive in 1975.

The PCI's claim to be honest rests on its record in parliament and in local and regional government. One of its most effective electoral slogans in 1975–6 was its claim to have "clean hands" (*mani pulite*), in contrast to the DC which at that time was racked by scandals. It is of course easier to keep one's hands clean in opposition than in power, and communist local government has not been entirely free of petty corruption. The violence of March 1977 in Bologna was also damaging to the image of communist good government. But since 1976 the PCI has fought hard, and not unsuccessfully, for the adoption of professional competence rather than party loyalty as the criterion for appointment to public office. Andreotti's complicity in what the PCI regarded as a disreputable reversion to the past practice of an inter-party share-out (*lotizzazione*) of top jobs was one of the immediate causes of the party's withdrawal from the majority in January 1979.

During its period on the threshold of power, the PCI can reasonably claim to have substantiated its claim to be national, democratic and honest. But few benefits have resulted. In the partial local elections of May 1978 the PCI's share of votes fell almost 8 per cent below that of June 1976. A further shock came in the June 1978 referendums, which were used by a surprisingly large number of voters to express disgust with the government and its five-party majority.[6] In July Berlinguer admonished an assembly of his regional and provincial secretaries for excessive "rubbing shoulders" with the DC, and for allowing the party to lapse into inertia.

> We have been very generous these past two months [he told them], generous perhaps to the limits of ingenuousness – for our generosity and trust has not been paid back in kind by the other parties, least of all by the DC.

The criticism was hardly fair, for "rubbing shoulders" with the DC was exactly what Berlinguer and his colleagues had been doing in Rome. Many of the rank and file, it was apparent, had lost their sense of identity and felt that the party had lost its way. Some even expressed nostalgia for the days of police repression in the 1950s, when the nature of the enemy against whom to struggle was clear. This dismay was reflected in a fall of 23,000 in party membership.

In his Congress speech of March 1979 Berlinguer declared that he had no regrets at the decision of 1976 and described the balance sheet as "impressive and positive". Nevertheless expectations had not been fulfilled. The belief that admission into the majority would accelerate reform, and that the right legislation could solve Italy's problems, had proved an illusion. The style of Italian politics had not changed, and the massive strength of DC power, entrenched in every sector of Italian society, had become painfully apparent. Some commentators have even suggested that Berlinguer was personally mesmerised by Moro. But even if that were true, the problem went much deeper. The DC's tactics were to wear the PCI out[7] by involving it in the responsibilities of power and forcing it to share the blame for failure, while retaining its own hegemony intact. In a press interview just before the June election, Berlinguer declared that the DC's motives for so resolutely excluding the PCI from government were not ideological, nor inspired by international considerations, but based on fear that the DC's "system of power" might be endangered.[8] So by the spring of 1979, having used the PCI to weather the storm of economic crisis and terrorism, the DC, especially its increasingly vocal and influential right wing, was ready to astonish the PCI by its ingratitude and to cast it out again into the ghetto of opposition.

The results of the election of 3 June have intensified the PCI's disillusionment and disarray. The drop in its vote from 34.5 per cent to 30.4 per cent was large by Italian standards, and it was small consolation that the DC's vote, despite its grandiose expectations, also dropped, by 0.4 per cent. It was the first election for 26 years in which the PCI could not claim an advance. The victors this time were the small parties of the centre, which had been severely squeezed in 1976, and the Radical party, champion of minority causes, outflanking the PCI on its left, which trebled its vote and increased its representation in parliament from 4 to 18. The PCI's electoral slogan was "Either in government or in opposition"; the DC pledged itself to keep the PCI out. In Italy it is unwise to take such statements at their face value. Nevertheless it is hard to escape the conclusion that the PCI has been roughly pushed back from the threshold of power.

The party has now started on what will be a long and painful process of self-criticism. There are likely to be some changes in the leadership, though Berlinguer's position seems to be in no danger. Already the PCI has identified three areas where its loss of support has been exceptionally severe: in the South, among the young, and in the impoverished peripheries of the great cities. In the South the gains of 1976 have been almost wiped out, mainly because nothing seemed to have changed in the regions and towns where the PCI had been in power. The alienation of youth has been the party's concern ever since it was taken by surprise by the explosion of student militancy in 1967–8. But perhaps the greatest shock came in the industrial cities of the north: whereas the PCI's vote held up well in the more affluent districts, in the most impoverished it dropped sharply. On 14 June the party's *direzione* resolved to launch a massive campaign of reclamation in these three areas.

To the outside observer it must seem obvious that a major cause of the DC's survival in power has been the disunity of the Left. Relations between the PCI and the PSI have been tense since 1976, mainly because of the PSI's aggressive attempts to establish its own separate identity and to win back lost ground from the PCI. But there are now signs from both parties of a desire to heal the wounds. The figures speak for themselves: the combined socialist and communist vote in 1979 was 40.2 per cent, and working together they might well attract additional votes and alliance partners on both their right and their left. But the process of healing will not be easy. A major obstacle is that the PSI's programme (provided it can resist temptation by the DC to return to the centre–left) is the "socialist alternative" of a PSI–PCI alliance, whereas the PCI remains attached to its historic compromise with the Catholics, in which the PSI seems to have no place. In his congress speech Berlinguer denied that the historic compromise could ever be just a "power-deal between the DC and the PCI", and stated that "it does not exclude the possibility of various governmental formulas". He continued,

> But what we regard as indispensable, for the salvation and the renovation of the country, are the convergence and collaboration of the great masses of socialist, communist and catholic orientation, and of their political and social organisations.

In a press interview in May he elaborated the point: "The historic compromise is a political strategy, not a formula of government." There would therefore seem to be a basis for reconciliation: in the short and medium terms a union of the left, and in the longer term an historic compromise between a united left and the forces of democratic catholicism. This might also turn out to be the elusive "third way".

But whether or not the PCI and PSI can work out a common programme, it seems likely that for the foreseeable future (which in Italy is not long) the PCI will be back in opposition. It will be a "responsible" opposition, to use the British phrase, for as one acute observer of the Italian scene has noted, the PCI has over the past three years acquired *réflexes gouvernementaux* which it would find hard to discard even if it wished.[9] There is no sign of a new line, nor of a new leader to formulate it. The PCI seems to have no alternative but to continue furbishing its democratic credentials and striving to convince a few more million Italians that "Italy can no longer be governed without us".

POSTSCRIPT (September 1980)

This chapter was completed in July 1979. Since then the DC's shift to the right has been confirmed by its congress in March

1980, the PSI has returned to partnership in government under a DC prime minister, Francesco Cossiga, and the PCI has moved from 'constructive' to 'intransigent' opposition. This last has taken the form of an abortive attempt to impeach Cossiga for alleged toleration of terrorism, and uncompromising criticism of the government's latest version of *austerità*. The PCI has nevertheless condemned the Soviet intervention in Afghanistan and maintained its positive Western European policy. It seems that its return to isolation has comforted, and even enthused, many of its members, especially its working class militants. But there is no evidence that its long-term objective – call it 'historic compromise' or anything you like – of forming part of a broad national consensus and sharing the responsibility of government, has been abandoned.

NOTES

1. The Liberal (PLI), Christian Democratic (DC), Republican (PRI), Social Democratic (PSDI), Socialist (PSI) and Communist (PCI) parties.
2. The PLI stayed outside.
3. Notably at the CPSU's XXV Congress in Moscow in February 1976, at the East Berlin Conference of European communist parties in July 1976, and at the Moscow celebrations of the 60th anniversary of the Bolshevik Revolution in November 1977.
4. Marxist professor of philosophy, one of the founders of the Italian Socialist Party in 1892.
5. Notably General Pasti, who had formerly held high command in NATO; Altiero Spinelli, a former EEC Commissioner; Luigi Spaventa, one of Italy's most distinguished economists; and several Catholic intellectuals who broke with the DC over divorce in 1974.
6. The subject of the referendums, which had been initiated by the Radicals, was the abrogation of the 1974 law for the public financing of parties and the 1975 anti-terrorist legislation. The PCI campaigned against abrogation with greater vigour than any of its partners of the majority, and abrogation was rejected; but the votes for abrogation were 43 per cent and 23 per cent respectively.
7. The word used is *logorare*, which has no exact English equivalent. Some observers with an historical sense have noted an analogy between Moro's dealings with the PCI and Giolitti's strategy of "taming" and integrating (and, his enemies of the left would have added, corrupting) the Socialist Party between 1901 and 1914.
8. *Panorama*, 29 May 1979.
9. Robert Solé in *Le Monde*, 16 June 1979.

8 Eurocommunism and the New Party

BRANKO PRIBIĆEVIĆ

I WHAT IS CHANGING?

The last 20 years have seen many significant, profound and far-reaching changes in the development of the communist movement, involving the doctrinal positions and policies of many communist parties. There has been a basic shift in the relations between a large number of communist parties. Changes of this kind are so substantial that one may reasonably ask whether the traditional and conventional expression "international communist movement" can still be used to describe the sum of organised communist party forces today.

In this period of major changes it might appear that the parties themselves have changed slowest of all. Moreover there is a good deal of scepticism at large about the possibility of such changes; and the view that changes are unnecessary is equally widespread. In Western countries many experts on these problems hold that a communist party is an organism resistant to all demands for change. They emphasise that a communist party cannot change its structure, internal relationships or mode of action without ceasing to be a communist party;[1] and there are a good many supporters of a very similar view in the communist movement itself. A fairly large number of parties – let us call them the protagonists of the orthodox line – often assert that there is nothing to be changed, and even that changes are unnecessary. For these parties the traditional concept and model, which they call Leninist, offers in every way the best solution, and is accorded lasting and universal significance.

Discussions of the possibility of, or need for, certain changes in communist parties have been particularly topical in the last few years with the affirmation of the Eurocommunist position in a number of developed Western countries. In this paper we shall try to show that such changes are not only theoretically possible, but that there are already important new elements in the structure and mode of action of certain Eurocommunist parties. It is our opinion that a communist party not only can, but must, change if it is to keep in step with times and conditions which are altering quickly and profoundly. Parties which do not change sooner or later begin to suffer the consequences of fossilisation and functional and political sclerosis.

It is true, however, that the idea that the party can and should adapt itself has made slow progress in the ranks of the communist movement. For a number of years the Yugoslav communists were almost isolated in their warnings that changes were necessary. One important document of the League of Communists of Yugoslavia stated that: "Existing forms of organisation of the working class frequently show signs of fossilisation and therewith a high degree of social obsolescence . . .".[2]

There have been serious theoretical differences and political arguments in the communist movement about the need or possibility of changes in the structure, internal relationships, and especially definition of the role of revolutionary parties. On one side the forces which favour these changes have increased their influence while on the other there is an ever-increasing resistance to proposals of this kind. The most powerful resistance comes from conservative trends and groups. Such positions are frequently taken by representatives of "orthodox" tendencies in communist parties, who are unable "in principle" to reconcile themselves to a change in, or abandonment of, certain earlier theoretical propositions and political solutions. These forces particularly attack those concepts and projects which aim at a deeper democratisation of internal relations in communist parties and a different way of playing their part in contemporary class and political struggles.

In their resistance to democratic change and to the various proposals for bringing the structure and mode of action of communist parties into line with changing historical and social circumstances, these conservative forces most frequently adduce two arguments. According to the first argument, any proposal which calls for substantial changes from the inherited traditional concept of a communist party is a deviation from the Leninist theory of the party. The second, which is very similar, holds that there is, and in principle can be, only one "correct" historically tested concept of a communist party: the type of party which is rooted in the ideas worked out by Lenin at the beginning of this century. Any departure from this concept is therefore an ideological and political "deviation".

In our view both propositions are theoretically indefensible. Two particularly important arguments may be advanced against them. First, the view that any form or type of political organisations can have universal and lasting significance is historically untenable. The political party of the working class is not an end in itself, or in any case should not be so. In Marx's and Engels' understanding it was always postulated as a means to the realisation of the essential historical interests and aims of the working class. This approach is particularly characteristic of Lenin. His theory of the party is linked with a definite conception and strategy of the socialist revolution. But just as there can be no universal strategies of the socialist revolution, so there can be no universal model of the party.

In Lenin's theory of the revolutionary vanguard, some elements have broader international and therefore lasting significance, but there are others which reflect the specific conditions in which the Russian revolutionary movement was then acting. The special quality and value of this concept of the party represents a successful synthesis of these two elements. The Bolshevik party would not have succeeded in its epoch-making achievement if it had represented only an incarnation of the general principles of organisation of a revolutionary vanguard without simultaneously adapting them to the particular circumstances of the class struggle in the Russian conditions of the time. Later interpretations of the Leninist theory of the party, which became official doctrine in the communist movement, often proclaimed as equally lasting and universal also those elements which reflected the specific conditions in which the theory was formed. This is particularly true of the organisational principles of the party, which are in the nature of things extremely liable to the influence of the specific environment and circumstances.

Secondly, in what is today often called the traditional or "universal" conception of the communist party, which many communist parties adopt as their theory and practice, there are a good many elements which were introduced later and which represent an alteration, supplementation and sometimes even deformation of Lenin's original theory of the revolutionary party. Now some of these alterations were certainly necessary as a response to the changed conditions in which communist parties were acting and the new problems which they had to resolve. There was also new knowledge which required certain modifications. Let us recall that even in Lenin's lifetime certain changes were introduced into the original conception. At the VI Congress of the party, held in July 1917, significant changes were made in the statute, especially in the definition of the principle of democratic centralism. Much more important changes were adopted at the X Congress (March 1921) which significantly narrowed the range of free expression of different political attitudes within the party. Enrico Berlinguer emphasised in a recent interview that: "a certain restriction of internal disagreement [that is, disagreement within the party] begins to appear towards the end of Lenin's life, i.e. before Stalin came to power. We do not therefore hesitate to criticise it . . .".[3]

Much more important and far-reaching changes came with the later development of the communist party. The most important of these came in the second half of the 1920s and in the early 1930s. In the guise of a struggle for the unity of the party, or for the elimination of divisions on fractional lines, a major limitation of the democratic rights of the party members was carried out. The democratic component of democratic centralism became severely atrophied in favour of bureaucratic and authoritarian centralism. By means of the Comintern these defects were internationalised. Thus, in one way or another, this form of Stalinism was to be found in almost all parts of the international movement, though not, of course, always to the same degree. These later additions modified Lenin's original concept of the communist party to such an extent that today, when we speak of the inherited or traditional model of a communist party, it would be more accurate to characterise it as the "Comintern" than the Leninist type of party. We shall try to show that the Eurocommunists, in their efforts to build a new type of party, are abandoning to some extent even certain features characteristic of Lenin's theory of the party, as well as – much more decisively – those later essential components of that type of political organisation which we here call the Comintern model of a revolutionary workers' party.

2 A NEW STRATEGY REQUIRES A NEW PARTY

The new ideas about the working-class party put forward by representatives of Eurocommunism have their roots in the changed strategic orientation of the parties. The rejection of the earlier belief in a violent socialist revolution as the only possible form of radical social change has inevitably brought into question the traditional Comintern concept of a communist party. The same consequences follow from the denial that the model of socialism which is dominant in most East European socialist countries has universal validity. The type of party which answers more or less successfully the requirements and needs of the one-party form of political system is less and less acceptable for those socialist forces which have accepted a pluralist concept of the political system.

The changed conditions in which these parties now act (which differ not only from the conditions in which ruling communist parties act but also from those in which they themselves acted some decades ago); changes in the position of the working class and other working strata; and particularly the adoption of a new strategy of social transformation and a new concept of socialism – all these required innovations in the structure, mode of action and internal relationships of the party.

The new strategy of the Eurocommunist parties is to a large extent rooted in a critical reassessment of their earlier policies. It is now fairly widely accepted in these parties that their policy was then in many respects inadequate.[4] As a result, at least some of these parties have come to the conclusion that in most of the developed Western countries there are good prospects for the realisation of radical social change by peaceful means, and particularly that this change does not imply the establishment of the communist party's monopoly of power.

The emergence of new conceptions of the party was particularly influenced by those elements of the new strategy which emphasise the importance of democracy and political freedom; party pluralism and the struggle for broad social alliances and political coalitions; the possibility of using the existing state as a means of change, at any rate in the initial stages, rejecting the idea that the existing state must inevitably be smashed; and finally the secular character of the state and society which these forces adopt as their goal. The Eurocommunists often emphasise that social progress is possible in these countries only in so far as such changes are supported by a powerful popular majority. The PCF, for instance, has asserted that "social changes must be a matter of common action and desire on the part of the majority".[5] The link between socialism and democracy, or socialism and political freedom, is constantly underlined in all the important new documents of these parties and in statements by their prominent representatives. The joint communiqué by the PCI and PCF in 1975 stated that:

> The French and Italian communists consider that the way to socialism . . . must be realised in a framework of constant democratisation of economic, social and political life. Socialism will be the highest stage of democracy and freedom, democracy taken to the limit.

The two parties expressed their allegiance to all the traditional freedoms of Western societies such as freedom of thought, expression, press and association and particularly the right of opposition and plurality of political parties.[6] Very similar ideas are expressed in the joint statements signed by the PCI and the PCE, and the PCI and the Japanese party.

The Eurocommunist parties frequently emphasise that their conception of democracy is inseparable from party pluralism; that is, that they now adopt that conception of democracy which is today the dominant feature of the political culture of these societies. In the polemical discussion in 1975 between the PCI's daily *L'Unitá* and the Czechoslovak party organ *Rude Pravo* the former stated that "the democracy of which we speak is of course the democracy which we know and in which we are living".[7] Marchais said very plainly:

> There is no democracy and liberty if there is no pluralism of political parties, and if there is no freedom of speech. . . . We consider that the principles we enunciate concerning socialist democracy are of universal value. It is clear we have a disagreement with the Soviet Communist Party about this question.[8]

Enrico Berlinguer also emphasised the universal value of democracy as practised in Western countries.[9] In his speech at the Moscow celebrations of the 60th anniversary of the October revolution Berlinguer said:

> The experience we have gained has led us to the conclusion . . . that democracy is not only the terrain on which the class enemy is compelled to retreat but also a historically universal value which must be at the basis of the construction of an authentic socialist society.

Hence there are regular references to "socialism in democratic colours" or "socialism in freedom".

The new strategy for socialist transformation entails certain changes in the structure, role and mode of action of Eurocommunist parties. Parties which want existing society, and especially other democratic forces, to become more open towards them, must themselves become much more open towards society and towards their present or potential partners. Parties which hold that socialism can be realised only by the stable support of a convincing majority must equip themselves to win such a majority. Parties which assert that the social transformation presupposes broad and stable political alliances must adapt their policy and mode of action to the establishment of such alliances. Parties which consider that the radical transformation presupposes the formation of very wide class and social alliances linking the working class with numerous and very various social strata – from agricultural producers to various categories of the urban middle class (the idea of the "historic bloc" developed by the PCI) – must prepare themselves to form such alliances. Parties which stress the decisive significance of direct democracy in all areas of social and political life must ensure a greater degree of political participation by their own members.

Many of these requirements can not be satisfied by a traditional party of the Comintern type. Thus, for instance, the traditional type of party always carries the risk of certain introversion and of a sectarian attitude to broad stata of potential fighters for socialism. Certain features of this type of party made it very difficult for it to gain a mass following. The sort of party which can gather a relatively small revolutionary elite, composed of utterly devoted and deeply involved militants, may offer too narrow a framework to attract a more numerous membership and various categories of potential supporters of radical social change. The earlier insistence that the communist party, as the paramount vanguard of the working class, must also have a special status among organised workers' and socialist forces was a prohibitive barrier to the establishment of lasting cooperation with other workers' parties.

3 THE SEARCH FOR A NEW PARTY AFTER THE SECOND WORLD WAR

As they gradually took account of some of the internal contradictions mentioned above, communist parties in some developed capitalist countries began to search for new solutions in many areas of party organisation and activity, including the principles determining their global role.

The first signs of a critical rethinking of the traditional Comintern model of the revolutionary party and of a search for new solutions appear with the end of the Second World War. These efforts were prompted by the Communist movement's broad anti-fascist platform and by the general political climate of those years. For many communist parties this was the first opportunity for them to break through the walls of their own isolation and to establish themselves as a serious national political organisation. It came to be seen that the Comintern type of party was unsuitable for the new conditions in which many communist parties in developed capitalist countries were then placed. Some very radical ideas appeared. The President of the CPUSA, Earl Browder, proposed that his party should be disbanded and replaced by a new political party of the left, much broader and better adapted to the American political climate. (Browder's proposal met with a very sharp reaction from the "international centre" of the communist movement, which qualified it as an expression of "capitulation to the class enemy". Browder was quickly expelled from the party and therewith all attempts to bring this party out of its traditional isolation came to an end.) Because of the very marginal status of the CPUSA, Browder's initiative had no broad international repercussions; but moves made by the Italian and French parties at that time carried much greater weight. The leadership of these two parties did not propose such radical changes as Browder's, but they succeeded in putting certain innovations into practice. Involved as they were in a fairly broad resistance movement against nazism and fascism they had to make an opening towards their political allies. Inevitably, too, they had to go beyond the traditional bounds of a cadre party. Both parties in those years threw themselves into a struggle for mass membership which brought results never since then surpassed: the PCI reached the impressive figure of nearly two and a half million members, and the PCF about one million.

In the PCI there were powerful demands for profound internal changes. Soon after his return to Italy in 1944 Palmiro Togliatti began to press for the building of "a new working class party". In a speech in 1944 he said:

> First of all – and this is essential – the new party is a party of the working class and the people. It does not confine its activity to criticism and propaganda but participates positively and constructively in the life of the country. . . . When we speak of a new party we are thinking primarily of a party which must be capable of reflecting in its policy and in its everyday activity that profound change which has come about in the position of the working class.[10]

Togliatti's appeal did not remain without response. In the next few years the PCI underwent some fairly important changes. There was a significant democratisation of internal relations. The party opened its doors to broad strata of the left. It became to a great extent a "mass party". Its role in the coalition government was both "positive and constructive".

However, with the coming of the Cold War, this tendency ran into increasing resistance. Togliatti later said that his idea of a "new party" was from the very beginning received with a good deal of misunderstanding and that there was resistance. The course laid down in the first years after the war was not consistently followed.[11] The traditional Comintern model of the party was re-affirmed and in some places crudely imposed. In all parties, including those in developed capitalist countries, a sectarian and dogmatist line was re-enforced, and the parties turned in upon themselves. Stalinism was an impassable obstacle to the democratisation of communist parties. All parties subjected to the domination of Stalinism had to continue to move in the framework of the so-called general laws and universal model of a communist party.

The historic breakthrough made by the Yugoslav communists in 1948 and the condemnation of some aspects of Stalinism at the XX Congress of the CPSU laid the foundations for a more serious reassessment of the Comintern concept and for more lasting changes in many communist parties. Among parties in developed capitalist countries, the PCI again took the initiative. Cautiously but fairly decisively the parties returned to the line which was broken by the opening of the Cold War in 1947. Characteristically, intra-party problems did not at first occupy the centre of attention; the accent was rather on the creation of a new global strategy. In this context there appeared ideas of an "Italian way to socialism" and a specific theory of structural reforms. In the early 1960s, when the new line was finally and widely accepted, a debate on the party was opened. This debate became particularly lively when in the late summer of 1964 Giorgio Amendola made some very substantial criticisms and drew far-reaching conclusions on the possibility of renewal of existing communist and socialist parties. Amendola surprised most of his colleagues from the party leadership when he recommended the foundation of a "new united workers party" which would be a direct continuation of neither of the prevailing types of workers' party, i.e. communist and socialist or social democratic.[12] The proposal was very radical: Amendola advocated creation of a quite new type of workers' party differing from the traditional model in the conceptualisation of its role, mode of action and internal structure and relations.

Amendola's ideas aroused a very lively and sometimes stormy polemic. The most responsible party leaders took the view that he had to some extent "exaggerated" or had "spoken too early" (Longo) or that his proposals were "premature". However, this stormy debate finished without any condemnations or ideological name-callings, which was very indicative of the new atmosphere in the party. It was concluded that the struggle for the democratisation of the party must be continued. In the PCI the conviction prevailed that a solution should be sought in modifying the existing party and not in building a new one. It was held that favourable conditions did not yet exist for the formation of a new united working class socialist party which could embrace all socialist forces in Italy.

4 THE MOST IMPORTANT CHANGES IN EUROCOMMUNIST PARTIES

Discussions on the party are still under way. Indeed it could be said that they have become a good deal more lively just recently. The subject of discussion is various aspects of the theory of the revolutionary party. There are some fairly important new approaches and ideas. On the whole, the proponents of these ideas do not go as far as Amendola did in the mid-1960s. The view has prevailed that necessary changes can be implemented within the existing communist party model. In this sense solutions are sought for certain problems in the field of intra-party relations, the party's mode of action and in the definition of its role in the workers' movement and in the political life of the country concerned. In all these fields there are not only new ideas but also new phenomena in party practice.

It must be said at once that the new tendencies are not equally represented in all Eurocommunist parties. On the contrary, there are sometimes important differences of approach to particular aspects of the creation of the "new" party. Nevertheless, it is true to say that the basic direction of evolution is similar. The same is true of the changes which have been realised so far. There is a firm foundation for the statement that in all the more important Eurocommunist parties we find, in one form or another, an effort to carry out a definite democratisation of internal relationships as well as an adaptation of the parties' structure, role and mode of action to the specific social and historical environment of developed capitalist countries. What is most noticeable is the effort to create a type of party which will be in much greater measure appropriate to the strategy of the peaceful path to socialism and to a lasting commitment to action in the framework of a democratic pluralist political system.

The following features may be cited as the most important innovations in party theory and practice which have so far been carried out:

(i) THE ROLE OF THE PARTY

The role of the communist party in the working class movement and in the struggle for radical social change has to some extent been redefined. This includes particularly the relationship between the working class and the communist party. There are some indications that the problem of the political vanguard of the working class is now formulated in a rather more flexible way. The actual idea of the vanguard is not brought into question. Here it is emphasised that radical social change cannot be realised without a political force of the vanguard type. The communist parties of these countries see themselves as providing that force in the future as in the past. Numerous party documents emphasise that these parties are by their social essence working-class parties, and their leading position, or leading role, in the process of social change is no less firmly asserted.

The new approach finds expression in three essential points. First, the idea that a communist party is by definition a vanguard – that is, that *every* communist party must have the vanguard role – is abandoned. It is now emphasised among Eurocommunists that this role is not derived from the name of the party or from the doctrine which it professes, but exclusively from the nature of its links with the working class and the real part which it plays in the political life of the country concerned. In other words the role of vanguard is not pre-ordained for anyone, nor is it guaranteed for all time. It has to be constantly won and confirmed anew. The vanguard character of a workers' party can be measured only by the depth, breadth and firmness of the support which it has in the working mass. It is untenable to claim a vanguard character in cases where there is no such support. It is further emphasised that the vanguard character is expressed in the capacity both to contribute to the solution of certain current problems of the social existence of the working masses and at the same time to point the way to radical social change. Thus a successful synthesis of these two roles is essential. Secondly, it is now allowed that the communist party should *share* this role with certain other political forces. It is explicitly said that other parties may also represent the legitimate interests of particular strata of the working class and that they have an important role in the social revolution. Thirdly, the political implications of the role of vanguard are now interpreted in an essentially different fashion. Whereas previously there was a regular insistence that the vanguard party must have a special, that is privileged, status among workers' organisations and other democratic political forces, there is now much more emphasis on its obligations. Sometimes it is even said plainly that the leading or vanguard workers' party has not and cannot have any special, greater or higher rights than other workers' parties and trades unions.

This new approach has been fairly comprehensively formulated by Santiago Carrillo in his book *"Eurocommunism" and the State:*

> The new ideas about the road to socialism in the developed countries allow certain diversification with regard to the role and function of the communist party. It continues to be the vanguard party, inasmuch as it truly embodies a creative Marxist attitude. But it no longer considers itself the *only* representative of the working class, of the working people and the forces of culture. It recognises in theory and practice, that other parties which are socialist in tendency can also be representative of particular sections of the working population . . . it has no hesitation in accepting, when circumstances warrant, that others may be more accurate than it in analysing a particular situation. . . . The role of the vanguard is not now a privilege derived from a name or a programme. Nor is it some sort of providential mission with which we have been entrusted by the grace of our teachers or through some authorisation from on high. It is a position which has to be earned every day, every hour and sometimes, I repeat, by going against the stream. Either we turn our role as vanguard into a reality in that way, or that role is reduced to an ideological fantasy which may serve to console us from time to time for our ineffectiveness.[13]

This approach is also found in the PCI. According to a recent important party document, "We have already abandoned the view of the communist party as a prototype of the state and of socialist society." A similar message is found in the following passage from the same document: "Parties are bound to definite class interests, but do not represent the unqualified automatic expression of these interests."[14] Today there is more and more readiness to accept that the communist party has no monopoly in the representation of the interests of the working class and other working strata. Equally, it has been repeatedly stated in the PCI that the communist party can have no monopoly not only of truth and wisdom but also of social progress.

There are similar ideas in the PCF. Although the party leadership often emphasises its vanguard character, this role is newly defined. To the question "Are you ready to admit that the plan for socialism is no longer a preserve of one party alone"? Jean Elleinstein recently answered: "Certainly. The PCF cannot and should not have the monopoly in any area."[15]

The very term vanguard and vanguardism are much less used today than previously. The PCI's official documents more and more use the expression "guiding party" instead of the traditional term. In the PCF it is often said that the process of social revolution implies its "directing influence".[16]

In support of the thesis that the traditional interpretation of the communist party as a pre-ordained and exclusive vanguard is gradually being abandoned, one may mention the Eurocommunists' approach to the problem of political alliances. Whereas previously communist parties generally accepted only those alliances in which they had the leading role (although there were exceptions to this general rule in certain alliances of the popular-front type which were made in some countries in the mid-1930s and at the end of the Second World War), it is now understood that this conception is quite unrealistic and even incompatible with the idea of the "peaceful, democratic, legal and gradual way to socialism". No concept of alliances has any prospects of success except that which is based on the absolute and unconditional equality of all partners. It is our impression that today these parties not only assert in principle the thesis of equality of potential partners, but behave in practice in this way. There is a real and increasing tendency towards dialogue and cooperation between equal partners.

Even more important, these alliances are no longer seen as merely a temporary and palliative instrument, useful in solving certain current social and economic or political problems. On the contrary, nowadays it is more often emphasised that these alliances are the most appropriate – and it is sometimes said (for instance in the PCI) the only possible – political framework for the realisation of long-term aims and tasks of social change. Whereas previously it was considered possible that the communist party itself should be the agent of radical changes in society, it is now seen that this is unrealistic. It is openly said that the establishment of broad political coalitions is a *conditio sine qua non* of the implementation of the new strategy of socialist transformation.

The impression may have been gained that the PCF is more inclined to try to preserve some elements of the earlier approach, and some authors consider that the repeated statement that there can be no socialist transformation in France without the PCF's "directing influence" is evidence of this old approach. The term "directing influence" has not been elaborated and is therefore subject to various interpretations including those which hold it to be no more than a euphemism or another way of expressing the wish to retain vanguard status in the workers' movement in any case. It is our impression, however, that the PCF is nevertheless gradually having to face the logic and implications of the pluralist concept of the path to socialism and also of a socialist goal in which there is no room for a vanguard of the Comintern type.

Closely related to this are certain innovations in the relations between the party and trades unions in countries where the Eurocommunist line has won acceptance and the influence of the communist party in the trades unions is traditionally fairly strong. Previously in these countries the well-known "transmission-belt" model of the party–trades union relationship was applied. The unions with strong communist influence were treated as junior partners – they were in every respect controlled by the party. Their subordination was not only political; it involved also functional, organisational and even personal aspects. This relationship has been subjected to a good deal of re-examination and revision. The general rethinking of the role of the communist party was reflected in this sphere as well. From the trades union side came demands which at least some of these parties were prepared to comply with. These trends emerged particularly strongly in Italy. De Vittorio, the prominent leader of the communist-led trades union federation (CGIL) stated as early as 1956 that "trades union unity requires complete independence not only from the employers and the state but also from all political parties".[17] Agostino Novella, who succeeded De Vittorio as President of the CGIL, urged the separation of the trades union movement from political party control in his speech to the 1961 Congress of the World

Federation of Trades Unions.[18] The result of these efforts was the decision made at the CGIL Congress in 1969 to rule out the possibility that the same persons should hold important positions in the trades unions and the party. In practice this meant that communists holding leading posts in the CGIL could no longer be elected to the ruling bodies of the PCI. In the joint PCI–PCF communique of 1975 it is said that the two parties had decided to guarantee the "free activity and autonomy of trades unions".[19] In the PCE's theses prepared for the IX Congress it was stated as follows: "The PCE rejects the idea of trades unions as a cogwheel for mechanical transmission and proclaims strict respect for the independence of the trades unions."[20]

When these parties support trades union autonomy, that is the abandonment of the unions' earlier role as party "transmission-belts", this is not merely an expression of their choice of a new conception of the role of the party as a matter of principle. There are also important practical motives here which found, and still find, particularly marked expression in the trades unions of these countries. These unions have been much weakened by the division of the union movement on party-political and ideological lines. Time has made it clear that the close connection of unions with particular parties had become an insuperable barrier to trades union unity. The "emancipation" of the unions from party domination is the first condition for more successful cooperation between existing trades union groups, and even more for their ultimate unification.

(ii) THE PARTY AND SOCIETY

The next important innovation is found in the gradual and increasingly emphasised "opening" of the Eurocommunist parties towards the existing class society in which they act. This is in fact a two-way process: not only do the parties open themselves towards society and its leading political forces, but these forces, in spite of all their reserves and inhibitions, adopt a different attitude towards the communists. Some authors have quite felicitously described this as "interpenetration". The walls of isolation surrounding the communists have begun to crack, and the political ghetto in which they lived for years is largely a thing of the past. Communist parties which in earlier conditions had to react by closing in on themselves, by creating the so-called "counter-society", which were driven to defend themselves with a "fortress mentality" (and it must be added that this position was not only imposed by the ruling forces of the existing order but was also largely determined by the Comintern concept of the role of a communist party in class society) are now overcoming these constraints.

Whereas previously the attitude of the communist parties of these countries, and also of all others acting in class society, was by definition emphatically critical and negative, and sometimes captious and nihilistic, their approach is now much more balanced. Increasingly the conviction is to be found among Eurocommunists that the societies and system in which they act contain not only things to be criticised but also a good deal to be defended and endorsed. We find also a readiness to take on major and direct responsibilities for the regulation and functioning of existing society. It is significant and characteristic that the PCI insists that it no longer accepts the status of an opposition party. It considers that it already now has the character of a "party of government" even though it is not in the government.

Another symptom of the new era is that the activity of Eurocommunist parties is much more open to the inspection of the public at large than hitherto. There have been occasions when the PCF and PCI invited non-members to attend the meetings of party cells and sections, and sometimes some broader party gatherings. Journalists are also often allowed to attend such gatherings.

Closely linked with this is what some authors call the emergence from the complex of a special party or communist "sub-culture". This is understood to mean that Eurocommunist parties no longer claim the right to direct and check all spheres of interest and activity of their members. Whereas previously many parties tried to influence effectively such matters as the artistic and cultural attitudes, the philosophical and aesthetic views of their members, such claims are now increasingly renounced. It is particularly emphasised that the party should not interfere in the personal life of its members. This too can be seen as an element in the party's opening to society.

This opening of the Eurocommunist parties to the societies and systems in which they act should not be interpreted as "growing into" these systems. When the leaders of the PCI state their determination to follow the so-called "third road", they mean, among other things, that they reject both the previous sterile dogmatism and sectarianism on one hand and any "growing in" of a social-democratic type on the other hand. The ambition of the Eurocommunists can certainly not be reduced to a desire to manage the existing capitalist order. Their aim is that the order should be changed.

(iii) MASS MEMBERSHIP AND CADRES

Almost all the Eurocommunist parties have rejected the traditional concept of a cadre party. The view is now widely accepted that the conditions in which these parties act, and in particular the new strategy for socialist transformation, require an essentially different type of party: what is needed is a mass party, or as it is sometimes called a true people's party or a party of the broad and democratic masses. This does not of course mean that cadres do not have a great significance for these parties. In one of the latest programme documents of the PCE the importance of both mass membership and the creation of a core of cadres is emphasised: "The PCE, as a mass party of a new type, must pay much attention to the formation and development of cadres . . .".[21]

The decision to go for a mass type of party has involved a revision of earlier criteria and procedures for the acceptance for new members. In all the parties these criteria have inevitably become much less stringent than hitherto. In practice the previously fairly detailed checking of the political, ideological and other qualities of potential members has been abandoned. The procedures for acceptance have been greatly simplified. It is now possible to proceed to a decision on enrolment as soon as an application has been made. (Already at the end of the Second World War the practice of the so-called candidate period was dropped.) The decisions of basic organisations on the enrolment of new members no longer require ratification by higher party organs.

The struggle of these parties for a mass membership dates back some time. The PCI and PCF had already grown into mass political organisations at the end of the Second World War, and in fact, together with the British Labour party, had become the largest political parties in Western Europe. Recently, however, new efforts have been made to extend the party ranks still further. In this respect the greatest success has been achieved by the PCF which between 1973 and 1978 increased its membership from 410,000 members to 630,000. In the same period the PCI registered almost 200,000 new members, reaching a total of approximately 1,820,000 members. The main source of new members is most frequently to be found in the category of so-called sympathisers, that is, people who by voting for communist candidates and by cooperating in some of their initiatives have expressed their support for these parties.

(iv) DEMOCRATIC CENTRALISM

The principle of democratic centralism has had, and still has today, a key importance for communist parties. A good deal has been said about this principle in the discussions carried on in recent years in these parties. In some cases there were proposals that the principle should be basically revised, or even abandoned: the Communist Party of Sweden, in which some groups made such proposals in the mid-1960s, went further than any other in this respect. The basic forces of Eurocommunism, however, do not accept such drastic suggestions. They reject the view that the principle is incompatible with party democracy, and that it inevitably breeds bureaucratic and authoritarian tendencies. On the other hand they accept that in practice this principle has often served as a screen and cover for major defects in the internal life of many communist parties. Rather than abandon democratic centralism, they propose to free it from some elements which have been conducive to such bureaucratic deformations. Romano Ledda, a prominent member of the PCI, admitted in one statement the possibility that the principle should be revised, and his view that the acceptance of political pluralism involves such a revision is of some interest.[22] The PCI has defined its position as follows:

> The method of democratic centralism corresponds to the aims of the party which wishes to change the basis or class character of a society and state. . . . This method has made it possible . . . for the PCI to carry out its obligation towards the country through its own democracy and unity. Nevertheless progress

> should be made by means of appropriate organizational changes. The popular mass character of the party . . . requires a closer organic link between the factors of democracy and unity. This is why the party should further develop profound mass democracy, the habits of free discussions and of free expression of a critical position, and the initiative of every member and every cell. At the same time one must strengthen the spirit of unity, creativity, unselfishness, loyalty in comradely relationships and the rejection of the method of "currents" which involve divisions and corrupt the life of the party, hindering or making impossible true democratic dialectic.[23]

The PCE's position is similar: "The principle of democratic centralism to which we adhere, but which is today adapted to conditions of legal work, will help internal democracy to flourish".[24]

It is, we believe, a tenable view that at least some, if not all, Eurocommunist parties have achieved definite results in the "democratisation" of the principle of democratic centralism. To some extent at least the democratic component of this traditional formula for the organisation and structure of a revolutionary workers' party has been rehabilitated. Even some authors who are very sceptical of the possibility of a renewal of democracy in communist parties have to recognise certain changes. According to Neil McInnes:

> There have been retreats from the rigors of centralism as practised during the Cold War, in all the western parties. Debate in the cells has become more frank, and at the level above, the section, there is open discussion, in which disagreement does not invite reprobation.[25]

Moreover, there are recently more and more instances of prominent party personalities expressing distinctly different emphases and attitudes.

The internal democratisation of the Eurocommunist parties is manifest in various ways, of which the most important are the following:

(a) The principle of monolithic unity which is practically incompatible with internal party democracy has been dropped. The legitimacy of different views within these parties has been accepted. In some cases they are officially recognised and even "advertised"; in others they are merely tolerated. Some parties do their best to discourage such groupings. The PCE seems to be quite liberal on this score. In a statement to a Madrid newspaper about the forthcoming IX Party Congress Santiago Carrillo said that it would "reflect currents which now exist in the party".[26] As it turned out he was right – the currents did emerge at the congress. The PCI does not officially recognise the existence of different tendencies but there is some evidence that they are present. Some leaders of the PCI have on a number of occasions mentioned "correnti" as a fact of life.

In sum, there is no doubt that in these two parties such phenomena are accepted with a great deal more tolerance. The PCF, on the other hand, has made efforts to discourage the formation of distinct tendencies. Not long ago a prominent official of the PCF specially underlined that the general democratic line of the party does not mean that different political positions can be represented "because it is essentially a matter of efficiency: if half-a-dozen different positions co-exist in a single party; how are the workers to find their way?". And then he went on to say:

> We have no ambition to be a "party of the whole people". The PCF is not a Tower of Babel. It is not a place of dialogue for people to express opposed views on France and France's future. No; it is a gathering point for citizens who share the same ideals, and the same aims, and who belong to the CP in order to contribute together . . . to the triumph of its policy. In these conditions it is only natural that we are seeking a form of intra-party life which will make possible at once the broadest confrontation of views [!], the clearest definition of political decisions and the greatest efficiency in carrying them out.[27]

The PCF's rejection of the existence in practice and even more of the legitimation of distinct tendencies does not, however, mean that it disallows the expression of differing views or even criticism of the leadership's policy. The open discussion which took place after the electoral failure of spring 1978 confirms that significant changes are under way in this party too. The leadership reacted to the public criticism of a large group of intellectuals by rejecting their assessments and arguments, but refrained from applying any disciplinary measures. It seems that the days are passing when notorious *affaires* could result in the expulsion of party members, including some prominent officials, because they criticised aspects of party policy or doctrine. This does not of course mean that the party will in future tolerate *every* sort of internal opposition. The expression of completely contrary attitudes cannot be tolerated, not only in a Communist party but in most other parties too. The toleration of the convergence of individuals with similar views in "correnti" does not necessarily imply a readiness to tolerate fractions, or to legitimise oppositional activity in the party.

(b) It seems that the influence of party congresses has increased somewhat, making them more like gatherings where effective political debate is conducted and influences the formation of party policy. The importance of the central committee as a policy-making body also seems to have grown relative to narrower executive organs such as the secretariat, directorates, executive committees and so forth.

(c) There is reason to conclude that at least to some extent the role of party members has increased. The opportunities for intra-party communication from the base to the top are now certainly greater than before. The increasingly free discussions in party organisations create a *sui generis* "party public opinion" to which the political leadership must pay attention.

The Eurocommunists are sometimes criticised for not going further in their democratisation and for not allowing the formation of party fractions. Sometimes it is even suggested that this is the acid test of their democratic intention, in the sense that only those parties which tolerate fractions can be accepted as democratic. The Eurocommunist parties, for understandable reasons, do not accept this sort of judgement. They say that fractions are quite acceptable for parties whose role is exhausted by gathering votes or by running the existing order. Parties which aim at radical social change must have a much higher degree of internal cohesion and capacity for action. It is quite certain that fractions are incompatible with these requirements.

The fact that fractions are not accepted in principle does not mean that they have not occurred in Eurocommunist and indeed in some other communist parties. It is, however, true that they have not lasted long, except in the Finnish party. The fractions in the Communist Party of Sweden in the mid-1960s are well known. Towards the end of the same decade similar groups appeared in the PCE (García, Líster and Gómez). The Finnish "exception" – two fractions coexisting in the party for some ten years – is to be explained more by certain specific peculiarities of the international position of Finland than by particular features of Finnish communists.

A further reproach levelled at Eurocommunists is that elections still do not have a proper weight in the formation of leading party structures. It is said that the procedure of adopting candidates, which takes place in the framework of the leading organs, is more important than the elections themselves. Some analysts consider that the candidature procedure is often still much more influenced by party leaderships than by the rank and file and basic organisations. It has sometimes been suggested in these parties that the number of names on the list of candidates should be increased, i.e. that there should be more candidates than places to be filled. These suggestions are not usually accepted when it is a matter of elections to leading party organs. This attitude is usually supported by the argument that the practice would introduce into party life elements of politicking, bidding for popularity and cheap demagogy. On the other hand the possibility of nominating a larger number of candidates in elections to less important party functions is accepted. It is our view that the future will bring a further democratisation of the electoral process. The general trend of development of these parties is in that direction.

One of the most controversial aspects of internal development in the Eurocommunist parties is the role of the party apparat, especially its professional element. This apparat has on the whole retained the significance and role which it had in the past. It is widely accepted today that the enormous concentration of power in the hands of the party apparat was an important source of the numerous deformations which affected most communist parties in the Stalinist period. Amendola recently laid particular emphasis on the great concentration of power which took place in the organisational and cadre sector of the party apparat headed at that time (that is, till 1953) by Secchia, and said that this concentration left even the party secretariat and the PCI directorate at a disadvantage.[28] The struggle against concentration of power in the apparat and in some executive bodies cannot, in the Eurocommunists' view, be identified with the struggle against a strong leadership. In fact a communist party does presuppose a strong leadership. This leadership must have a competent and efficient apparat. No doubt this is an inherent contradiction of the revolutionary party of this type. The way out is obviously not to scrap the mechanism but to make it responsible to the membership. This is the course taken by most Eurocommunist parties.

This is of course a problem faced not only by communist parties. Party leaderships and apparats in many other types of party try to monopolise the right to political initiative and the power of decision. This deserves some emphasis because some criticisms directed at Eurocommunists try to make out that there are no such problems in other parties, and that communist parties are some sort of exception in this respect. It may be accepted that in many communist parties this problem was indeed particularly serious and acute, especially in the years of Stalinist domination, but not that it is a problem for them alone.

(v) IDEOLOGY

There are important innovations in the approach to party ideology. The role of ideology in the formation and internal life of the party has been changed. In the first place, the basic approach to party ideology has been largely freed from the ballast of rigid dogmatic interpretations. All these communist parties emphasise their basic Marxist position. They accept Marxism as the source of ideological inspiration and the basis of their view of the world, but some earlier forms of exclusiveness have been abandoned. The possibility of other influences is acceptable. The official position of the PCI is characteristic:

> The communist party takes as a model the tradition of ideas and culture which, beginning from a basic Marxist inspiration, has been created in the course of its history by a lasting and fruitful contact with the living currents of Italian and world culture. . . . We have long since held that the formula "Marxism–Leninism" does not reflect the whole richness of our theoretical and ideological heritage.[29]

In the PCI openness towards changes in society, and therefore readiness to revise certain theoretical positions is held to be in the spirit of Marxist tradition. Lucio Lombardo Radice has said that in this sense Lenin too was a "revisionist", and continues: "We are all revisionists, or, if you like, Marxist–Leninists, in the sense that we have all adapted, changed or ignored the texts according to the demands of concrete situations."[30]

There is a similar message in the statements of some prominent representatives of Eurocommunism that their parties' ideology is not an incarnation, or emanation, of universal and absolute truth. Berlinguer has in this sense several times emphasised that "part of the truth" is always to be found in other political forces. Jean Kanapa, a member of the PCF Politburo, pointed out in an interview that the official party ideology and "scientific theory is not absolute truth. We do not think that we have the sole possession of such truth."[31] Another significant innovation is that Eurocommunists emphasise their decisive opposition to the establishment of any state ideology.[32] There are more and more statements in favour of ideological pluralism as a lasting feature of the society which these parties favour and for which they struggle. PCI representatives have more than once emphasised that they are equally opposed to state religion and state ideology. When they say that they are struggling for a secular society they include the ideological aspect of this secularisation. Moreover, the PCI emphasises that it not only stands for the secular character of modern society but considers that the party itself should have such a character.

In line with this position in principle, the PCI (and also the other two big Eurocommunist parties of western Europe) have abandoned the traditional demand that only someone who adopts the official party ideology can be made a party member. The first breakthrough in this direction came in the PCI. As early as 1946 at its VI Congress the PCI adopted a statute which opened the doors of the party to people of other philosophical and ideological views. In article 2 of this statute it was stated that membership is open to "all citizens who are 18 years old without regard to their . . . religious or philosophical denomination who accept the party programme". This was certainly a major change compared with the traditional criteria for enrolment which were defined for all communist parties in the "Twenty-one conditions" of the Comintern in 1920.

The sense of this approach lies not only in a desire to carry out a sort of de-ideologisation of the criteria for enrolment and thereby a secularisation of these parties as a matter of principle. There is also a political motive connected with the desire of these parties to open their doors to that section of the working class and other working people which is under the powerful influence of Christian ethics and the Christian world view as a whole. Practice has confirmed that the earlier atheism of these parties was a great and sometimes impassable barrier to their efforts to approach these strata of the population. After this opening took place, tens of thousands of Christians joined the communist parties in these countries. It is important to note that nowadays Christian convictions are no longer considered primarily as an "error" which is "magnanimously" and "benevolently" tolerated. There are more and more statements which recognise certain essential values of the Christian view of man and society. Togliatti was one of the first prominent personalities in the communist movement to say this openly. In a speech in 1963 in Bergamo he said:

> We have stated, and we insist on the statement, that the aspiration towards a socialist society can not only find support in people with a religious belief, but can find encouragement in religious consciousness itself.[33]

More recently such judgements have become fairly common. A religious, or, more precisely, Christian outlook is treated as an important source of socialist inspiration.[34] It is of interest to note that a considerable number of Christians have won important reputations in some of these parties. Today there are a fairly large number of communist Christians in important positions in the PCI and PCE.

5 WHAT POINT HAS BEEN REACHED?

On the whole, the Eurocommunist parties have had considerable success in their democratisation and particularly in their efforts to bring their structure, role and internal relationships into harmony with the conditions in which they act and the most important tasks which they face. Their experience, like that of many other parties, shows that difficulties, obstacles and resistances in this area are particularly serious. However, the periods of stagnation and vacillation in the process of democratisation cannot be reduced simply to internal resistances and misunderstandings. These certainly exist but the problems extend beyond them. There are also certain objective difficulties and contradictions. It is not easy to get away from forms of organisation and political action which are the outcome of accumulated customs and traditions. It should be said at this point that resistance to the challenge of the time and to demands for change is present also in most other working-class parties (socialist and social-democratic) and trades unions.

One must also reckon with the pressure of forces which, in the guise of a struggle for innovation and modernisation of communist parties, in fact try to deprive them of some of their most essential features as revolutionary organisations. There have been very marked efforts by the Eurocommunists' present or potential partners to make them agree that if they accept pluralism as the framework and essential feature of the political system in which they have to implement their policy, they must also adopt a kind of intra-party pluralism. Quite a few people today stress that only two choices are possible – either the traditional Comintern party of monolithic unity and a dominant apparat or, on the other hand, the traditional bourgeois or social-democratic party with a loose structure, ill-defined programme and especially with developed internal, and most often fractional, divisions.

The Eurocommunists do not accept these appraisals, which are sometimes a form of blackmail by their political partners and opponents. They emphasise that pluralism in the political system of a country does not presuppose the *same kind* of pluralism in parties as the subjects of its political life. They decisively reject the thesis that the only choice is between a Comintern or a social-democratic type of party. The innovations which they have already introduced have shown that a "third" solution might be possible. The new type of party which they favour, quite understandably, runs into many difficulties and unknowns. Most of the problems are entirely new. The enterprise is thus largely a pioneering one, and it is in that sense that the difficulties, weaknesses and contradictions which appear from time to time must be understood. Breaking new ground and searching for new forms of revolutionary organisation and action was never an easy, simple, one-dimensional operation. The important thing is the basic direction of this enterprise. Here there can be no doubt: the Eurocommunist parties are searching for a conception of a revolutionary party adapted to the conditions of the milieu in which they work and demands imposed on them by the last quarter of the twentieth century. Those who reproach the Eurocommunists that democracy in their parties is still insufficient or faulty should be made aware that contemporary political parties in general are not sterling examples of democracy. Parties which do not accept the essential imperative of capacity for action cannot put to communist parties such demands as they do not meet themselves.

Translated by Richard Kindersley

NOTES

1. In his well-known essay "The prospects for pluralistic communism", published in the early 1960s, Richard Lowenthal defends the view that departure from the traditional Leninist model can lead only in two directions – either to the social-democratisation of the communist parties or to their degeneration into utopian sects. See also his article "Communism as an historical force", in *International Journal*, vol. 32, no. 1 (1976). Neil McInnes emphasises that ". . . it is in respect of their internal organization that the western parties have evolved least from the original model" – *Eurocommunism*, The Washington Papers, no. 37 (1976), p. 43.
2. *Platform for the Tenth Congress of the League of Communists of Yugoslavia* (Belgrade, 1974), p. 182.
3. *Repubblica*, 2 August 1978.
4. Giorgio Amendola wrote in 1964:

   Neither of the two solutions which have been offered to the working class of the West European capitalist countries in the last fifty years – the social-democratic solution and the communist solution – has so far proved adequate for the task of realizing the socialist transformation of society . . . . (*Rinascità*, 28 November 1964).
5. Declaration of the PCF Central Committee prepared for the XXII Congress of the Party (February 1976), "Ce que veulent les communistes pour la France", *L'Humanité*, 12 November 1975.
6. *L'Unità*, 18 November 1975.
7. Quoted in *Politika* (Belgrade), 3 September 1975.
8. *L'Humanité*, 15 January 1976.
9. See, for instance, his speech published in *L'Unità*, 25 July 1978.
10. Speech of 24 September 1944 at a meeting of the Rome federation of the PCI, *Rinascità*, vol. 1, no. 4. See also his speech to the Naples PCI *aktiv* published in *Critica Marxista*, 1964, nos. 4–5, and the speech made in Florence in October 1944, *Rinascità* 29 August 1964.

11. Speech at the VIII Congress of the PCI: *Osmi Kongres KPI* (Belgrade 1957), p. 44.
12. *Rinascità*, 28 November 1964.
13. *"Eurocommunism" and the State* (London, 1977), pp. 99–100.
14. Theses for the XV Congress of the PCI, 20–5 March 1978 (theses 15 and 12). A similar view was expressed by Giorgio Napolitano, who said in one statement that no one party or group could claim exclusive representation of the working class. Napolitano expressly says that "other parties" such as the Socialist and Catholic parties, the trades unions, cooperatives and some other organisations "also play a role in expressing legitimate needs of the working class". R. Tőkés (ed.), *Eurocommunism and Détente* (New York, 1978), pp. 121–2.
15. *Nouvel Observateur*, 25 September 1978.
16. Georges Marchais emphasised in his report at the XXII Congress of the PCF, ". . . the possibility of building socialism in France is linked to the Communist Party's capacity to exercise a directing influence in the popular movement" – *Cahiers du Communisme* (February–March 1976), p. 60.
17. De Vittorio, speech at the VIII Congress of the PCI, 1956.
18. Tőkés, op. cit., p. 101.
19. *L'Unità*, 18 November 1975.
20. Resolutions of the IX Congress of the PCE, thesis no. 7.
21. Ibid., thesis no. 15.
22. Interview given to *L'Europeo*, 16 July 1976.
23. Theses for the XV Congress of the PCI, thesis no. 15.
24. Resolutions of the IX Congress of the PCE, thesis no. 15.
25. McInnes, op. cit., p. 44.
26. *Politika*, 23 January 1978.
27. Paul Laurent to *France Nouvelle*, quoted in *Politika*, 22 June 1977.
28. *L'Unità*, 11 February 1978.
29. Theses for the XV National Congress of the PCI, Thesis no. 15.
30. Quoted in Norman Kogan, "The Italian Communist Party: the modern prince at the crossroads", in Tőkés, op. cit., p. 119.
31. *Nouvel Observateur*, 5 February 1978.
32. In the theses for the XV Congress of the PCI it is stated: "The democratic–secular state must not take as its own any particular current of ideology or religious belief" (thesis no. 15).
33. Quoted from *Rinascità*, 30 March 1964.
34. See the very significant passage in the Draft Theses for the XV Congress of the PCI: "Experience teaches us that in the dramatic situation of our time Christian belief can be a motive to join the struggle for the socialist transformation of society" (thesis no. 14).

    Santiago Carrillo argues that in Spanish conditions the communist party can only gain, and be enriched, by Christians joining it: "We say that with the entry of Christians our party has gained a new dimension; one could perhaps add that the same has happened to the faith of our Christian members". Carrillo in fact holds that the entry of Christians into the communist party leads to mutual enrichment. (*"Eurocommunism" and the State*, pp. 32–3.)

9 In Lieu of a Conclusion: Eurocommunism and "the Crisis of Capitalism"

RICHARD KINDERSLEY

Euratom, Eurodollar, Eurovision – by 1975, when the "Euro-" prefix was first attached to communism, it was already familiar and carried a distinctly positive overtone. (Even "Eurocrat" is, at least in prestige, a cut above "bureaucrat" – who ever heard of a "petty Eurocrat"?) So it is not difficult to see why the Italian, Spanish and French Communist Parties, with varying degrees of hesitation, took up what must have seemed (to put it no higher) a good sales pitch. The disclaimer of inverted commas, retained by Carrillo in 1977, is not always discarded even today – as the title of Giuseppe Vacca's contribution to this volume shows. By 1978, when Manuel Azcárate gave the talk reproduced in this book, it was no longer considered necessary by the Spanish Party. For Jean Elleinstein, in spite of some initial conceptual doubts, Eurocommunism becomes, in the end, almost an ideal: something to which the PCF should aspire.[1]

Of course, there were certain risks involved. Regionalisation has not been an accepted practice in the world communist movement. Moscow has tolerated no formal regional groupings of communist parties: even the Cominform, in any case totally under Soviet control, was European in practice rather than in principle. Chinese suggestions that there might be such a thing as an Asian road to communism, distinct from the Soviet way, played some small part in the great schism. The Eurocommunists must have known that they would provoke Soviet disapproval.[2] Moreover, the three parties had to become convinced that they had enough in common to justify the adoption of a single label. Their histories, as parties, exhibit major differences: the PCI with its years of illegality under fascism, but blessed with an intellectual heritage in Gramsci and an independent-minded (if for many years prudently cautious) leader in Togliatti who, albeit with Stalin's approval, brought the party into constitutionalism and indeed government from 1944 to 1947; the PCF, *ouvriériste* and persistently Stalinist in the legacy of Thorez, *fils du Peuple*, but – alone of the three – disposing of a *national* revolutionary mythology dating back before 1917, which helped it to adjust to the Popular Front of the mid-thirties, as well as to government after the Second World War, and now fuels what has been called "gaullo-communisme";[3] and the PCE, a participant – and not just a supporter like the PCF – in a Popular Front government under the Republic, but only now emerging from forty years of clandestinity and émigré leadership, mainly from Moscow and Paris.[4]

Nor – except in one important particular – were the parties' immediate political circumstances much more similar: in Italy there was virtually a two-party system (in which the Christian Democrats were always the government and the communists always the opposition) in a state of advanced demoralisation, accentuated by terrorism on right and left; in France, the disarray of Gaullism without the General, but a still powerful centralised state and a startlingly revived socialist party; in Spain, a surprisingly auspicious beginning to parliamentary democracy, threatened chiefly by regionalist tensions and terrorism.

The important similarity lay in the fact that all three parties seemed to their leaders to have a chance of sharing power: in Italy with the Christian Democrats, in France with the Socialists, and in Spain in a "Government of National Concentration". That this coincidence of opportunity has an important explanatory value is not to be doubted;[5] but it does not define what features combine together to make a party Eurocommunist.

What, then, are the common features? According to a Russian legend, the earth rests on three whales. Likewise Eurocommunism's claim to a distinct identity has a triple basis. First, the presentation of a new analysis of the society in which it exists, from which flows a new prospect of "democratic" transition to socialism and even a new outline of socialism itself; secondly, a critical attitude to the Soviet Union, which is no longer to be accepted as *the*, or even – some Eurocommunists have dared to say – *a* model for socialism; and thirdly, a new concept of what a communist party should be and do.[6] Now whales, though large, are mainly made of blubber, and move about a good deal – and anyway it is only a legend: much of the discussion of Eurocommunism concerns the degree of solidity, stability and indeed reality of the three points on which it claims to rest. Do the Eurocommunists "really" believe in a peaceful transition to a pluralist society? Are they "really" independent of the CPSU? Are they "really" democratising themselves?

Put like that, the questions could boil down to the sincerity of politicians, or the value of their promises, and would scarcely be worth asking; certainly no attempt will be made to answer them in those terms here. They do, however, help to define Eurocommunism – for there is a sense in which politicians are what they say, even if they do not always do what they say – and so to provide the framework in which it has been discussed.

EUROCOMMUNISM AND THE CRISIS

It may be instructive to relate these three bases of Eurocommunism to a paradox in the present situation, namely that what is diagnosed as the "general crisis of capitalism", which might have been expected to produce more revolutionary attitudes and activity in communist parties – since the opportunities for revolution are, canonically at least, greater in times of crisis – has in fact apparently made them more "revisionist", "reformist" and "moderate" in their statements and programmes.

How far is it true to say, with Santiago Carrillo, that Eurocommunism is "first of all and above all a reply to a decadent capitalist system at the height of a crisis . . ."?[7] Several contributors to this book have been at pains to point out that the ideas of Eurocommunism can be traced well into the past; not only before the present crisis, but before the sociological changes inherent in the approach to "post-industrial society" which constitute the empirical material for Eurocommunist political economy. It is however the coincidence of these changes and the crisis which has given Eurocommunism its present influence and credibility, and the paradox still requires some elucidation.

When it was first perceived, the relative decline in the number of blue-collar workers in society, and the concomitant increase in salaried white-collar employees, especially in service trades, was thought to present Marxists with a problem. These developments, it seemed, would alter the political attitudes of those moving out of the proletariat *sensu stricto*, giving them a stake in the existing order and reducing their interest in changing it, let alone by revolution, with which the communist parties were still identified. *Embourgeoisement*, as it was called, seemed to go with the consumer society, affluence, motor-cars, refrigerators and washing-machines: if more and more people were getting more and more of these things, why should they risk not only them, but the additional pleasures of parliamentary government and civil liberties for the untested promises of socialism?

This question does not, of course, lie at the root of the theory of "state monopoly capitalism" which has a lineage from Lenin, Hilferding and Bukharin; but the theory was developed and re-popularised among Western communist parties, particularly in France, in the 1960s.[8] Not that this theory, even outside Soviet usage, is peculiar to the Eurocommunists. In Western Germany, where there is no Eurocommunist party, the radical "Young Socialist" movement (Jusos) in the SPD has appropriated it – under the acronym *Stamokap* – as a road back from the Godesberg Programme to a new form of Marxist orthodoxy; and although their sociological analysis is much the same, the programmatic conclusions which they draw from it are not those of the Eurocommunists, but point to something much more like a DDR-type one-party state.[9] For Eurocommunists, however, it offered some sort of solution to the problem of capitalist prosperity. The present version did not, like its predecessor of the 1920s, go with a catastrophist and apocalyptic view of the coming end of capitalism. On the contrary, it recognised that state intervention could make capitalism work better, and even postpone the inevitable transformation into socialism. But its emphasis on the power of big business allied with government defined a new enemy against which not only the proletariat but everyone living mainly from earned income should be able to unite. To be sure, there was more than an echo in this of the *deux cent familles* of the 1930s, and some of the old slogans were exhumed. But the evident threat of fascist states and movements supported by them, which justified the Popular Fronts at that time, was absent now, and the implication that the dividing line of the class struggle should be raised to a much higher level in society, leaving below it a broad alliance of blue- and white-collar workers, peasants, technicians, intellectuals and even small businessmen, took some time to sink in. While prosperity lasted, *embourgeoisement* did put a brake on all but the most extreme forms of radicalism.

The onset of crisis might well have led to a reversion from this strategy to a more traditional revolutionism. That it did not do so may perhaps be attributed to two peculiarities of the present crisis. Its first unprecedented feature (unprecedented except for a brief episode in central Europe after the First World War) is simultaneous unemployment and inflation, a dilemma which apparently cannot be resolved by Keynesian methods: impossible to prime the pump without the whole thing overflowing. Whereas in the 1930s people suffered almost exclusively as producers, through unemployment and depressed wages, the concurrent inflation now attacks them no less as consumers. It is this factor, by which not only factory workers but all income-earners suffer, which gives credibility to the Eurocommunist appeal. There may be a few gaps in the picture (on which side of the class division are the employees – or even the proletariat, possibly exploited but certainly well-paid – of the "monopolies" to be found? or can stockbrokers' clerks really be expected to see their social and political interests in the same way as miners or dustmen?), but it is sufficiently plausible to have prompted the re-thinking of communist strategy and tactics which has been called Eurocommunist. If, in Marx's words, all history is the history of class struggles, some part of the history of Marxism is the successive redefinitions of those struggles, a process to which Eurocommunism is now making its own contribution.

The second relevant peculiarity is to be found in the energy crisis, in particular the oil price rise, which increases the insecurity of Europeans by the feeling that they are at the mercy, not – as in previous crises – of impersonal market conditions, in which, according to an historically and psychologically established pattern, "bad times" would eventually be succeeded by "good", but of a more or less coherent group of people who have no particular reason to want good times in Western Europe, whose interest may rather lie in prolonging the crisis at a level short of complete collapse, and who have the power to bring this about. High oil prices are unlikely to go away, and France, Spain and Italy are not protected by the cushion of North Sea oil. The direct political (as distinct from economic) effects of this situation have hardly been felt so far, but if and when they come they are likely to include a resurgence of nationalism – either on a competitive basis, with each country grabbing at scarce energy resources, or on a co-operative European basis, with the oil-deficitary EEC opposed to the oil producers. Either way, the opportunities for xenophobia are obvious, and may be exploited to increase social cohesion in the oil-consuming countries. The day of proletarian revolution is thus once again postponed, the slogans of revolution once again lose their relevance, and the Eurocommunist view gains support.

This second feature of the crisis plays little or no part in the Eurocommunists' own thinking, which does not stray much beyond a class analysis of their own societies, except where the hand of imperialism is detected. (For all the Eurocommunists' recent criticism of particular features of the Soviet Union, and in spite of such experiences as the Soviet attempt to displace Carrillo in the PCE, the danger of Soviet "hegemonism" still generally weighs lighter with them than American expressions of distaste for the accession of communists to NATO governments: Berlinguer comes nearest to explicit neutrality on this point.)

The concept of revolution is thus replaced by something rather less precise: the "peaceful transition to socialism". It is important to insist on this imprecision, because it makes it more difficult to frame certain questions. With revolutionary parties, the question (more often asked than answered) was "After the revolution, what then?" But the Eurocommunist scenario offers no such dividing line. After what? Not "the revolution"; not "the seizure of power". The "transition", certainly; but what does this mean? Participation in power? Entry into a coalition government? As minority or majority? Outright victory in unrigged elections? Would this lead to a "Communist government" in the same sense as a Gaullist or Christian Democrat government? It is this imprecision which prompted Annie Kriegel, in her book *Un autre communisme?*, to entitle the last chapter "Qu'arriverait-il si . . .?" without finishing the sentence.[10] "Post-capitalist society" is a phrase already in use; must we learn to dodge the issue even more widely by saying "post-transitional" society? To little avail, it seems: Fernando Claudín notes that "socialism" is itself a transitional concept, and that the Eurocommunist parties have in fact introduced a new phrase: "the transition to the transition".[11]

Be that as it may, the idea of peaceful transition, in the present political circumstances in France, Italy and Spain – though not necessarily elsewhere or at other times – involves the communists in more or less ambivalent combinations with other parties, ranging from the *compromesso storico* in Italy, through the unstable *Union de la gauche* in France, to the PCE's efforts to "push the PSOE to the right in order to keep the monopoly of Marxism in Spain".[12] How has the current crisis affected these combinations? In Italy, far from driving the communists back from their non-revolutionary position, it has positively accentuated it: they alone of the influential communist parties of the capitalist world, are prepared explicitly to accept some responsibility for "managing the crisis". In France, where the PCF clung stubbornly to the theory of "pauperisation", denying the very fact of prosperity, but where the Common Programme of Government was signed nevertheless, in 1972, before the economic crisis broke, it has helped the socialists, rather than the communists, to gain popular support, and has led to intensified competition between the two main parties of the Left. In Spain the same thing has happened, but the PCE has been more flexible. Its call for a "government of national concentration", with PCE support but not participation, seems to move some way towards the Italian position (and is accompanied by much Gramscian terminology), but could equally well be used to exercise power without responsibility; however, the PCE has been ready to recognise a role even for multi-national capital in Spain's economic development.[13] In no case has there been a reversion to revolutionism, not even in France, although the value attached by the PCF to the preservation of ideological integrity suggests that there is less security against such a reversion there than elsewhere.[14] One important reason is doubtless that each of the three parties has had, or has seen the chance of, a taste of power with support of people afflicted as consumers, as well as producers, and realises that to preach revolution would lose them this support indefinitely. These are, moreover, often the same people who were alarmed by the students' movements in France and Italy in 1968–9, when the sudden appearance of groups to the left of the CPs gave the latter a chance to earn a measure of respectability. "Smashing the bourgeois state machine" is a much more frightening prospect than "hegemony"; indeed the recognition by some liberal-democratic critics of Eurocommunism that anti-communism has declined in the past few years[15] suggests that hegemony pays off where revolutionism has failed, and that this process has not been interrupted by the crisis.

If questions of revolutionary-reformist strategy have tended to accentuate differences between Eurocommunist parties in the present crisis, the issue of relations with the CPSU and attitudes to the USSR has been somewhat less divisive. For one thing, given the logic of détente, the Soviet attitude to the crisis is carefully modulated: not for them a paean of triumph at the coming of a revolutionary wave which would throw their Western *interlocuteurs valables* into an indefinite period of chaos. This has, of course, suited the Eurocommunist book well, for pro-Sovietism in their ranks has been a form of romantic conservatism, an unwillingness to renounce the myth of Utopia realised, or at least on the way to realisation.

As H. T. Willetts points out earlier in this book, the development of autonomy and independence in Western communist parties is a secular trend of which the Eurocommunist polemics with Moscow are merely one of the more spectacular episodes so far. The acceleration of this trend came not with the crisis but before, with the invasion of Czechoslovakia in 1968, and the culminating moment – so far – with the symbolic omission at Berlin in 1976 of the standard reference to "proletarian internationalism". Given that the Eurocommunist parties have met the current crisis not – as the Comintern met the crisis of 1929 – with a theory requiring a withdrawal of the united front strategy, but with one implying a policy of broad alliances, then autonomy and independence from the CPSU are all of a piece with the aim of winning such allies in their own societies. The crisis has not produced the drive for autonomy but merely increased its urgency. The fact that on occasion socialist parties, such as the PSI and the PSOE, have profited from the crisis to take up positions outflanking the communists on the left has only increased the latter's need for *enracinement*, and therefore for distancing from Moscow.

All the Eurocommunist parties have to cope with pro-Soviet elements within their ranks. For the PCI, Togliatti's inheritance has made the process relatively easy, at the intellectual level, as witness the party's quasi-official support for certain forms of Soviet dissidence. Moreover, the increased protection of wages and employment in Italy, by the *scala mobile* and the *statuto dei lavoratori*, may have done something to reduce the need to idealise "realised socialism" in the USSR and Eastern Europe. The PCE not only saw immediate popular advantage in *New Times*' attack on Carrillo, but, seeking a "solution" to the crisis in Spain, understood the need for every possible economic assistance, and therefore not only supported Spanish accession to the Common Market, but also as we have seen above, accepted, at least for the time being, the multi-nationals in Spain (as has the PCI in Italy). On the first of these points the PCE found itself at odds not only with the Soviet Union but also with the PCF, which flew its national colours in the hands of Jean Kanapa.[16] On the second issue, there might be no difference with the Soviet Union if the latter could admit openly that it has its own crisis, which can be alleviated only by the importation of American capital and American grain; but in the absence of any such admission, the difference is there. Just as it is the PCF which has been least willing to shake off the Leninist ideological heritage, so the PCF's refusal to *gérer la crise* has left it most closely aligned with the Soviet Union's public position. Nevertheless, these are nuances, and it is probably this aspect of Eurocommunism which has been least affected by the crisis.

The third point of distinction of the Eurocommunist parties lies in the parties themselves, their role and internal organisation. In this context Branko Pribićević[17] identifies five new developments. These are the role adopted by the party in the working-class movement; its relationship to society as a whole; the relations between rank-and-file and cadres; the interpretation of democratic centralism; and the party's attitude to ideology. In all these, Pribićević finds statements and declarations which indicate a more flexible, less exclusive, more democratic and – in the traditional sense at least – less "revolutionary" type of party. Now while it would be unreasonable to dismiss such statements as of no importance – for they may be used by liberalisers and democratisers within the parties to further their cause – it is also fair to ask for evidence that practice is following precept. On some of these points, at least, such evidence is forthcoming: as Pribićević points out, the PCE and PCI have both tolerated diverse "currents" of opinion, and if the PCF has not moved so far in this direction, at least the era of notorious *affaires* appears to be over, and even the electoral disaster of 1978 did not result in disciplinary measures against party leaders, as it surely would have done some years ago: scapegoats, it seems, are no longer as necessary as they used to be. Paul Preston concludes[18] that even if Santiago Carrillo defeated his opponents in the PCE by undemocratic methods, the result has been a democratisation of the party from which it will find it hard to retreat. Against this, readers of Jean Elleinstein's contribution to this volume can only think that there is a good deal further to go before democratisers in the PCF will be satisfied, particularly as regards horizontal communications and the "unwritten rules" of party discipline, while Isaac Aviv reminds us of the "incredible" unanimity (to borrow Semprún's phrase) with which the PCF Central Committee voted to support Marchais after the 1978 elections.[19] Duhamel and Weber, introducing a collection of interviews covering the main trends of thought in the PCF after the electoral defeat of 1978, record the PCF leadership's response to their invitation to participate: "If we do not allow a public debate in *L'Humanité* with those of our comrades who have strayed into fractional activities . . . we certainly do not intend to conduct it in a miscellany of this sort."[20]

This present crisis has had an ambivalent effect on the party aspects of Eurocommunism. On the one hand, Pribićević argues that it is difficult for parties claiming legitimacy in an open and democratic society not to become more open and democratic themselves, and that their interest in forming alliances with other parties whose tradition, at least, is democratic rather than centralist (and who have sometimes resisted such alliances on the ground that the proposed communist partner is undemocratic), can only favour this trend. This motive dates from before the crisis, but is likely to be strengthened by it. On the other hand, the proliferation of ultra-left groups and parties, which appeared before the crisis, but have derived much impetus from it, is more likely to be seen by the Eurocommunists as potential subversion, and to be dealt with by such methods as most organisations of any sort use to treat subversion. Maria-Antonietta Macciocchi's account of her expulsion from the PCI[21] suggests that disciplinary procedures against such activities in the PCI are still a matter for manipulation rather than fair hearing. (Macciocchi's book also contains the statement, interesting if true, that Gramsci was once expelled from the Communist Party of Italy.)[22] Whether the use of undemocratic procedures against ultra-left infiltration would put off potential allies among socialist, radical or centre parties is, of course, another question.

The question we may reasonably ask is whether continuation or deepening of the crisis is likely to push the parties further on their liberalising path: will they, for instance, formally abandon democratic centralism and legitimise "fractions"? As Pribićević reminds us, there have been cases of fractions tolerated for years on end in some communist parties, though not in any major European party since the 1920s. The advantage – possibly the only political advantage – of that degree of liberalisation is that it gives some guarantee against political sclerosis. Fractions, groups, clubs – the Tribune and Manifesto groups in the British Labour Party, the Bow Group and the Monday Club in the Conservative Party, the CERES group in the French Socialist Party – all these offer an arena for manoeuvre, which democratic centralism, strictly applied, would preclude. Political and ideological innovation is, of course, possible in parties which do not formally tolerate fractions: the Yugoslav Party since 1948 is a prime example. But rigidity is a disease of monolithic rather than divided parties. Secondly, internal liberalisation may help to convince a sceptical electorate that a vote for the party would not be a vote for tyranny.[23] Lastly, the need for alliances, enhanced by the crisis, may, as we have already suggested, prompt the argument that "democratic" parties will not willingly ally themselves with "undemocratic" ones. Against this, given that such alliances are now concerted by what used to be damned as the "united front from above" (that is, agreement between the party leaderships) internal stability becomes a virtue. Each side – socialist, radical, liberal or Christian Democrat as much as communist – will want to know that the other can deliver the goods; and a leadership harassed by divisions in the ranks is that much less able to give this assurance. A still more serious consideration, perhaps, is one to which Pribićević alludes briefly: that "the essential imperative of capacity for action" is a reason for stopping short of legitimising fractions. If this means action in government, or indeed in opposition, it would be hard to find a party which would deny the imperative, though many would question the conclusion; but if – as it might also be thought – it means extra-parliamentary action, the conclusion is inescapable, though many would reject the premise. The question is then: have the Eurocommunist parties "really" renounced extra-parliamentary (which means, in a parliamentary democracy, extra-constitutional) methods? The ultra-left, as we shall see below, reproaches them with having done so. The crisis has not, so far, induced them to give the lie to these reproaches; but it is possible to imagine circumstances of social chaos from which a monolithic party could profit and for which even Eurocommunist parties may feel that they should hold some preparations in reserve.

From another point of view, it may be argued that internal party organisation need be of little concern provided that the commitment to multi-party pluralism is not in doubt. Pribićević rightly remarks that not all "democratic" political parties are sterling examples of internal democracy (some would cite the British Conservative Party as one in which, to say the least, democracy is tempered by oligarchy); but this need not matter very much so long as the electorate can be sure of its ability to throw the party out of office if it wants to. The danger of tyranny, according to this view, arises if an undemocratically-organised party, democratically elected to power, then fails to observe the "rules of the game", as did, for example, the Nazi Party in Germany. All the Eurocommunist parties profess adherence to these rules, and assert that if voted out of office they would indeed relinquish it and go into opposition. However, as Berlinguer for one has recognised, it is impossible for such a party to give any *formal* guarantee of its commitment; and remarks (such as those of Lombardo Radice)[24] to the effect that it is unthinkable that the electorate would wish to reverse the achievements of socialism, to "retreat from a higher form of society to a lower" can only feed the doubts of liberal–democratic sceptics on this score. (Radice is referring to Eastern Europe, but his words are presumably applicable, *a fortiori*, to "post-transitional" society in the West.) There is, on the face of it, a contradiction between the Eurocommunists' commitment to parliamentarianism both during and after the transition and the assertion that parties aiming at radical social change cannot be measured by the same yardstick as those whose role is limited to vote-gathering for elections and managing the system. Do the

Eurocommunists, in fact, interpret the rules of the game in the same way?

Nor are sceptics wholly satisfied by the thought that even if the unthinkability of reversing socialist legislation so qualifies party pluralism as to make it meaningless, internal changes in the party will offer some guarantee of freedom and democracy. Ample, free debate; genuine election and recall of officials; responsibility of higher organs to lower – all these democratic sides of democratic centralism are not accepted as a substitute for the right to organise an opposition with the avowed object of changing the leadership of the party which, in the situation we are considering, will in effect be the government of the country.

A more serious argument, perhaps, is that based on the idea of political culture. Lombardo Radice has said that

> It is, in a democratic society, impossible to advocate, year in, year out, a pluralistic, free, democratic type of socialism, and then, as soon as we are put in power by the votes of the people, to repudiate it, to suppress freedom and set up the dictatorship of the proletariat. . . . It is quite unreasonable to suppose that you can say one thing on Monday and do the opposite on Tuesday. . . . You cannot manipulate millions of workers. They have voted for you because you have given them a certain programme. You can't suddenly choose to do the opposite.[25]

This is to argue that certain political acts are impossible because of the established public attitudes, "subjective" factors which would not tolerate such acts. Pribićević, too, points out that the conception of democracy adopted by Eurocommunist parties is "the dominant feature of the political culture" of their societies.[26] Now the malleability of political culture is a subject on its own, but it is fair to say that most authors considering radical change in this context tend to assert the persistence of habits and attitudes in spite of such change.[27] However, it is also true that these habits and attitudes can be suppressed for a more or less lengthy period. Even if we assume – and it can only be a qualified assumption – that the basic political cultures of Italy and Spain are democratic, we are bound to admit that they could be virtually extinguished, under Mussolini and Franco, for decades. What is to say that, *mutato nomine*, it could not happen again? In the short or medium term, political culture may be a fragile guarantee of pluralist democracy; and in the long term, as Keynes said, we are all dead.

EUROCOMMUNISM, ITS CRITICS AND THE CRISIS

The Eurocommunists' uneasy relationship with the Soviet and East European parties and states has been well covered both in this volume and elsewhere.[28] It may therefore be more useful here to look at some of the attitudes which have been adopted towards Eurocommunism by critics and observers outside the Soviet orbit.

Various attitudes towards Eurocommunism have been taken up on the right, centre and left. Seen from the right – mainly exemplified by certain spokesmen in the United States – Eurocommunism is "Stalinism in a mask and tyranny in disguise", covered by a "deceit of democratic pretensions".[29] Not unnaturally, strategic considerations strongly colour some Western attitudes to Eurocommunism. These were succinctly stated by General Haig at the Western European Union Assembly on 29 November 1977 and turn on the issues of security of information in NATO and of the likely effect of Eurocommunist participation in government on the priority given to defence spending. From the strategic point of view, these arguments can hardly be denied. The PCF's abrupt espousal of the *force de frappe* is directed against both superpowers, the USA as much as the Soviet Union, and must be seen as a "Gaullo-communist" rather than Eurocommunist gesture. This attitude may well be mirrored in the Soviet defence establishment, for whom Eurocommunist participation could only mean a weakening of Western defence efforts and security. Soviet politicians may see matters rather differently. Both Robert Legvold on the one hand, and Fernando Claudín, on the other, have given convincing reasons why the Soviet leadership may prefer, at least for the time being, powerful communist parties in opposition rather than either coalition-hobbled parties in government or a full "transition to socialism"; but Legvold underlines the present similarity between Eurocommunist and Soviet foreign policy objectives.[30] As we have seen, the Eurocommunists' efforts to achieve re-integration have been increased by the present crisis; but the crisis has not altered Soviet foreign policy aims, which the Eurocommunists' contribution to the weakening of Western defence can only advance. What the crisis has done is to lend more political weight to the arguments of the Eurocommunists and the Western left in general against defence as opposed to other forms of public spending.

Some Western socialists, especially those on the right or at the centre of parties not involved in dealings with communists, express similar concerns. Sir Harold Wilson has evoked the danger to the EEC and NATO if one of its members were to "go Communist or become a socialist-diluted communist state", condemning "Mitterrandisme" and calling, in historically evocative terms, for "vigilance and resolution" to guard against Eurocommunism – "this latest of threats".[31] For some on the left wing of socialist parties, the Eurocommunists' differences with Moscow have seemed to offer a promise that the breach of 1920 might be healed, leading to a new regenerated European democratic socialist movement.[32] For most socialists, however, the crucial question has been not defence but democracy, embodied in free elections; could "a political phenomenon which draws its support from the ballot box . . . at the end of the day, prove to be the instrument which closed the ballot boxes for good"?[33] Others have seen the Eurocommunists "detaching themselves from centralist dogma", proving the strength of social-democratic concepts, and – ultimately perhaps, for only time would show whether the Eurocommunist conversion was tactical or fundamental – ready to be welcomed back into the social democratic fold.[34] The Eurocommunists, of course, deny any such thing, and attack, in particular, Helmut Schmidt, with whom the other socialists are associated in the Socialist International.

Criticism of Eurocommunism from the left is conducted on a rather different theoretical level, though it shares some points of view, adventitiously or not, with that of the right: a belief in the Eurocommunist parties' kinship with Stalinism and their insufficient democratisation. Nor is it only Western liberal critics of Eurocommunism who question the adequacy of its critique of the Soviet Union. Such critics may warn us that "occasional Eurocommunist criticisms of the lack of freedoms in the USSR must be set against their generalised support for Moscow",[35] but Ernest Mandel, a leader of the Fourth International, maintains that it is Eurocommunist criticisms of Soviet internal affairs, not their general political and strategic attitudes, which disturb the "Soviet bureaucracy".[36] For him, even the "timid criticisms" of the Soviet Union by the Eurocommunists have "great objective explosive potential".[37] Mandel interprets the position of *New Times vis-à-vis* Santiago Carrillo as follows:

> We can easily accept and live with all the "rightist" excesses of Eurocommunism; but what we cannot accept are public criticisms of the political régime in the USSR and the People's Democracies, much less "calls to fight against the existing order of things" in the USSR, that is, calls to political revolution.[38]

Thus, to blame the Eurocommunists, as Mandel does, for their failure "to break definitively and irrevocably with the Soviet bureaucracy"[39] offers an ironic point of contact between the Trotskyist left and Western liberals. Another major critic of the Eurocommunists from the left, Fernando Claudín, charges them with inconsistency: on the one hand they declare that freedom and democracy are indivisible from socialism, while on the other they accept as socialist the countries of the Soviet bloc in which they find freedom and democracy totally lacking. (Claudín, moreover, rejects the Trotskyist argument that the system of production in these countries is socialist but not the political superstructure.)[40] Claudín's conclusion, that so long as the Eurocommunists continue to accept – even with qualifications – that the Soviet system is socialist, they will remain to some extent under Soviet hegemony[41] parallels that of writers of a very different colour who also see "the break with Moscow" as a crucial issue for a true judgement of the Eurocommunist movement.[42]

For Mandel, Eurocommunism is a hopelessly corrupted child of both Stalin and Kautsky, an oddly-matched pair, but here conjoined as arch-betrayers of internationalism. Not all critics on the left go as far as this. Claudín (who was, after all, expelled from the PCE for premature Eurocommunism)[43] credits the Eurocommunists with "re-discovering . . . the interdependence of democracy and socialism" which had been lost to sight in the communist parties when the left split into social-democratic and communist movements; but fears that the Eurocommunist scenario of first "advanced" or "progressive" democracy, to be followed by socialism (i.e. one transition after another) will concentrate attention too much on the electoral and political arena and too little on "working class self-organisation and struggles which might upset alliances with the 'non-monopoly bourgeoisie'".[44] It is in this connection that Mandel accuses the Eurocommunist, and particularly PCI, leaders of fraudulently claiming the heritage of Gramsci,[45] while some French critics on the left of Eurocommunism deplore the appearance of what they call *le gramscisme mou*.[46] These critics might well classify Giuseppe Vacca's contribution to this volume under this heading; but as H. T. Willetts hints,[47] the Gramscian treasury is large enough to provide a *gramscisme dur* with no less claim to orthodoxy. Claudín, for his part, finds the PCI guilty of failure to

> use those areas of power which it has won within the institutions of representative democracy and the State machine to assist the organisation of the struggle among . . . the unemployed, students, women; to unify those struggles with the struggles of the employed workers; to develop organs of rank and file democracy through which the masses could play a more active and direct part in solving their own problems; or to co-ordinate such organs with the institutions of representative democracy so that an electoral majority could become an active fighting majority, with a growing awareness of its social role and tasks.[48]

The role assigned, in this outline, to "the institutions of representative democracy" is indeed rather more instrumental than Eurocommunists usually make out; there is more than a suggestion of soviets in the "organs of rank and file democracy"; and the ghost of "dual power" hovers not very far behind the "co-ordination" of these organs with those institutions. There will, according to Claudín, be a "*period of uncertainty*, of extreme agitation in the class struggle during which the question not merely of government but of power comes to the fore".[49] The distinction is important: Claudín anticipates that "the ruling classes and their state machine" will use force – or at least undemocratic methods – to reverse an Eurocommunist electoral victory, and concludes that the electoral majority must be "organised. . .into a solid, non-atomised force . . . a socio-political bloc":[50]

> The basic difference between a revolution in a backward country and a revolution in one of the advanced countries of Western

> Europe lies in the fact that if there is to be a revolution at all in the latter it will only be made when there is a majority that is both objectively and subjectively committed to socialism. That requires the existence of a social bloc which is able, because it comprises all the essential vital elements of society, to impose the kind of democratic process we have described.[51]

Possibly the most useful contribution made to the discussion by critics on the left is their effort to relate it to the present crisis. As Claudín has put it:

> In a country such as France or Italy, the high rate of economic growth during the fifties and sixties might have lent some degree of credibility to the perspective of an "advanced democracy", though it would have implied a reformist co-existence with monopoly capitalism . . . on the Swedish or West German model rather than its defeat. It would also have implied the complete social-democratisation of the Communist Parties. But in the present conjuncture of a global capitalist crisis such a perspective is absurd. Either the forces that are fighting for socialism will decisively establish their hegemony or there will inevitably be a counter-revolutionary reversal.[52]

Seen from this angle, the Eurocommunists have not adapted, but have failed to adapt, to the changed conditions of the late 1970s; they are at fault not for innovation but for conservatism. For such critics, the crisis is also "the phase of rising mass struggle",[53] and that "pre-revolutionary and revolutionary explosions" are just round the corner; which leads them to accuse the Eurocommunists – specifically the PCI – of "playing the role of saviour of a threatened capitalist system".[54] However, whereas Mandel agrees with the Eurocommunists on the principle of a multi-party system,[55] he makes it clear that this has nothing to do with parliament, but with "power truly in the hands of the masses" as in Paris 1871, Russia 1917 and Portugal 1974;[56] the Eurocommunists stand accused of parliamentary cretinism.

Some parts of the far left in Italy, on the other hand, while accusing the PCI of a "reformism" which prevented it from exploiting the crisis except as a "claimant", within the existing structure of society,[57] put forward a programme which not only recognises the need for "austerity" in much the same terms as the PCI, but is to be borne "by the upper and middle layers of the population (that is, not only by a handful of monopolists. . .) and imposed by adequate instruments: direct taxation of inheritance and rationing (not only of petrol but of all imported mass consumption commodities, energy, meat etc.)" Such frankness is refreshing, and it is not surprising that such measures are said to require "the full development of organs of control at the base", and the transformation of the role of the great structures of society such as Education, Health, Transport, Justice, Public Administration.[58]

All these critics on the left assume that the crisis is such as to give rise to a revolutionary wave which they think the Eurocommunists neglect or even fear. They and the Eurocommunists agree on the need for a transition to socialism: they differ as to the means. But will it ever happen? Some of the authors in this study offer, even from the Eurocommunist point of view, an outlook of guarded pessimism: in France, a continuance in opposition corresponding to the internal ethos of the PCF; in Italy a relapse into opposition for the "foreseeable future, which in Italy is not long", followed by a remoter prospect of re-alignments on the left and a new "historic compromise" including the socialists; Spain is in an altogether earlier phase. Those who accuse the Eurocommunists of a lack of confidence in the masses may be right to do so; but if they are, it does not mean that the Eurocommunists are wrong. "The masses" may even be a bad bet in advanced capitalist societies. The only moments at which it could be argued (and not all would accept the argument) that mass politics played a significant role in Western Europe since the Second World War are France in 1968, Italy in 1969, and the end of the dictatorships in Greece, Spain and Portugal. The first two of these came while the economic boom was at its height; the others were aimed at targets which no longer exist and did not exist outside those southern European countries.

Perhaps one little-regarded fact may be mentioned here, namely this: the unemployed cannot strike, and are much harder to organise than workers employed in factories; they can, however, vote. Now although Eurocommunism's critics on the left emphasise the relative strength of the working class in the present crisis compared with earlier ones, they also recognise the possibility of working-class division and demoralisation if what they see as present opportunities are missed. Should they not go further and admit that recession may carry within it a small "objective" brake on revolution? It would doubtless be too simple to say that this is why there has never been a socialist revolution in an advanced capitalist country. However, it does seem to be the case that the greatest economic crisis for forty-five years has been accompanied by a wave of hermetic terrorism, both right and left, but shows little sign of engendering a mass revolutionary movement in "developed capitalist states". The political aim of terrorism, apart from self-advertisement, is to make people lose their nerve – in this case the supporters of liberal democracy, the rule of law, and parliamentarianism. The Gramscian concept of hegemony, increasingly accepted in other Eurocommunist parties,[59] puts the issue squarely as a struggle for the hearts and minds of men, rather than the inexorable workings of history, and in such a struggle morale is crucial. Western liberal-democratic critics of Eurocommunism have emphasised the way in which the *sense* of communist growth and the "decline of anti-communism"[60] can contribute to the outcome of this struggle, notably through the mass media. (Mandel recommends that the first investment to be made by a "workers' government" in France, Spain, Italy and Portugal should be "the world's most powerful television broadcasting system," able to reach an audience in other pre-transitional countries and appeal for international solidarity.)[61] Few would dispute the view, attributed to the Trilateral Commission,[62] that the best way to counter Eurocommunism's bid for power would be to overcome the present economic crisis. If this came about – say, by the early discovery and application of new sources of energy[63] – it would doubtless improve the morale of almost all parties to the struggle; it would also lessen the discontents of all but those who favour *la politique du pire* and reduce pressure for a change in the social status quo. But it has been argued in this essay that Eurocommunism is not a product of the crisis, but has rather been lent credibility by it. In so far as it is the communism of advanced capitalist prosperity, the recovery of that prosperity, to a greater or lesser degree and in one form or another, is unlikely to deal it a death-blow.

NOTES

1. See p.79.
2. See p.5.
3. See Ronald Tiersky in Olivier Duhamel and Charles Weber (eds.), *Changer le P.C.?* (Paris, 1979), pp. 220f.
4. On the importance of the "Paris Centre", see pp. 45–7.
5. See p.3.
6. Only the second and third of these three points have been treated as separate themes in this book, but the first, more or less explicitly, informs all the papers devoted to individual countries.
7. Santiago Carrillo in *El País*, 6 November 1977.
8. See Ronald Tiersky in Rudolf L. Tőkés (ed.), *Eurocommunism and Détente* (Oxford, 1979), pp. 172ff; Stuart Holland in Filo de la Torre *et al.* (eds), *Eurocommunism – Myth or Reality?* (London, 1979), pp. 212ff. For the political role of this phrase in the mouth of Thorez in the 1950s, see Pierre Daix, *La Crise du PCF* (Paris, 1978), p. 32. Cf. p. 89.
9. See Alexander and Gesine Schwan, *Sozialdemokratie und Marxismus* (Hamburg, 1974), pp. 265–70.
10. Annie Kriegel, *Un autre communisme?* (Paris, 1977), pp. 140ff.
11. Fernando Claudín, *Eurocommunism and Socialism* (London, 1978), p. 101. For a discussion of the current Soviet analysis of the successive "phases of the revolution" see Robert Legvold's contribution to Tőkés (ed.), op. cit., pp. 528ff.
12. F. L. Agudín, quoted in C.-E. Diaz Lopez, "The Eurocommunist alternative in Spain", *Political Quarterly*, vol. 50, no. 3, July–September 1979, p.357.
13. Santiago Carrillo, *"Eurocommunism" and the State* (London, 1977), p. 106.
14. See Isaac Aviv, ch. 5; Daix, op. cit., pp. 165ff.
15. Roy Godson and Stephen Haseler, *"Eurocommunism", Implications for East and West* (London, 1978), p. 10.
16. See Daix, op. cit., p. 224.
17. See ch. 8.
18. See ch. 3.
19. See ch. 4 and ch. 5, p. 99. See also, on this point, Henri Fiszbin, *Les Bouches s'ouvrent* (Paris, 1980).
20. Duhamel and Weber, op. cit., p. 10.
21. M.-A. Macciocchi, *Après Marx, avril* (Paris, 1978).
22. Ibid., p. 134. It is, of course, known that Gramsci was excluded from the PCd'I *leadership*. See A. Pozzolini, *Antonio Gramsci* (London, 1970), p. xix.
23. See the data quoted by Norman Kogan in Tőkés (ed.), op. cit., p. 79, which show that this has been a factor in the past.
24. Lombardo Radice in G. R. Urban (ed.), *Eurocommunism* (London, 1978), p. 48.
25. Ibid., p. 43.
26. See p. 162.
27. See for instance, Archie Brown and Jack Gray (eds), *Political Culture and Political Change in Communist States* (London, 1977).

28. See ch. 1; Robert Legvold, William E. Griffith and Rudolf Tőkés in Tőkés (ed.), op. cit., Part II; Archie Brown and George Schöpflin in de la Torre *et al.* (eds), op. cit., ch. 8; Zorica Priklmajer-Tomanović, *Evrokomunizam* (Belgrade, 1978), pp. 98ff; Leonard Schapiro, "The Soviet reaction to 'Eurocommunism'", *West European Politics*, vol. 2, May 1979, no. 2., pp. 160–77.
29. Former President Gerald Ford, at Fulton, Missouri, *Sunday Telegraph*, 30 October 1977.
30. Legvold, op. cit., pp. 353ff; Claudín, op. cit., p. 141.
31. Sir Harold Wilson, Labour and Trades Union Press Service, *The Guardian*, 7 November 1977.
32. Eric Heffer, *The Times*, 7 November 1977. These remarks led to a public exchange of view between left and right in the British Labour Party, culminating in a suggestion from the right that the Labour Party was itself on the road to Eurocommunism. See Stephen Haseler in *The Times*, 27 October 1978.
33. Dr David Owen, Hugh Anderson Memorial Lecture, Cambridge Union Society, 18 November 1977.
34. Bruno Kreisky in *L'Unità*, 14 October 1977; Brandt, Palme and Soares have expressed similar views. See Priklmajer-Tomanović, op. cit., pp. 88ff.
35. Godson and Haseler, op. cit., p. 95.
36. Ernest Mandel, *From Stalinism to Eurocommunism* (London, 1978), p. 97.
37. Ibid., p. 48.
38. Ibid., p. 97. Although the Soviet Union has indeed shown itself sensitive to Eurocommunist "anti-Sovietism", it is easy to exaggerate the length to which Eurocommunists (especially the PCF) are willing to carry their criticism: we need only remember that although the measured and largely abstract historical revision of *L'URSS et nous* was approved for publication by the PCF, a book by two young French communists who lived in Moscow describing the de-humanisation of personal relations which they found there in everyday life (Nina and Jean Kéhayan, *Rue du Prolétaire Rouge*, Paris, 1978) which was far more likely to be read by the party rank-and-file, had to be published under a "bourgeois imprint" and was banned at the PCF's *fête de la Marseillaise* (C. Buci-Glucksmann in Duhamel and Weber, op. cit., p.136).
39. Mandel, op. cit., p. 85.
40. Claudín, op. cit., p. 61.
41. Ibid., p. 63.
42. Godson and Haseler, op. cit., ch. 3; Schapiro, op. cit., p. 176.
43. See pp. 52–3.
44. Claudín, op. cit., p. 109. For a similar view, with reference to France, see Duhamel and Weber, 'L'Électoralisme, ou comment perdre les élections', op. cit., pp. 13ff.
45. Mandel, op. cit., pp. 201ff.
46. Georges Labica and Christine Buci-Glucksmann in Duhamel and Weber (eds), op. cit., pp. 83, 146.
47. See p. 13.

48. Claudín, op. cit., p. 116.
49. Ibid., p. 117.
50. Ibid., p. 122.
51. Ibid., p. 127.
52. Ibid., p. 107.
53. Mandel, op. cit., pp. 54, 81, 124, 186; cf. pp. 59, 196, etc. This is not, of course, to suggest that Mandel believes in spontaneity without mobilisation by "revolutionary Marxists".
54. Ibid., p. 125.
55. Ibid.
56. Ibid., p. 65.
57. Lucio Magri in Henri Weber (ed.), *Parti communiste italien: aux sources de 'l "eurocommunisme"* (Paris, 1977), pp. 188f.
58. Ibid., pp. 209ff.
59. See Azcárate, p. 31, or Duhamel and Weber, op. cit., pp. 125–46, 272f.
60. Godson and Haseler, op. cit., p. 10.
61. Mandel, op. cit., p. 217.
62. Priklmajer-Tomanović, op. cit., p. 95.
63. Claudín, op cit., p. 18, lists several other ways of "capitalist reconstruction".

Index

Note: Entries relating to the four main communist parties discussed will be found under their initials, as in the text, i.e. CPSU (Soviet Union), PCE (Spain), PCF (France) and PCI (Italy). References to the communist parties of countries other than these are to be found under the names of those countries.